S0-BRR-763

Praise for **Big Intel**

"What if you combined the dark, anti-human politics of the academic left with the unfettered power and impenetrable secrecy of the national security state? You'd have pretty much what we have now, which is the end of America as we know it. Mike Waller explains how we got there in this wise book."

—**Tucker Carlson,** host of *Tucker on X*

"Waller tracks the fall of the FBI and CIA from their heyday as the legendary scourge of bank robbers and commies everywhere to their current, degraded state as a shabby collection of political button men doing the domestic dirty work of their Democrat masters. Waller's devastating portrait of these simultaneously corrupt and incompetent bureaucracies, and his suggestions for rebuilding our intelligence and counterintelligence organizations up to at least a minimal level of competency, make for essential reading for conservative policymakers and citizens alike."

—**Kurt Schlichter,** Townhall columnist and bestselling author of *We'll Be Back: The Fall and Rise of America* and *People's Republic*

"It's the worst strategic intelligence disaster in American history—the CIA and FBI's decades of failure to detect and defend the country against a relentless Kremlin active measures campaign that survived the Soviet collapse and took on a life of its own. Waller chronicles how the Communist enemy spawned cultural Marxism and critical theory, and how that alien worldview has corrupted the entire American intelligence community."

—**Peter Schweizer,** nationally bestselling author of *Red-Handed: How American Elites Get Rich Helping China Win* and cofounder and president of the Government Accountability Institute

"Like real Wizards of Oz, the FBI and CIA have amassed and weaponized unthinkable powers against the American people hidden behind the facade of serving the national interest. Mike Waller pulls the curtain back to show us how great and terrible these agencies have truly become."

—**Stephen Friend,** FBI former special agent and author of *True Blue: My Journey from Beat Cop to Suspended FBI Whistleblower*

"Michael Waller earned well-deserved credibility as a scholar-investigator of the counterintelligence and intelligence craft with his *Secret Empire: The KGB in Russia Today*. Now Waller has turned his scholarly focus on the security bureaucracies closer to home: the U.S. intelligence community. The self-referential counterintelligence/intelligence bureaucracies are not confined merely to the eastern marches of Western civilization. I'll venture that Waller's earlier probe of the counterintelligence state's reincarnation in post-Soviet Russia led him to this unsettling opus on that state's appearance here in America today."

—**John J. Dziak,** author of *Chekisty: A History of the KGB* and former senior intelligence official in the Department of Defense

"Waller takes you step-by-step through the historical circumstances that allowed the ideological capture of the Deep State's most powerful weapons: U.S. foreign and domestic intelligence agencies. His personal connections to critical players on the timeline will make you wonder if you picked up a Ludlum or Clancy novel."

—**Kyle Seraphin,** former FBI agent

"After decades of our agencies and bureaus abusing power to politicize intelligence and meddle in American politics and U.S. presidential elections, the reputation of the U.S. intelligence community has sunk to a new low. In *Big Intel*, Dr. Waller provides a fascinating and detailed analysis of the fall of America's intelligence services and how they might be salvaged to protect American security and freedom."

—**Fred Fleitz,** senior vice chair of the American First Policy Institute, former National Security Council chief of staff, and former CIA analyst

"Spellbinding. Provocative. Essential. We are at war, and the enemy long ago made its way inside the wire. We are betrayed at the highest levels, and the fate of the republic hangs in the balance."

—**Sam Faddis,** editor-in-chief of AND Magazine and retired senior CIA operations officer

"Well researched and accessible, this timely account is not just for historians and intellectuals, but for all decent Americans who want to know the real story behind the extreme leftward drift of our institutions, particularly those organized to prevent that very foundational shift from occurring. Why the primary organizations Americans have relied on to lead us away from this country-ending path—the CIA and the FBI—have failed in this regard is Waller's great subject. Dr. Waller argues that we still have time to stop them. The Communists, radical left, and enemies of America will hate it."

—**Phillip Jennings,** retired U.S. intelligence operative and Marine officer

"If you've got a nagging feeling America is being systematically dismantled and destroyed by obscure forces from within, J. Michael Waller's book shows this is indeed what is happening. And the attack is far along. Based on his historian's eye and his own long experience taking on Marxists over decades, Waller lays out the hundred-year, multi-generational Marxist effort to destroy America's capitalist and Judeo-Christian foundations. His is a frightening book but a necessary one."

—**Grant Newsham,** author of *When China Attacks: A Warning to America*

"Mike Waller takes us on a deep dive into the reasons behind how the once testosterone-laden, mission-oriented FBI and CIA have morphed over the years into ineffective, bloated, unfocused government bureaucracies. He begins with their origins under J. Edgar Hoover and 'Wild Bill' Donovan and shows how what he calls 'insidious Kremlin active measures' evidenced by the Venona intercepts of Soviet coded messages, and continuing Communist influence have served to bring down so many of our institutions, including the FBI and CIA."

—**F. W. Rustmann Jr.**, retired senior CIA clandestine services officer and author of popular spy trilogy *The Case Officer*, *Plausible Denial*, and *False Flag*

Big Intel

Big Intel

How the CIA and FBI Went from Cold War Heroes to Deep State Villains

J. Michael Waller

Regnery Publishing
WASHINGTON, D.C.

ISBN: 978-1-68451-353-6
eISBN: 978-1-68451-433-5
Library of Congress Control Number: 2023944067

Cataloging-in-Publication data on file with the Library of Congress

Published in the United States by
Regnery Publishing
A Division of Salem Media Group
Washington, D.C.
www.Regnery.com

Manufactured in the United States of America

10 9 8 7 6 5 4 3 2 1

For Allison

"Only a virtuous people are capable of freedom. As nations become more corrupt and vicious, they have more need of masters."

—Benjamin Franklin, 1787[1]

"It is a characteristic of any decaying civilization that the great masses of the people are unconscious of the tragedy."

—Fulton J. Sheen, 1948[2]

Contents

Introduction

He had the look of a madman as he sat in the heavy wood and leather chair. His contorted face shifted from side to side and up and down as if disembodied from the neck. Beady eyes never broke their stare into the camera lens. A creepy, tight-lipped grin sneered contempt. In one short video, he exuded the disturbed, sadistic mania of a nightmarish bad clown.

He was the FBI's chief of counterintelligence, America's top spy-hunter. At least that was his position. His name was Peter Strzok. Apart from the reptilian movement of his head, he sat still in his chair, smirking as he avoided answering questions of the congressional oversight panel.

With people like Strzok running the FBI's bloated headquarters, the bureau's most influential work in recent years had little to do with finding real spies. Its most impactful counterintelligence operation was Crossfire Hurricane, which wasn't a spy hunt at all, but a fake exercise to push the idea that the brash Donald Trump, as candidate and as president, was a willful Russian collaborator and traitor to his country.

It was all a lie. Special Counsel Robert S. Mueller III, a former FBI director, issued a lengthy report in 2019 stating that the premises of Crossfire Hurricane were unsubstantiated and fabricated.[1] In 2023, seven years after Crossfire Hurricane further polarized the nation almost to a breaking point, Special Counsel John H. Durham led a team to find out who in government was responsible for the reckless disinformation and why. Durham and his investigators conducted more than 480 interviews, issued 190 grand jury subpoenas, and collected 6 million pages of documents.[2] Some important objects of his probe, including former FBI directors and FBI counterintelligence agents, refused to cooperate.[3]

Durham issued a blistering three-hundred-page document showing how the intelligence community, and the FBI in particular, threw all standards of professionalism out the window to spread these reports—every word of them unsubstantiated or false. They were instead cooked up by the Clinton campaign, a foreign former intelligence officer, and a Russian citizen who the FBI believed all along had been a Kremlin spy.

This book isn't about the heroic, creative, patriotic men and women of the FBI and CIA who faithfully executed their oaths as public servants and literally saved the country from foreign enemies. It isn't about the magnificent successes against cartel gangsters, terrorists, child traffickers, and spies. It isn't about the failures and terrible judgment of those who tried mightily, usually with good intentions, but whose actions continue to haunt the country. It doesn't reveal who "really" shot JFK.

All utopian movements and societies require enforcers. *Big Intel* is about how these former protectors of American founding principles have followed societal trends to become the secret services of critical theory and fonts of the democracy-demolishing wokeness that the theory animates.

This is a counterintelligence story—a chronicle of a battle the FBI and CIA fought for decades before they succumbed to a generations-old hostile foreign intelligence operation to destroy the United States and Western civilization from within. It's about how American foreign intelligence was targeted and attacked as soon as it was founded. These attacks were not about partisan politics—yes, the FBI and CIA did meddle in domestic politics and still do—but something far deeper: they were meant to turn American instruments of power into enforcers of the vanguards spearheading the fundamental transformation of our country. *Big Intel* seeks to answer how it happened. And to do that, we go to Moscow more than a century ago, before there was an FBI by that name, or a CIA at all.

Like the virus that caused COVID-19, the critical theory pandemic infecting America's institutions is a foreign import with traceable origins. From its beginnings in and around the Kremlin, we can follow what journalist Diana West calls an unbroken "chain of ideological custody," a "red thread," from the launch of two brilliant Bolshevik strategic active measures offensives that its designers intended to unfold over generations.[4] As with the people who conceived them, those operations begat their own spores or strains, which developed lives of their own and succeeded beyond their founders' imagination. The successor spawn are well on the way to imposing their own hegemony over American life and the lives of nations around the world. Here I focus on the infection of the CIA and FBI, the very institutions designed to defend against hostile foreign covert subversion.

The early Soviets' strategic cultivation of seeds in Europe grew into a taproot called the Frankfurt School. Moscow's plan a century ago was to use the Frankfurt School to destroy Weimar Germany from within after World War I, and then collapse the rest of Europe by poisoning its culture and destroying its history. The United States was barely part of the picture then.

The rise of Adolf Hitler and his National Socialist German Workers' Party inadvertently gave the Frankfurt School an unplanned boost. The Nazis caused the leaders and operatives to flee to free parts of Europe, and ultimately to export the Frankfurt School across the Atlantic and anchor itself on both coasts of the United States. The good-natured American people welcomed them. Their naïve hospitality was used against them. Rather than becoming good fellow Americans, these intellectuals of the Frankfurt School and other Soviet agents and fellow travelers would bring their Central European ideological baggage with them to subvert and ruin, not strengthen, the country that gave them sanctuary. Some of them hit on a formula that had wide appeal and quickly spread like a prairie fire.

After a century, the net results of that active measures strategy would fundamentally transform the way many American politicians, influencers, lawyers, judges, law enforcement officers, intelligence analysts, and intelligence operatives viewed their own country and its founding constitutional principles. The strategy ditched the stodgy and dull driving principle of established Marxism—the economic determinism that pits the proletarian economic class of toiling masses irreconcilably against the bourgeoisie toward a "dictatorship of the proletariat"—and returned to Marx to divide, polarize, and destroy by other means.

Marxism's permanent warfare would ravage the culture, starting with education and family and spreading through the arts, deeply held religious beliefs and values, ethnicity, sexuality, patriotism, and law. We can trace the rise of cultural Marxism from its beginnings in early Soviet Russia, through interwar Germany, during World War II when it first penetrated American foreign intelligence, through the Cold War when the FBI led the country against such subversion, right up to the present when the CIA and then the FBI embraced it, wrapped it in lovely packaging called diversity, equity, and inclusion, and placed it at the core of their missions. The term "cultural Marxism" was too inflammatory to use in government and always denied. But the agencies internalized the train of thought to induce people to think and behave as cultural Marxists, usually without even realizing it. That intellectual construct or thought process is called critical theory.

More than a century ago, FBI director J. Edgar Hoover recognized this red thread and understood where it would lead. Hoover was trained as a lawyer. He portrayed himself as America's lawman, but first and foremost he fought foreign subversion of American values and society. Federal lawmakers of both parties never enacted laws to wage the fight effectively, so Hoover and his FBI, usually with a wink or diverted eye from presidents and from Congress, dove into that gray area and built the FBI into a domestic intelligence agency with police powers.

Though not known to have used the term critical theory, Hoover worked tirelessly to act against it and warn the country about it. He tracked the red thread as it stitched and wove through educational and activist institutions, to the creation of the administrative state under President Franklin D. Roosevelt's New Deal, the great OSS of World War II, and the CIA. Hoover wasn't perfect. Like none before or since, he had decades to compound his mistakes and few opponents to challenge him. His permanence in power, with almost no congressional oversight, often presented a public menace in the name of the public good.

But he was right in identifying the institutional, individual, and ideological drivers of destructive change in America. He fairly predicted the social trends at work to fundamentally transform the country. History may have reviled him. So has the FBI itself. But the twenty-first-century FBI, as with the CIA, became a greater threat to the constitutional system and American society than the surprisingly restrained Hoover ever could have been.

My Beginning

Chapter 1

The grandfatherly OSS veteran sat with me over a cup of tea. "You're a Catholic, aren't you." It was more of a statement than a question.

"Well, yes. But not a very good one."

"Go to the five o'clock vigil Mass at Saint Matthew's Cathedral on Saturday. Sit in one of the back pews on the left side. Don't leave until someone speaks to you."

That was an odd way to get me back to church, I thought. But I did as he suggested.

He went by Jim. Just Jim. I never knew his last name, but I'd been told by a friend, Constantine Menges on the White House National Security Council (NSC) staff, to go and meet the OSS gent and tell him about myself. There wasn't much to tell. It was in the fall of 1983. I was just a kid, a junior at the George Washington University. What made me different was my interest in fighting Communism and supporting

President Reagan's strategy to push Soviet-backed revolutionaries out of Central America. I tried Army ROTC at Georgetown but bailed before officially signing.

Weird Way around Reagan's White House

At the time I was national secretary of Young Americans for Freedom (YAF), Reagan's favorite youth organization, and doubled as a coordinator at the College Republican National Committee on Capitol Hill to promote the president's takedown of the Soviet bloc.

Earlier I'd interned for United States senator Gordon Humphrey from my home state of New Hampshire, where I met his policy director, Morton Blackwell, who himself had been active for decades in youth politics. That was in the fall of 1980, when I voted for the first time, casting an absentee ballot from my dorm for Reagan as president. The day after the election, Morton was gone. He joined the Reagan transition team to prepare for the incoming administration.

Morton was a networker. Before Reagan's election he had told me to go to the next CPAC, the annual Conservative Political Action Conference. At the Reagan White House, he was responsible for outreach to conservatives. I kept in contact with him, and he put me in touch with Faith Whittlesey, back in Washington from her first stint as ambassador to Switzerland and then, in 1983, doing public outreach at the White House. Faith and I became friends right away. By then I had become interested in student journalism and was angling to go to Soviet-occupied Afghanistan with *Soldier of Fortune* magazine, whose correspondent I had met at a YAF meeting.

"That would be a very bad idea," Faith warned sternly. "You can do better. You speak Spanish. You should cover the wars in Central America."

At that time in 1983, Nicaragua was in its fourth year of Communist rule under the Sandinista National Liberation Front. The Sandinistas turned Nicaragua into a staging area to export Soviet-sponsored subversion and violence across Central America. Their main immediate target was neighboring El Salvador, where their allied Farabundo Martí National Liberation Front (FMLN) was waging a murderous campaign to overthrow the Salvadoran government. True to their ways, the Salvadorans responded in kind, causing diplomatic and political nightmares for their American allies. It was an ugly time.

"You should meet Constantine," Faith said.

I had heard of Constantine Menges, the CIA man who served as a national intelligence officer on the White House National Security Council staff. Constantine was a profound, learned scholar handling parts of the extremely controversial Latin America portfolio for Reagan. Friends and detractors, for different reasons, called him "Constant Menace." He was also CIA director William J. Casey's designated person, or at least one of them, on the NSC staff. Reagan and Casey didn't trust the CIA, or at least most of the intelligence officers and analysts who had risen to the top, so they needed trustworthy eyes and ears like Constantine who knew the agency inside and out.

"They'll Grind You Down or Spit You Out," or "You Will Hate It and It Will Hate You"

That fall at the university, I took a course on the history of Soviet intelligence services. My professor, John J. Dziak, was a civilian officer attached to the Defense Intelligence Agency. He taught the country's only unclassified course on the subject. I developed a friendship with him and told him that I'd like to go into the CIA. "Don't do it," he warned. "Not with your views and your personality. They'll grind you down or spit you out, or you'll leave broken and disillusioned."

In making my rounds on Capitol Hill to network with people, I met an intensely energetic Senate Select Committee on Intelligence staff member. His name was Angelo Codevilla. He patiently listened with morbid amusement to my plans to join the CIA. With a penetrating stare and a grimace both fierce and amiable, he intoned, "Intelligence is a vital function of government. Don't be so impressed with the CIA. It's a bureaucracy that isn't doing its job. You will hate it and it will hate you. The CIA is about perpetuating itself as a bureaucracy. It is not for mission-oriented people like you. Not anymore."

That came as a discouragement, since Casey was supposedly rejuvenating the CIA. The agency had been in a state of demoralization following the Vietnam War collapse, the congressional oversight revelations after Watergate, and the wholesale overturning of the agency under the Carter administration. The CIA was recruiting other young people as it expanded and rebounded. While the agency was indeed hiring conservative people as operations officers and analysts, my temperament was not suited to becoming part of a permanent bureaucratic machine. So I never applied.

Constantine shared my views and independence, but he had been within, but not part of, the establishment for a long time. As a college student he had marched in the civil rights movement with Rev. Martin Luther King Jr. and made networks of friends and contacts across the political spectrum. With Faith's recommendation, he met me for what became a long if challenging friendship for the rest of his life. He liked that I was a YAF leader and one of the few Spanish-speaking young conservatives on the Reagan team. He liked that, earlier that year, I had been a U.S. delegate to the United Nations International Youth Year preparatory commission in Costa Rica. He especially liked that—using that week-long UN delegate credential—I had tried to sneak into Nicaragua on my own with the anti-Sandinista forces of former Sandinista guerrilla leader Edén Pastora.

"My Friend Jim" from the OSS

Known as Commander Zero, Pastora had become world-famous leading a Sandinista insurrection against the Nicaraguan congress controlled by then strongman Anastasio Somoza. Once the Sandinistas took power, Pastora joined their regime only to quit or be forced out. He took up arms because they betrayed the revolution's alleged democratic ideals. The Communists couldn't control Commander Zero, and neither could the CIA. Sadly, the charismatic leader couldn't control himself either, and he hindered rather than advanced the Nicaraguan resistance.

Constantine had endless intellect, energy, and stamina. He is said to have been the first, in the 1960s, to design a plan to collapse the Soviet empire without fighting a war. He constantly sought opportunities to exploit against the Soviet enemy. In the Reagan White House, while I was befriending him, he took advantage of deadly infighting within the Communist regime of Grenada, a small Caribbean island, and pushed a plan to use the opportunity to spark the strategic reversal of Soviet expansion, what he called the Reagan Doctrine. That was in October 1983, when President Reagan launched Operation Urgent Fury, both to rescue American medical students in Grenada and to overthrow the Soviet-backed regime to start a rollback against Communism. Some of Reagan's critics accused him of invading Grenada to divert attention from a massive terrorist attack on U.S. Marine barracks in Beirut. They denied that Grenada's regime was really Communist or Soviet-allied and was building an airstrip that could accommodate Soviet bombers. These critics were wrong.

Busy as he was, Constantine took the trouble to talk to me a few more times that fall. I told him of the work I wanted to do on the ground in Central America, doing something meaningful against the Communists and exposing their American support networks. "Talk to my friend Jim," he said. Jim was a World War II veteran of the Office of

Strategic Services, the OSS. A few times in late 1983, Jim took me out for a casual tea or coffee, wanting to know all about me and my background, my interests, my likes and dislikes, my views of the world, and my future plans, some of which he already seemed to know. But he never told me much about himself. He certainly never told me his real name.

Through Constantine I got in touch with the leadership of the Nicaraguan Democratic Force (FDN), a large anti-Communist guerrilla army backed by the CIA to overthrow the Sandinistas. The official government line was that the FDN was fighting to interdict Soviet bloc arms shipments to the FMLN Marxist guerrillas in El Salvador, and to pressure the Sandinistas to democratize. I wasn't interested in that, and neither was the FDN. The real purpose, of course, was to overthrow the Communist regime, and I was all for it.

Constantine had two warnings for me. "Never say 'CIA,' because people's ears perk up. That's how things get in the *Washington Post*. Call it 'ABC' and nobody else will pay attention."

His second warning was more emphatic: "Stay away from that lieutenant colonel. He's going to get somebody in trouble."

I heeded Constantine's advice but never knew of any lieutenant colonel until a while later, when the headlines blared about a Marine of that rank, also on the NSC staff, named Oliver North. I immediately admired Colonel North, but kept my compartmentation pledge to Constantine. During the course of events another old OSS veteran working with the Contras took me under his wing: Major General John Singlaub, the former commander of U.S. Army forces in South Korea. Singlaub had a notch in his ear from a Waffen-SS sniper bullet. He had retired a few years earlier after differing publicly with President Jimmy Carter's plan to reduce the American presence against the North Korean regime. He quietly warned me to avoid certain private individuals who were unduly profiteering from arms sales to the Contras. Singlaub was in it for the fight, not the money.

Anti-Communist Solidarity Forever

Meanwhile I linked up with an international group of anti-Soviet scholars and activists, all private citizens who had their own personal intelligence networks. They were somewhat like the OSS recruits in the early days of World War II. Indeed, some had worked at one time or another for OSS or MI6 or their Australian, Belgian, Canadian, nationalist Chinese, Danish, Dutch, French, German, Israeli, Italian, Norwegian, Polish, Turkish, or other counterparts. Some were Ukrainian nationalists. A few were very elderly White Russians who had fought the Bolsheviks, their Cheka secret police, and the Red Army. All, one way or another, had fought the Communists and the Nazis and their allies.

That private network was called the 61. Its leader was Brian Crozier, an Australian-born Brit who had been close to French general Charles de Gaulle during World War II. The 61 provided alternate sources of intelligence for British prime minister Margaret Thatcher, for President Reagan, and for other leaders around the world. It also "did things," political warfare work for its members' own countries and in solidarity with others worldwide. Here I learned the value of building lifelong personal international networks, and about the world of private, parallel intelligence collection and analysis for the mission-oriented—not publicity- or career-minded—in the land of misfit toys.

Through Constantine's intercession, the FDN agreed to meet me in Honduras, take me to their main base just over the border from Nicaragua, and tell their story to American college students and the public. If someone had something else in mind for me, I was unaware. The week before I was to fly from Miami to Tegucigalpa, Jim asked me to see him. That's when he told me to go to church. He also slipped me two envelopes of $500 each for "walking-around money" to cover my expenses and those of a fellow student journalist, Michael Johns, of the *Miami Tribune* at the University of Miami. I had already raised money on my own for the trip through Young America's Foundation, but the cash would come in handy to get out of a jam in Central America.

Jim never mentioned why he wanted me to go to church. I thought that maybe it was an awkward way to clean me up spiritually before spending a week in a dangerous combat area with no training or preparation of any kind. He admonished me to tell no one. Forty years later, now that everyone concerned but Mike Johns is deceased and I won't be violating anyone's confidence, I can tell the story for the first time. Plus I'm not subject to any CIA pre-publication review.

Chapter 2

Going to Church

Constantine expressed interest in my trip, which I thought was odd for a very busy White House NSC official, given that I was just a college undergrad. For me, at age twenty-one, having such a White House connection was a really neat thing, and I enjoyed the friendship. Constantine was also a Catholic.

Following Jim's advice, I went by myself to the sparsely attended Saturday afternoon vigil Mass at Saint Matthew's. Perhaps it was a test of something. I didn't know. But I did see, about ten or fifteen pews ahead of me, a familiar-looking, stooped figure. Jim had told me to stay put until someone approached me, so I didn't go to Communion. I wasn't in any spiritual shape to go at that time in my life anyway, so it would have been wrong. But the stooped man went. He looked exactly like CIA director William Casey.

After the priest concluded that the Mass had ended and bid us go in peace, I stood and sang as the organ played the recessional hymn. A stern-looking woman blocked me by the pew. "Are you Waller?"

That was odd. "Yes."

"Stay here. Don't move."

Obviously Jim had sent her. What a coincidence that I went to the same Mass as Bill Casey just before my trip with the Contras!

But it was no coincidence. The woman motioned to a man at Casey's side as the CIA director shuffled to the organ music up the center aisle. The man gestured up to Casey, who stopped next to the woman and looked right at me.

My right hand shot out, stupidly. "Nice to meet you, Mr. Director." I felt like a jerk.

Casey ignored my greeting and leaned toward my face. "Cap-ee-tan Loo-kay," he mumbled. Or something like that.

"Excuse me?"

"Cap-ee-tan Loo-kay." Casey shuffled away.

In an unforgettable barking whisper, the man escorting Casey issued five commanding words: "*Capitán Luque*. Remember that name."

As the organist keyed the second verse of the recessional hymn, Casey and his entourage disappeared through the cathedral's massive bronze doors and down the steps to a waiting car on Rhode Island Avenue.

I didn't have a clue what had just happened.

Later I called Jim, but he didn't get back to me. We never spoke again. I never learned who he was.

Just an Amateur Tourist in Tegucigalpa Looking for Contras

Skipping the beginning of spring semester a few days later, I flew to Tegucigalpa, met Mike Johns at the shabby plate-glass and cinder-block airport, and got questioned. "What is the purpose of your visit?" the immigration guard asked.

"Tourism."

"Where will you be staying?"

I had no idea where we would be staying, so I said, "Holiday Inn." The Contras had merely told me that they would have someone greet us at the airport. I didn't know their names or what they looked like. I knew nobody in Honduras, and of course there were no cell phones or internet back then. My answers were most unsatisfactory. With my longish hair and jeans, I might have been one of those Yankee Sandinista fellow travelers set up for some revolutionary useful idiot tour. We were told to wait.

And wait we did. It took a long time. Turns out there was indeed a Holiday Inn in Tegucigalpa, but they had no reservation for me. I couldn't tell the Hondurans what I was really doing, and Constantine had told me to stay away from the American embassy. So I had nothing to say to my local inquisitors. That was unhelpful. I thought we'd be taken away as suspected Communists and interrogated. So I decided to pull rank. I would ask for the only officer whose name I knew.

In Spanish I told a uniformed bureaucrat, "I want to see Capitán Luque." The bureaucrat looked puzzled, muttered something I didn't understand, disappeared into a grimy office, and closed the door. Several minutes went by. Finally a very fat uniformed officer, whose insignia I didn't recognize, waddled out to talk to us. "Capitán Luque?" I asked.

"*Capitán Luque. Bienvenidos. Vengan conmigo.*" Captain Luque. Welcome. Come with me.

Nothing more. The portly officer helpfully escorted us through a private side door of the primitive airport terminal to the parking lot and gestured toward a beat-up, twin-cab Toyota pickup full of Contras. And so began an adventure that would span seven years on and off, through the entire fight of the Nicaraguan resistance and the counterinsurgency against the Communist guerrillas in El Salvador.

It was one of those exciting times at the beginning of adult life, and I didn't really pay much attention to detail at the time, but over the years I wondered why CIA director Casey would know the name of a heavy Honduran captain during a still-unexplained encounter at church. Especially because that first trip down there was as legitimate student journalists. I ended up writing a three-part series that ran on the front page of the newest daily newspaper in the nation's capital, the *Washington Times*.

Constantine never explained why Casey said those words to me, and I never asked. Nobody told me. I just trusted these older spooks and prayed, for real, that everything would turn out well. Then, during the Iran-Contra hearings a few years later, word got out that Casey would meet people at Mass because he couldn't legally be forced to testify to Congress about what happened in church during a religious service. And with the cathedral organ still playing the recessional hymn, under some law or interpretation thereof to protect citizens' freedom of religion, Mass was still in session even if the priest had already said it was ended and we could go in peace. But I wouldn't understand the significance of this for many years.

A Cryptonym and a Pat on the Back

I figured out that Jim was probably a friend of Casey from the OSS days, making sure I'd be at church on time.

Thirty years later, Casey's son-in-law, Owen Smith, told me that in the early 1980s Casey had deployed him to buy fax machines and other communications gear for Lech Walesa's Solidarity movement in Soviet-occupied Poland. Smith, a private citizen, then ran the equipment to a Vatican nunciature for delivery under diplomatic seal to Warsaw.

One or more of Casey's trusted friends had given Smith cash to buy the equipment in a third country.

When I told him about my Contra story, Smith, an enthusiastic man with a friendly laugh, exclaimed, "That's how Bill did it! 'Jim' was certainly one of his old OSS buddies. He gave you some cash, right? Yeah, that came straight out of Bill's pocket. Bill used his own money to fund these sorts of things. Congress couldn't control that. He gave me the money to buy the fax machines for Poland. He would meet people in church to give them instructions or get information. He'd always pick a different church. He went almost daily. As long as Mass was in session, nobody could force him to testify. That's how he protected his people."

I asked why Casey would have told me, "Capitán Luque."

"That's all he said to you? That was probably your cryptonym," Smith said, thinking it over. "Yeah, Bill personally gave you your cryptonym. That's how he kept it out of the CIA records. No paper trail. That guy in Honduras wasn't Captain Luque. *You* were Captain Luque."

And so I served as an asset for CIA director Bill Casey in Central America. Total amateur. The first trip was just to get my feet wet. The Grenada invasion had supplied a haul of secret documents which, made public, would provide proof of Soviet plans to take over the Caribbean and Central America—something Reagan's liberal opponents in Congress were downplaying or denying. The CIA was uncovering more in Central America, mostly from FMLN guerrillas in El Salvador, but few were truly useful to provide the public proof that Reagan wanted.

During Constantine's time in the Reagan White House, we talked a few times a year, with him giving me guidance on intelligence he hoped I would collect on the ground in Central America. By then I was going back and forth as often as I could. Constantine was specifically interested in Soviet and Soviet-bloc material support for El Salvador's

FMLN, and about Latin American youth leaders supportive of Fidel Castro or local Communists.

One day I was invited to the Roosevelt Room at the White House with other Central America–oriented people. We all wore name tags. President Reagan walked in to greet us individually. He shook my hand strongly, gripped my shoulder, and looked me straight in the eye. "Mike, what you're doing is very important to me," the president said with that famous Reagan smile. "Keep up the good work."

Didn't Trust the CIA Then, Either

I didn't become a CIA asset, because I was working in a parallel channel through a White House detailee who reported straight to Bill Casey and at his personal expense. I collected documentation of Soviet-bloc weapons and subversion, and on Cuban- and Soviet-controlled human assets and targets.

As long as those humans were not Americans.

When I discovered documentation of U.S. congressional staff who worked with the Sandinistas and FMLN or the Cuban regime—people like Jim McGovern, then an aide to Congressman Joe Moakley (D-MA)—Constantine waved me off and said he wouldn't touch it. But he told me who legally could. Still nothing was done. McGovern got elected to succeed Moakley and still represents the district in Worcester, Massachusetts. And he still supports the same old causes.

Constantine was thrilled with the cache of secret documents that American forces had captured in Grenada. Such documents, he said, should be examined and made available for all to see, to show the nation and the world what the USSR was doing in the American hemisphere.

Ultimately, the Grenada documents were sorted and released jointly, along with an analytical report, in a very public way by the Departments of State and Defense, and provided to anyone who wanted them. With no editing or alteration. In their pure form, the documents proved the ongoing covert Soviet invasion of the Americas.

Constantine believed that the CIA had grown too large, and after the 1970s turmoil too ineffective, to run operations that should properly be left to non-intelligence agencies, non-governmental organizations, and the private sector. People in captive nations risked compromise or arrest if they took money or instruction in a CIA covert political operation, but by the 1980s risked few such dangers if the funds were openly provided by a non-intelligence entity. Just as Radio Free Europe/Radio Liberty had been spun off from the CIA into independent corporate entities funded by Congress in the 1950s, so should American support for foreign political parties, media outlets, social movements, and so forth in the fight against Soviet international subversion. The covert became overt.

Meanwhile, my relationship with the Salvadoran army grew to the point that I gained unusual access to battlefield intelligence, including documents captured from the backpacks of captured or killed FMLN members, even at times when the Salvadorans had grown tense with the U.S. embassy. Constantine wasn't interested in tactical minutiae, only in Soviet big-picture evidence. I had no knowing contact with any CIA officer anywhere except for Constantine in his role as a senior White House official who reported outside official channels directly to Casey.

And with good reason: Constantine didn't trust many of his colleagues at the CIA. Nor did Angelo Codevilla. Nor did Casey, who had engaged in a public battle with CIA analysts miraculously unable to link the Soviet Union to the sponsorship of international terrorism.

Amateurs against Traitors

So by the mid-1980s I operated as a privately funded amateur collecting documentation of Soviet support for terrorists and insurgents. I infiltrated and attempted to disrupt the World Peace Council, a Soviet front organization, and took part in a few other activities, because for some reason the official channels weren't always working. I was told just to collect the latest Kremlin propaganda materials and not to be disruptive. But when I saw some British friends from the Crozier network who were organizing a massive disruption to wreck the $50 million event, I jumped right in.

As a part of the United States Peace Council delegation, I met a Communist operative from California named Barbara Lee, then a congressional aide. She called herself "Comrade Barbara" and went around affectionately addressing certain others as "Comrade," which I understood to be a mutual recognition of loyal party membership. She gushed over a short, oily man from India whom she called Comrade Romesh. It was Romesh Chandra, a high-level KGB agent who headed the World Peace Council. Comrade Barbara is now a senior member of Congress.[1]

It was never clear during this freewheeling adventure why the CIA didn't have its own human assets to do this fairly easy and fun activity, or why the unclassified intelligence products that I'd seen missed a lot of the obvious. Part of the problem was the nature of bureaucracies. Part was institutional turf-fighting. Part ideological or political bias. Part simply poor analysis and the groupthink that reinforced it. And part was far more sinister.

At that same time, in Defense Intelligence Agency headquarters in Washington, the lead analyst for Nicaragua and El Salvador toiled busily day and night on the Central American wars. She was a dour, spindly woman born at a U.S. military base in Germany. Four of her family members reportedly worked for the FBI. She lived alone by the National Zoo. She never got my information because I had circumvented official channels.

This DIA analyst also worked for the other side. She passed American secrets to an intelligence officer for the Cuban government. She was an ideological Communist spy.

Her name was Ana Belén Montes.[2]

She wasn't the only traitor. There were more in the FBI, CIA, and elsewhere. But the attitude at both the FBI and CIA in those years was one of smug invincibility. They believed themselves clever and careful, and this belief propagating through their bureaucratic culture convinced them that no hostile spies could penetrate them. And if I said any differently at the time, I was obviously terribly misinformed, if not maliciously set against the bureau or the agency. These institutions were sacred and could not be challenged. Because they had the secrets. And I did not.

Chapter 3

"Most Irregular" Research on Soviet Intelligence

After I spent two years studying how to recognize and combat Soviet disinformation under former Soviet-bloc intelligence officer Ladislav Bittman at Boston University's Disinformation Documentation Center, and then three years studying the real-time changes in the Soviet KGB under Professor Uri Ra'anan at BU's Institute for the Study of Conflict, Ideology, and Policy, an academic press published my doctoral dissertation.

My research methodology was "most irregular" but always brought a smile to the somberly serious Professor Ra'anan. It involved several trips to Moscow during the Soviet collapse of 1991 and the aftermath in 1992 and 1993, with rare interviews and discussions with dozens of active and former Soviet KGB foreign intelligence, internal security, political police, and other officers and their victims. Former Soviet dissidents and political prisoners, human rights activists, elected members of the Supreme Soviet and the Russian State Duma, Russian investigative journalists, and foreign activists helped me in my work. It was primary source information. Many of them had ransacked or otherwise pillaged secret KGB and Soviet Communist Party documents from unsecured offices. I brought back bags of classified KGB documents and manuals, some of KGB chairman Yuri Andropov's briefings to the Politburo, and other material. I was one of the few Westerners at the time who got unofficial access into the ghostly Lubyanka headquarters of the KGB.

My dissertation, the first scholarly work of its kind, was published in 1994 as *Secret Empire: The KGB in Russia Today.*

Despite the book's new information, public interest had almost evaporated in anything except the warmest wishful thinking about Russia's future. My unpopular and sometimes ridiculed view was that the former KGB had positioned itself to take over the Russian economy and state. HarperCollins publishing house had bought Westview, the publisher of my dissertation, and the accountants ordered slow-selling books like mine to be recycled as pulp.

Secret Empire got some good endorsements, including a cover pitch by former national security adviser Zbigniew Brzezinski and my former professor Jack Dziak, and a scholarly review by General William Odom, a formidable Sovietologist and former director of the National Security Agency.

Of all the FBI agents and analysts assigned to watch the KGB, only one had actually read the book and sought me out to learn more. This fairly senior FBI man, a counterintelligence supervisory special agent named Bob, had become interested in my work. He also wanted to know about what I did *not* put in the book. He demonstrated an unusually deep and broad knowledge of the KGB. I was enthused to be able to put my academic experience in the service of FBI counterintelligence.

Bob invited me to his office at the State Department, where he served as the bureau's man overseeing foreign embassies and other diplomatic missions in Washington. He invited me many times to his house for lasagna dinner with his wife and children. He often took me out to lunch. Bob was a big, rather odd guy, with an awkward, toothy smile and a tendency to try to dominate physically. But he had a lot of stories and shared deep insights and information. And he asked endless questions, not interrogative but intellectual and philosophical. He handed me a couple of pocket-sized, unclassified State Department booklets with a key to all the prefixes of the diplomatic license plates issued to each foreign embassy in Washington, so I could tell which car was from which embassy.

Awkward Moment with FBI Director Freeh and an Agent Named Bob

A few years later, in December 2000, Bob and I chatted at a family Christmas party at the school that our sons attended. FBI director Louis Freeh's son studied at the same school. As Bob and I stood a few feet from the Christmas dinner buffet table talking shop once more about KGB stuff—it had now been almost a year since a Chekist named Vladimir Putin had taken control of Russia's government, confirming a warning in my academic research—Freeh walked into the room, alone. He was going to give a talk to all the dads and their sons. He saw Bob. Instead of saying hello, he made a beeline for the buffet.

"Louie's a good guy, but he doesn't know anything about CI," Bob said, using CI as shorthand for counterintelligence. I asked him to introduce me to Freeh before his presentation. He said I should just introduce myself. So I tried to strike up a conversation with Freeh at the buffet. We were the only two at the table. I stood two feet across from him. But Freeh kept his gaze fixed into the chafing dishes. He wouldn't even look at me.

Returning with my plate, I said to Bob, "Everyone always said that Freeh's a really nice guy. He's pretty rude."

Bob countered that, no, Freeh was indeed a nice guy, but agreed that tonight he did seem a little uptight and out of character. Again he said, rather smugly and gratuitously, "Louie doesn't know anything about CI."

A few weeks later, in January 2001 during a lunch break one day, Bob walked from the State Department on Twenty-third Street to my office on Sixteenth Street up from the White House, at the Institute of World Politics, a graduate school where I was the Annenberg Professor of International Communication. He seemed uncharacteristically happy—not in his usual smug and awkward way, but free and almost giddy.

"I've been reassigned to headquarters," he announced. He didn't know what his job would be, but he said that being back at the J. Edgar Hoover Building, where he claimed to have written the FBI's accounting software system years before, would look great on his resume before his planned retirement. "I don't have computer skills in my personnel record, so this will be beneficial," he said, noting the tech boom in the Washington, D.C., area and musing about a post-FBI career. The antiquated bureau wasn't known for its digital acumen. We both chatted in the lobby for five or ten minutes; then he abruptly announced it was time to walk back to the State Department.

That was the last time I ever saw Bob. Within days, while taking a different kind of walk in his northern Virginia neighborhood, he learned the hard way that Louis Freeh did know something about CI after all.

"What took you so long?" Bob taunted the FBI agents who arrested him. From that day, Bob would be known to the world by his full, now infamous name: Robert Philip Hanssen.[1]

Director Freeh's Side of the Story

Freeh would write about the Christmas father-son evening in his memoir. "There I was on the small stage, waiting to speak and knowing that the man sitting in front of me had sold his nation down the river; and there Bob Hanssen was, sitting by his son in the front row, not having the least idea that we had finally cracked his cover. I don't think I ever showed it that evening—I certainly hope I didn't—but the longer I sat, the angrier I got," Freeh recalled.

"His crimes were going to come crashing down not just on his own very deserving head but also on the head of the unsuspecting boy sitting next to him as well as his wife and the rest of his family. To me, that was almost as unforgivable as the espionage itself."[2]

No wonder the FBI director wasn't up for a Christmas buffet table chat.

After the Russian spy's arrest, an interagency Hanssen Damage Assessment Team scoured everything it could to get a handle on the full extent of the destruction from the FBI man's treason. By that time, late 2001 or 2002, in the aftermath of 9/11, Robert S. Mueller III was director.

Rude Awakening: What the FBI Didn't Want to Know

During my years as a working journalist at a weekly magazine published by the *Washington Times*, Hanssen had provided me material of an extremely sensitive nature. He did it, he said, to see if I could be trusted, and so I would know the terrible burdens of keeping secrets. I revealed none of it to anyone. After his arrest, I offered it all, including the physical laptop containing decrypted data received from Hanssen's at-home server, to the Hanssen Damage Assessment Team. Six times. At my employer's instructions, since I was a working journalist, I did it through Akin Gump Strauss Hauer & Feld, a major Washington law firm that represented the *Washington Times*. The FBI showed no interest. Separately, two teams of FBI special agents came to visit me, but they didn't seek the laptop.

I recounted this in 2004 at a McCormick Foundation counterintelligence conference during a chance meeting with the CIA's counterintelligence chief, Paul Redmond. Redmond had headed the Hanssen Damage Assessment Team. During a walk outside, I told him about my attempts to provide my computer to the FBI.

"So you're the guy with the laptop," Redmond said. The Hanssen Damage Assessment Team was closed down. He said cryptically, or so I understood him as saying, that Hanssen's betrayal was so devastating that the FBI didn't want to know its true cost after all. Too much to handle. The bureau just wanted to tidy things up and move on.

Spending Years with Living History

My first direct experience with FBI political correctness came after I helped start a jihadist awareness training program for the bureau in about 2005. Director Robert S. Mueller III presented each of us with a signed citation for our "extraordinary service" to the FBI. PC culture was seeping in. Under pressure from the Muslim Brotherhood and other jihadist sympathizers who felt offended and said the program was racist and bigoted, the FBI shut it down.

There's no school like the old school. For years during and after college, I took every opportunity possible to sit down with old-timers from the FBI, the CIA, the OSS, and friendly foreign intelligence services. These meetings were just conversations, always presumed to be off the record, so I took no notes. The many late nights with living history profoundly refined my worldview. I got to know the people who had worked for, and with, J. Edgar Hoover and "Wild Bill" Donovan.

Both the bureau, as built by Hoover, and the OSS with Donovan as its sole leader, emerged in times of world war and national emergency, of foreign-sponsored political subversion and covert manipulation of American politics and decision-making. They were as essential as they were imperfect. They were led by honorable men with human frailties. They served as America's eyes and ears against foreign enemies, and as the hands with which to defeat them.

Hoover built the FBI primarily as a domestic intelligence service with police powers, and secondarily as a law enforcement agency. The Bureau of Investigation had functioned since 1908 without an act of Congress or a legislative charter, its founding document a vague one-page memorandum about special agents by an attorney general named Bonaparte. The OSS would come decades later, as the United States entered World War II, only to be shut down after the war ended, to be replaced, with a few years' gap, by the new Central Intelligence Agency.

Hoover and Donovan were personal rivals before becoming the giants of their times. Both were patriots with very different views of national security threats to the United States. Those divergent outlooks mattered with the rise of the Soviet Union. Hoover saw the threats clearly—not simply as matters of upholding the law or combating foreign agents, but as matters of preserving America's national character and founding principles. He understood foreign subversion against the country was seeking to destroy Americans' belief in themselves.

Donovan understood subversion, too, but in an opposite way: against a foreign enemy in wartime. He seemed not to see domestic threats from the Soviet side at all. And so began the bipolarity of American foreign intelligence, the "no enemies on the left" mentality that foreign enemies would exploit then as now, the battlespace through subversion that would fundamentally transform America long after the

Soviet Union collapsed by injecting our society with critical theory and cultural Marxism.

CIA director Bill Casey's OSS experience showed him the need for alternate sources of intelligence outside official channels as a quality check against the existing bureaucracy of collectors and analysts. Like Donovan, he liked amateurs. He wanted the CIA to collect intelligence that the agency establishment, for whatever reason, would not. And to analyze that intelligence in ways that it could not. Just as inside critics accused him of politicizing intelligence, Casey himself saw that intelligence was already politicized and substandard. He had no way of knowing just how politicized his beloved agency, to say nothing of the FBI, would ultimately become.

Though Donovan was older than Hoover, both got their starts in security or intelligence at about the same time, during and after World War I and the Bolshevik Revolution in Russia. Donovan did so as a private citizen collecting intelligence, and Hoover as a government official making sense of dangers to the country.

Here begins the story of America's standing foreign intelligence and counterintelligence services, what would become the FBI and the CIA. This time also marks the beginning of the Soviets' strategy to destroy America from within, which Donovan seemed not to comprehend but which Hoover understood all along.

Part I

"Wild Bill" Donovan, the Bolsheviks, and J. Edgar Hoover

"I want you people here to organize and keep organizing until you are able to overthrow the damned rotten capitalistic government of this country."

—Leon Trotsky, New York City, March 1917

Chapter 4

Donovan, Pancho Villa, and German Secret Codes

William J. Donovan lived large as the ultimate warrior gentleman adventurer. The 1905 Columbia College graduate built an influential law practice from his hometown in Buffalo, New York. Grandson of Irish Catholic immigrants at a time when being Irish and Catholic was not socially acceptable in much of the country, the handsome and dashing Donovan married an attractive, socially networked wife whose personal attributes and well-to-do Protestant family took off some of prejudice's edge.

Donovan's fast mind and drive made him an extraordinarily high achiever. While building what would become a powerful firm, he founded a cavalry unit for the New York National Guard. Then, in 1914, the Great War broke out in Europe. This provided an opportunity to go international. With the war raging but the United States still neutral, Donovan steamed to Berlin on a Rockefeller Foundation contract to open routes for humanitarian aid to refugees in stricken countries.

But there was trouble closer to home. A revolution and civil war had been tearing Mexico apart, with various factions fighting for power. In the fall of 1915, President Woodrow Wilson unofficially recognized one faction as Mexico's legitimate government. The Germans had also backed that faction. Five months later, the audacious General Pancho Villa attacked the United States to provoke an American invasion to benefit his tactical position against the dominant, ruling faction.

Donovan returned home from Europe only to be called to active duty to lead his National Guard cavalry unit to the Mexican frontier. The United States Army was more of a constabulary force than an expeditionary force at the time, and relied on the National Guard against substantial Mexican forces. Donovan joined Brigadier General John "Black Jack" Pershing to hunt down Villa.

But Villa, with his trademark wide sombrero and machine gun bandolier belt crossing his chest, and a Hollywood film crew to record his escapades, drew the Americans deeper into Mexico and escaped. Wilson withdrew the troops and Donovan returned to New York.

For two more years, the British threw everything and everyone they had at the Central Powers of Germany, Austria-Hungary, and Turkey. The Western European countries lay crushed. Only Britain remained intact, but barely so.

Intel and Information Wars Transform the Twentieth Century

While Donovan and his cavalrymen were hunting Pancho Villa, Wilson was running for reelection under the slogan "He Kept Us Out of War"—even though he desperately wanted to invade Europe to spread democracy. During the campaign, in the summer of 1916, German agents blew up a huge military supply depot in New York, with a blast that would have measured higher than 5 on the Richter scale and was felt as far away as Maryland. Even this terrible act of war had not persuaded the public or Congress that it was in America's vital interest to send millions of troops to fight overseas. But German attacks and British pro-war propaganda—along with the president's own progressive idealism—made neutrality increasingly difficult. The British became more desperate for American intervention on their behalf. They needed to exploit a crisis or manufacture a provocation. This was where the clever use of intelligence came in.

London had long been able to intercept German diplomatic and military communications linking the world through undersea cables. Their codebreakers had cracked the German codes. The result of that persistent mathematical genius was one of Britain's deepest secrets.

The Germans were equally desperate to keep the United States out. They faced a two-front war against Britain and remaining continental allies to the west and the immense Russian Empire to the east. Like Mexico, Imperial Russia was tearing itself apart in revolution and civil war. The tsar's empire teetered on collapse.

The German leadership devised a plan to bog down America in its own hemisphere. Foreign Minister Arthur Zimmermann sent an encrypted telegram to his minister in Mexico in January of 1917, outlining an audacious strategy. Zimmermann informed his embassy in Mexico City that Berlin would arm the dominant Mexican faction to reclaim lost territories by invading the United States.

Germany would align militarily with Mexico and Imperial Japan. And it would resume unrestricted submarine warfare to sink American civilian ships.

By forcing the Americans to defend their own southern border and national territory with their small army, protect Atlantic shipping from German U-boats, and secure their vital trade routes with Asia, Berlin would foil British efforts to draw the United States into the war in Europe.

Meanwhile, exiled Russian revolutionaries worked Americans over whom they had influence to stay out of the war to allow the Germans to keep grinding away at the armies of Tsar Nicholas II. U.S. support for the British and their near-defeated Western European allies would strengthen the British, French, Belgian, neutral Dutch, and other "imperialists," potentially taking pressure off the Russian imperial government, a pressure that the Russian revolutionaries, like the German high command, wanted to maintain.

American public opinion became the battlespace of the warring European powers.

Bolshevism in New York

Many of the larger eastern coastal cities of the United States, especially New York, had become home to radicalized European exiles and "refugees" who had infiltrated among the cold, huddled masses. They brought their anarchist, socialist, Communist, and other anti-American politics with them. One of those exiles, a visitor who had arrived by steamer on January 13, 1917, already enjoyed notoriety among the most extremist immigrants, mainly among German, Jewish, Polish, and Russian newcomers. He had tried to overthrow the tsarist government a dozen years earlier.

His name was Lev Bronstein. He went by the name Leon Trotsky.

Trotsky visited New York not as an immigrant or refugee. "My only profession in New York was that of a revolutionary socialist," he later wrote.[1] The night of his arrival, he joined another Bolshevik, Leonid Bukharin, to visit the grand New York Public Library. Trotsky would use the library as a base for revolutionary research. The United States had little ability to screen violent extremist foreigners at the time, let alone deport them. That left Trotsky and other foreigners free to agitate for Wilson to honor his reelection promise to keep the United States out of the war in Europe.

A short, mustachioed man with wild, wavy hair who sported a goatee to conceal his cleft chin, Trotsky lived for three months in the Bronx. In that short time, he "became one of New York's leading voices against entering the World War," according to historian Kenneth D. Ackerman. He addressed "packed crowds at the Brooklyn Lyceum, Manhattan's Beethoven Hall, the Labor Temple near Union Square and similar venues."[2]

The U.S. Socialist Party gave Trotsky a formal post to shape the party position on what members should do in case of war. The party had intended to represent the American working class, but in New York its membership was mainly radical immigrants who combined Old World prejudices with no American identity. Trotsky shared platforms at an anti-war protest with American socialist leader Eugene Debs.

British intelligence agents in New York watched Trotsky's every move. Their Trotsky file began with warnings from the allied French secret service. While Trotsky and his Communist allies ran influence campaigns to reinforce the American people's tendency to stay out of the war, the British ran campaigns of their own for American boys to save the British empire (though the propaganda framed it very differently), reinforcing Wilson's idealistic and globalist words urging to "fight for democracy."

The Zimmermann Telegram and Leon Trotsky

Three days after Trotsky's arrival in New York, on January 16, German foreign minister Zimmermann sent what would become his infamous telegram to Mexico.

It took British cryptographers a while to break the coded message, one of many German cables being cracked at the time. The United Kingdom and United States did not enjoy the special relationship they would later develop. By this time, Britain's back was to the wall, the existence of the empire at stake.

With covert knowledge of Germany's plan to invite a world war against the United States if it supported its European enemies, the British made a last-ditch gamble. They decided to pass along one of their deepest secrets to the Americans and worse, to make it public, at the cost of alerting the enemy. The knowledge contained in the telegram was important, but the real secret was that Britain had broken the German code. The British could fire only one political shot such as this. They went for the kill.

In late February, British officials revealed to Wilson representatives in London that they had cracked the enemy's codes and that the decrypts revealed the German conspiracy to place the United States on a three-front defensive war on the Atlantic, Pacific, and Mexican border. The British reputation for ruthless cleverness was well earned.

With the tool he needed to justify a congressional declaration of war, Wilson had the Zimmermann telegram released to the press on March 1. The operative part of the German foreign minister's short message stated, "We make Mexico a proposal of alliance on the following basis: make war together, make peace together, generous financial support and an understanding on our part that Mexico is to reconquer the lost territory in Texas, New Mexico, and Arizona."[3]

Many Americans, including leaders in Washington, wondered if the secret message was a British fabrication to dupe the country into a foreign war. Then the Germans, with their famous formality, conveniently solved the mystery. The sincerely gentlemanly Foreign Minister Zimmermann confirmed that the decrypted telegram was real.

Marxist Meltdown

In New York, Trotsky foamed with rage. Some of his key American socialist allies suddenly broke their stance on neutrality, and now supported Wilson's desire for war with Germany. The Russian felt personally betrayed. He loudly attacked his American hosts. Fellow comrades, he thought, were in fact bourgeois imperialists. American intervention in France would divert more German troops to France and relieve the forces of his enemy, Imperial Russia.[4]

Then, just over a week later, came another blockbuster. Rival revolutionaries to Trotsky had overthrown Tsar Nicholas II and his imperial regime. The provisional democratic socialist government led by Alexander Kerensky took its place. But Kerensky wanted to continue Russia's war against Germany.

That was enough for Trotsky. A New York police agent wrote down the angry revolutionary's words: "I am going back to Russia to overthrow the Provisional Government there and stop the war with Germany. I want you people here to organize and keep organizing until you are able to overthrow the damned rotten capitalistic government of this country."[5]

New York City police had no arrest or deportation authority for matters like this. No federal institution existed to arrest Trotsky in New York for sedition or conspiracy to overthrow the Constitution and turn him over for prosecution and judgment. Indeed, almost no federal law existed in this regard. The Justice Department had some small offices far off in Washington: an Alien Enemy Bureau with the colossal job of identifying and rounding up hundreds of thousands of German nationals, and a handful of detectives in a little unit called the Bureau of Investigation. The "Federal" part would come much later.

Had there been a full-fledged FBI and a proper set of laws to enforce, the bureau could have changed history by nabbing the most important Russian Communist leader next to Vladimir Lenin before his revolution could take place. The would-be founder of the Red Army might have served a long sentence up the Hudson River at Sing Sing.

With the ultimate overthrow of the United States government still on his mind, Trotsky steamed back to Europe, by way of Nova Scotia, to wage his promised revolution.

Meanwhile, Germany resumed sinking American ships, each sinking an act of war. In April of 1917, President Wilson asked Congress to declare war on Germany and the other Central Powers. He signed executive orders for the Justice Department to monitor, detain, and imprison, without due process, any foreigner considered a threat to the United States.

While the Americans prepared to fortify the Allies in Western Europe, the Hun exploited Russia's internal turmoil. Germany would benefit from cutting a deal with Trotsky's comrades who were hiding out in Switzerland and across Europe. The German General Staff and Reichsbank stoked those fanatics led by the exiled Vladimir Lenin, put them on a train, and sent them to Russia.

That faction, which would call itself the Bolsheviks, agreed with its capitalist German patrons to a separate peace with Berlin. The Bolsheviks would enable Germany to focus on its Western Front and slaughter the fresh American liberators. Under Lenin, the Bolsheviks, giving deathly life to the civilization-destroying theories of Karl Marx, ousted Russia's fledgling socialist democracy in October and November of 1917, launching the revolution that Trotsky had promised in New York.

Trotsky became war commissar of Bolshevik Russia. Two months later, he founded and commanded the Red Army.

Chapter 5

Global Revolution

Taking over a country's domestic intelligence service and police powers, or creating an entirely new internal security apparat, is the first vital step for any revolutionary group to put the population under control. Before Trotsky created the Red Army, the Bolsheviks established a secret police, the All-Russian Extraordinary Commission for Combating Counterrevolution and Sabotage, the notorious Cheka, to root out opponents and murder everyone in their way. Feliks Dzerzhinsky and his Chekists, as the "sword and shield" of the Communist Party, would make war against the people under their domination, tear down Russian civilization, and within five years build the Union of Soviet Socialist Republics.

As they built their one-party state, Russia's Communist leaders always kept their eye on what they wanted the entire world to look like politically. Dzerzhinsky never let his internal war distract him from shaping the rest of the world once the great Western powers ended their hostilities. The Bolsheviks' separate peace with Germany allowed Berlin to move its forces from the Russian front to fight the Americans, Canadians, British, and French in the west. The Bolsheviks, in turn, could build their Soviet republic and empire without worrying about a German enemy. Indeed, a peaceful Germany weakened after the war would become a prize, or so the Soviets thought.

Within months of war's end, in early 1919, Lenin's Bolsheviks erected a huge global apparatus to spread Communist subversion and revolution and take advantage of postwar tensions to tear down entire civilizations worldwide. That apparat was called the Third International, or more popularly the Communist International, in Soviet shorthand the Comintern.

The Cheka would embed its foreign espionage and operational cadres into the Comintern's growing political network. In time, with its sword-and-shield crest to herald its weaponization on behalf of the ruling party, it would change its name and structure: the GPU/OGPU of Lenin and Stalin, the NKVD of Stalin, the Soviet KGB, and ultimately the Federal Security Service and Foreign Intelligence Service of post-Soviet Russia—Vladimir Putin's FSB and SVR. All with the same sword-and-shield coat of arms. Always calling themselves *Chekisti*, or Chekists.[1]

Before long, the Chekists would have their eyes on Wild Bill Donovan. And from Washington, a young Department of Justice official would have his eyes on Cheka and Comintern agents and assets in America. The young man was John Edgar Hoover.

Wild Bill and Hoover Fight World War I and Its Aftermath

Donovan left his New York law practice in early 1917 to deploy to France to fight the Germans. Just a couple years before, he had been in Berlin on the Rockefeller Foundation refugee relief account. Now, fresh from his horseback pursuits of Pancho Villa in Mexico, Donovan would lead infantry troops against formidable German forces in France.

Germany's industrialized war machine had ripped apart the fresh-faced Americans with ghastly casualties on the French battlefield. Under relentless enemy fire, Donovan reorganized his chopped-up men and joined them personally on the front lines. He led with no apparent regard for his own safety. An enemy gunner shot him in the knee, but the determined Donovan refused to leave the field until his men could find shelter from the murderous maelstrom of bullets and shrapnel. Donovan's brashness, courage, and superhuman endurance earned him the Medal of Honor and, perhaps more importantly, his nickname, "Wild Bill."

Tackling Sedition: The Rise of J. Edgar Hoover

As Donovan deployed that spring, back in Washington Congress passed the Espionage Act to empower the Justice Department to arrest, detain, and deport enemy spies and agents. Wilson's executive orders gave the department virtual free reign. The department's War Emergency Division, responsible for protecting against enemy sabotage of industries and critical infrastructure, would be in charge.

The Alien Enemy Bureau nested in the Justice Department's War Emergency Division. That small unit compiled lists, monitored, and arranged for the roundups of suspected foreigners from enemy nations. No due process needed.

J. Edgar Hoover, age twenty-two, graduated from law school that spring. He registered for the wartime draft. But he came to prominence as a civilian on the home front rather than as an infantryman in France. He received a job at the Alien Enemy Bureau.

It was a wartime domestic intelligence job, not law enforcement. The hardworking Hoover put in seven days a week with endless energy and precision. He impressed his superiors, who repeatedly promoted him, and quickly.

The Justice Department contained another small bureau of interest, too. At the time it was called the Bureau of Investigation.

Raised on Capitol Hill in the Age of "Manly Vigor"

Born in a row house in an integrated neighborhood on Capitol Hill, Hoover grew up in the shadow of the great neoclassical palace of Congress. That place and time prepared Hoover for his most unusual life. The Hoover family, descendants of German and Swiss immigrants to Pennsylvania, had lived in Washington since the British had burned the city in the War of 1812.

Most of the Hoovers worked in government service as messengers and clerks. Edgar's father was a printing plate maker for the U.S. Coast and Geodetic Survey. As a boy, Edgar delivered groceries from Eastern Market and learned that the faster and harder he worked, the more tips he earned.[2] He excelled in his studies. He taught Sunday school. Edgar pushed himself hard. His rapid pattern of speech or his efficiency as a messenger and delivery boy earned him the nickname "Speed." He led his high school cadet corps and graduated as valedictorian.

Washington was a growing but still small city. President Theodore Roosevelt, the former New York police commissioner, dominated politics during Hoover's childhood, with police reform a major political issue. So was the threat of terrorism and extremism; anarchist violence plagued big cities, and TR himself had become president after an anarchist gunned down President William McKinley. A would-be assassin later shot Roosevelt in the chest, the bullet ricocheting off a steel eyeglass case in the president's breast pocket. Roosevelt finished his speech.

The Hoover family joined the annual city tradition in which anyone could visit the White House unannounced on New Year's Day—Edgar's birthday—to drop in on the president. Roosevelt fascinated local children with his exotic pet zoo, including a bear, a hyena, and a macaw, on the White House grounds. Hoover once went as a teenager to meet President William Howard Taft.[3] The nation's political news was local. Roosevelt personified the virtues of a man's man, a self-reliant American who picked himself up from childhood sickliness to live a life of courage and what he called "manly vigor."

Edgar took it all in. As a boy, he ran a typewritten neighborhood children's newspaper. His *Weekly Review* featured profiles of virtuous, great men who had overcome adversity, collections of Benjamin Franklin's famous quotations for better living, announcements of prominent wedding engagements and retirement parties for public officials, and dry chronicles of local crime and sudden death.

He grew up watching the construction of the neoclassical marble wonders of the Senate and House office buildings flanking the Capitol, the House building just steps from his cramped family house. In high school, he developed a military-style discipline. He led his cadets in President Woodrow Wilson's first inauguration parade. Raised as a devout Presbyterian, Edgar showed a missionary streak. He almost followed in his brother's footsteps to become a Christian preacher on the Washington waterfront. But he found another calling.

Files, Archives, and Instruments of Power

The breathtaking, newly finished Library of Congress building, a splendidly ornate Greco-Roman temple of knowledge built of Massachusetts granite, fascinated Edgar as it would any visitor. It occupied an entire block across the street from the Capitol. Over time the library drew Edgar to the value of thorough files and extensive archives, all painstakingly indexed for easy reference. Three-by-five-inch index cards, each hand-typed or written in India ink, mounted securely on steel rods set in long hardwood drawers, each drawer arranged in tables and racks, and each of those in galleries, became his database.

Hoover got clerk and messenger jobs at the Library of Congress to work his way at night through the George Washington University Law School. The library taught him how to store and efficiently retrieve massive amounts of information through elaborate classification indices. The experience schooled him in the ways of Congress and the eccentricities of politicians and the legislative process. Hoover got to know lawmakers and their small staffs. At a time when members of Congress often lived in Capitol Hill boarding houses amid the working-class row houses, congressmen were Hoover's neighbors.

Edgar knew the federal government's whole political and administrative system and what made it tick. The system was minuscule compared to what it would become. Hoover understood that people with human failings formed the basis for upholding constitutional principles of a government by the consent of the governed. Those failings could be addressed or they could be exploited, for better or for worse.

Running the Alien Enemy Bureau

Without being part of any political group or power structure, and as a normal matter of course for someone raised on Capitol Hill, Hoover registered for the draft in the summer of 1917 and, with his new law degree, got a job at the Justice Department. His father, who had battled severe depression, became dysfunctional, making Edgar the breadwinner. Mental illness was a forbidden subject for most people at the time, and Edgar, like many, viewed it as a sign of weakness and moral failure. Long after his elder brother and sister moved away, he stayed home to care for both his parents. He maintained the family honor by keeping secret his father's mental health condition. Fidelity mattered. Bravery and integrity protected fidelity.

In 1918, Hoover earned a promotion to run the Alien Enemy Bureau to lead the fight against anarchists and Marxists. He was twenty-three years old. At least 6,500 German nationals sat confined in camps under his authority, with another 450,000 under some kind of monitoring.[4]

Weeks before the Bolsheviks swept over Russia in November 1917, and mindful of the influx of agitators from abroad, Congress amended immigration law to protect against foreign extremists wracking America.

All "aliens who disbelieve in or advocate or teach the overthrow by force or violence of the Government of the United States shall be deported," the law said, adding that "aliens who are members of or affiliated with any organization that entertains a belief in, teaches, or advocates the overthrow by force or violence of the Government of the United States shall be deported."[5] Then came the Sedition Act of 1918, which would ensnare socialist labor organizer Eugene Debs, who had shared the platform the year before with Trotsky.

The new wartime laws meant a huge amount of work at the relatively tiny Justice Department. Alien Enemy Bureau chief Hoover immersed himself completely in the mission.

DOJ Intelligence Unit with Police Powers

At age twenty-four, shortly after the Armistice of November 11, 1918, Hoover earned a promotion to head the Justice Department's General Intelligence Division, popularly known as the Radical Division. Its job was to hunt down extremists and others—mainly anarchists, radical socialists, and Communists, both American-born and foreign-born—who sought to subvert American constitutional government. Part of the job involved collecting information from local police departments. Hoover would then draw up lists of suspected anarchists and other subversives responsible for violence and other illegal agitation.

The Roaring Twenties had not yet arrived. Unemployment, inflation, vicious labor strikes, race riots, and terrorist bombings scarred the early postwar years. All made worse by a deadly influenza pandemic.

Terrorists mailed bombs to a U.S. senator and the mayor of Seattle, with a New York postal worker the next day finding sixteen more explosive packages bound for prominent political and business leaders. An anarchist terrorist bombed the home of Attorney General A. Mitchell Palmer in June 1919, shaking the neighbors, the young Franklin and Eleanor Roosevelt. That day, coordinated attacks struck political figures, judges, and police officers in eight cities across the country.[6]

The public demanded action. Hoover oversaw the deportation of 249 Russian-born anarchists and Communists back to their homeland. He arranged for a recently decommissioned troop transport, the *Buford*, to send them all from a holding center on Ellis Island in New York Harbor to Bolshevik Russia, and brought a group of congressmen with him to watch the deportation. One congressman described young Hoover that night as "a slender bundle of high-charged electric wire." With U.S. soldiers on board as guards, the *Buford* steamed to Helsinki, where Finnish and American troops would take the radicals across the border into Russia and hand them over to Trotsky's Red Army.[7]

That done, Attorney General Palmer and Hoover resolved to round up even more undesirable foreigners and other domestic extremists. Hoover anticipated as many as ten thousand. With the cooperation of local police, in early 1920 the Palmer Raids began to sweep up thousands of suspected subversives, deporting hundreds. But the Palmer Raids suffered from poor planning, often inadequate or wrong intelligence, and bad communication. Problems plagued the lawmen at every turn, from issuing warrants to making arrests. Innocent people, mostly immigrants who spoke little or no English, got swept up while bad ones got away. Many Americans thought the roundups had gone too far.

Some might say that the Palmer Raids failed to go far enough. The month before, in Moscow, at about the time the *Buford* was making its way to Finland, the Soviet regime began organizing its machinery for international aggression. It founded its global Comintern network that would send Kremlin agents and operatives into the United States and organize radicals into disciplined Soviet assets.

Inside the United States, the foreign enemies of the Constitution would mobilize immigrants and American citizens already predisposed toward the Bolsheviks, carefully recruiting hundreds or perhaps thousands as agents of the Red Army's GRU military intelligence and the Cheka and its successors. Those assets would organize. They would propagandize. They would agitate. They would infiltrate. They would subvert. They would spy. And they would influence far beyond their own small cadres.

Palmer hadn't commanded or controlled those raids. Hoover had. Faced with the backlash, Hoover learned valuable lessons and gained experience of how to survive every political crisis and transition.

Like a warrior monk, Hoover lived an ascetic life, wedded to the constant work of his unique mission. As a loyal son, he stayed at home to care for his parents, which he would continue to do until his mother died when he was forty-three.

Hoover Leads America's Fight against Marxism

In the months after the Palmer Raids, there were two notable developments. First, liberal and progressive jurists founded a group called the American Civil Liberties Union (ACLU) to defend accused foreign anarchists and Communists and protect their rights to agitate and subvert. Second, Hoover started to become a national figure as the vanguard against extremist subversion of the United States. Now twenty-five years old, Hoover made his first official report to Congress under a Great War–era anti-subversion law. In support of Attorney General Palmer's testimony, Hoover presented an intensive, well-organized, carefully detailed document that showed sophistication and nuance.

Under the simple signature "J. E. Hoover," he told Congress that the Socialist Party in the United States, composed largely of immigrants who had exported their Central European ideologies to their new home, had split. One branch advocated the Bolshevik tactics inspired by Trotsky in New York and reconstituted as the Communist Party USA. Hoover provided as evidence the revolutionary faction's 1918 manifesto, and quoted part in his narrative report:

> Revolutionary Socialists hold, with the founders of scientific Socialism, that there are two dominant classes in society—the bourgeoisie and the proletariat; that between these two classes a struggle must go on until the working class, through the seizure of the instruments of production and distribution, the abolition of the capitalist state, and the establishment of the dictatorship of the proletariat, creates a Socialist system. Revolutionary Socialists do not believe that they can be voted into power. They struggle for the conquest of power by the revolutionary proletariat.[8]

On the heels of the anarchist bombings and German sabotage, this new, existential threat to the American way of life captured the public imagination. Many—usually friends or allies of the targets—derided it as a Red Scare, an irrational fear, a phobia.

The German saboteurs undermined the American war effort but had never presented an existential danger to tear apart the country itself. But the Bolsheviks and their allies would overthrow everything, destroying not just the economy but the constitutional republic itself and, even worse, the Judeo-Christian culture upon which it was built. They would build networks of spies, agents, and collaborators in every sector of American society. They were doing it in the United States as they were in postwar Weimar Germany. The tactics of these revolutionary socialists would change over time, sometimes to conform to the Soviet Communist party line, and sometimes diverging or even breaking from it. But the general strategies would remain sound.

A century later, most historians, and a very different FBI in its own official history, would dismiss the Red Scare as "over-hyped."[9] The FBI's present official history never mentions the Cheka or GPU or Kremlin influence operations. These histories would have one believe that reactionary conspiracy theorists of the time had spooked America into a baseless, illogical state of fear.

Chapter 6

Cultural Marxism: An Enemy Like We've Never Seen

Hoover didn't conceive of the threat as a means of finding law-breakers, busting them, and handing them over to prosecutors for their day in court. That was law enforcement. He looked at the threat as a gifted counterintelligence officer would: an opportunity to uncover and neutralize foreign-sponsored attacks on the American Constitution and the country's founding principles, threats to the American way of life including the underlying values that upheld it all, and to smash them.

As socialists made common cause with well-to-do supporters and often became wealthy themselves, they would move from overthrowing the economic system to undermining the culture. The more successful would discard the rich-versus-poor, bourgeoisie-versus-proletariat model for another engine of total wreckage of society, community, church, and family. The battlespace would be not economic, but cultural. It would be an all-of-society attack.

There was also the practical matter of Marxist economic determinism being flat-out wrong, the fact that the working class in upwardly mobile industrialized societies would not "throw off their chains" in violent revolution. Adherents to that tired idea subscribed to the ravings in *The Communist Manifesto* of 1848.

The Original Marx Saw a Cultural Battlespace

Cultural Marxists, however, dug back to Marx's earlier 1843 writings about total war on culture. "I am speaking of a ruthless criticism of all that exists," Marx wrote,[1] or as another translator interpreted it, "the ruthless criticism of the existing order." Marx's goal was not to improve but to destroy: family, human relationships, economics, patriotism, loyalty, morals, religion, Western civilization. Destruction of the entire human existence.

In Marx's words, "Thus, the criticism of Heaven is transformed into a criticism of Earth, the *criticism of religion* into the *criticism of law*, and the *criticism of theology* into the *criticism of politics*," denigrating Western civilization and culture.[2]

That irreconcilable cultural warfare approach would become known as "cultural Marxism." Adherents called its philosophical basis—the logical trains of thought that would lead people to accept and pursue cultural Marxist conclusions—"critical theory." As opposed to the later Marx, the cultural Marxist originalists would tear apart societies not by economic class and the hard currency of capital, but by religion, law, race, family, tradition, knowledge, patriotism, and beliefs.

A "critical" theory is an intellectual set of guidelines to produce thought processes that program people to see the world as being between oppressors and the oppressed, and that the oppressed must rise up and defeat said oppressors.[3] Critical theory would be kneaded, reinvented, and refined over the decades, with help from the Marxist psychosexual interpretations of psychologist Sigmund Freud, to apply to sexuality, gender, race, ethnicity, and beyond.

Definitions are controversial, and critical theorists try to hide the real meaning, going so far as to call cultural Marxism a "right-wing conspiracy theory." So we will stick to the middle-of-the-road *Encyclopaedia Britannica* definition of critical theory: "Marxist-inspired movement in social and political philosophy originally associated with the work of the Frankfurt School. Drawing particularly on the thought of Karl Marx and Sigmund Freud, critical theorists maintain that a primary goal of philosophy is to understand and to help overcome the social structures through which people are dominated and oppressed. . . . Since the 1970s, critical theory has been immensely influential in the study of history, law, literature, and the social sciences."[4]

Under cultural Marxism or critical theory, the wealthy bourgeoisie were no longer the class enemy but, since they have the money in their big foundations to make things happen, a key ally. Economic determinism went out the window. The new class enemy, the new system to be overthrown, was Western society down to its foundations. Those foundations were hewn from the ideas and values of the dead white men of the ancient Hebrews, Greeks, Romans, European Christians, and the American Founding—men in general, white men in particular, and especially straight white men, and the entire "oppressive" society that they created plus anybody who believed in it. All would have to be torn down one way or another.

The working class or proletariat, under cultural Marxism (which was invented by straight white men), would become the "oppressed" minorities: women both natural and artificial, BIPOC (Black, Indigenous, People of Color), people with physical and mental handicaps—as long as they complied intellectually and avoided wrongthink—plus those with any number of lifestyles, genders, imaginary identities, mental illnesses, and fetishes. As their progeny, the cultural Marxists, would teach, the "oppressed" would launch the "seizure of the instruments of production and distribution" and resort to dictatorial means to create some sort of corporatist socialist system. Everything of the past, and everyone believing in the principles of that past, would be discredited, marginalized, and destroyed.

The goal of Marx then, as with his disciples now, demanded the destruction of Judeo-Christian civilization. The cultural Marxists would do this not as violent revolutionaries. That would get them repressed and killed. They would do it quietly within the existing system. They would infiltrate and subvert the system and channel it to attack itself.

Cultural Marxism had not been developed by the time J. Edgar Hoover delivered his first report to Congress in 1920, but the basic theory and strategic design was already understood. Hoover quoted the 1918 revolutionary party manifesto in his appendix to Attorney General Palmer's testimony: "Between the capitalist society and the Communist lies the period of revolutionary transformation of the one into the other."

"This corresponds to a political transition period, in which the state can not be anything else but a dictatorship of the proletariat," the manifesto said, per Hoover's report. Part of the "struggle," it declared, "is the direct struggle for government control. . . . This is a political act." Established Western governments are "nothing less than a machine for the oppression of one class by another and that no less so in a democratic republic than under a monarchy."[5]

Hoover told Congress, "Marx, the spokesman of Communists and the formulator of the original Communist manifesto, explains the class struggle as being an essentially political struggle in that its end is the destruction of the political state, but that the means of accomplishing such an end is not to be accomplished through political means, but by direct and mass action."[6] The Communists knew they could never win through free elections.

"Marx declared that 'the working class can not simply lay hold of the ready-made state machinery and wield it for its own purposes,'" Hoover said. "This machinery must be destroyed. But 'moderate socialism' makes the state the center of its action."[7]

Like none before and few since, Hoover sensed and understood the nature of subversion. Marxist operatives would use every subterfuge to undermine American laws, polarize the country, run influence operations and espionage, and destroy the American way of life. For the most part, it was a foreign enemy. Tracking, disrupting, and uprooting it was an obligatory function of the federal government.

America's defense in 1920 depended almost entirely on twenty-five-year-old J. Edgar Hoover.

Hoover started his lifelong Justice Department career as an intelligence collector, intelligence analyst, and intelligence officer with police powers. Only much later would he become known as a lawman.

High-Society Intelligence

The elegant Wild Bill and Ruth Donovan formed a socially formidable couple wherever they went. Bill had spent so much time away from home on business and on military duty in Mexico and France that, as a postwar consolation of sorts, he told Ruth he would take her on a working vacation anywhere in the world. She chose exotic Japan, Korea, and China.

Touring those countries, Donovan, with a magnetic charm, mingled with top officials, businessmen, and international diplomats. He enjoyed fine drink and fine cigars. He charmed the ladies wherever he went.

He had a distinguished air about him. Even on vacation, he collected business, political, and military intelligence for his law practice and clients. He took a strategic approach to everything.

Deep inland, across the steppes of the Siberian plains and the Russian Far East, fanatical bands of Bolsheviks—Trotsky's Red Army and Dzerzhinsky's Cheka—had murdered their way toward the Pacific to fight their countrymen to the death in the Russian Civil War. Donovan wanted to see for himself.

The civil war in Russia would permanently affect the future of East Asia. Donovan, like most, viewed the Bolsheviks as a strategic threat, not only to business but to the American way of life. Through his new friends in Tokyo and China, he made his way to Siberia to assess the anti-Bolshevik White Russians' ability to resist. Returning to the Japanese capital, the lawyer-adventurer argued to American diplomats that the Russian resisters could hold out with some help.

The diplomats agreed and telegrammed Washington, but the Wilson administration, which had just pulled American troops out of Siberia at the end of the world war, had other priorities. Before long, the Bolsheviks wiped out their internal enemies and turned their aggression outward.

The Donovans returned home. By the summer of 1920, Donovan saw the new and growing Comintern as impacting post–Great War recovery and the international businesses that would drive prosperity. The Bolsheviks and their global Comintern cadres were calling for the heads of political and business leaders in the United States. "The house of Rockefeller and the house of Morgan will fall as has the house of Romanoff in Russia!" an American radical had proclaimed with Trotsky at a Madison Square Garden rally celebrating the overthrow of the tsar.[8]

Donovan got a contract with the giant J. P. Morgan financial house to return to Europe and learn what he could about the Comintern and try to understand what the unprecedented international network meant for free enterprise.[9]

That brief job would be Donovan's first foray into foreign intelligence collection.

The Meeting in Moscow Where It All Began

Moscow, 1922: In the squat, boxy, four-story headquarters of the new Marx-Engels Institute, a small group of Bolshevik and European Communist leaders grappled with the mechanics of how to implant the Marxist idea globally. Their fondest hope was for it to take root quickly in an advanced but demoralized and politically polarized society. The postwar world stewed in fear and uncertainty.

Across Europe, statues came down, place names changed, violent extremists battled police and one another in the streets, and militants sought to overthrow the social order and rewrite history—especially in Russia's former enemy and the Bolsheviks' secret sponsor, Germany.

Leaders arose to challenge or stoke the negative energy for their own purposes. Unlike most individuals or movements of the time, the Bolsheviks possessed internationalist networks of human talent. Many created or controlled their own political parties loyal to the ruling vanguard Communist Party in Moscow. The Kremlin had built its functioning central command-and-control Comintern structure to administer and enforce those networks abroad. With storehouses of stolen treasures, it had access to money. It would set up the machinery in Berlin, where the new Weimar Republic had replaced the old imperial government.

Germany posed the greatest potential postwar threat to the new Soviet regime. It also presented the greatest Soviet opportunity. All of German society, unconditionally defeated with the old imperial order destroyed, sat in a state of profound demoralization. That demoralization splintered the fractious Weimar Republic, which was torn across economic and social class lines and amid an extreme cultural revolution of its own.

The men and women at Moscow's Marx-Engels Institute created something new for the occasion. Their Comintern needed something different to appeal not to the toiling masses of proletarian workers, but to the elites: the wealthy, bohemian, countercultural intellectuals, influencers, and poseurs of postwar Germany and beyond.

The Marx-Engels Institute gathering would create foreign subsidiary institutes, under prestigious academic cover, as a sophisticated social base to attract leaders of the arts, culture, and academia. The primary institute would incubate and grow a cadre to tear apart German culture—and any other culture that it could. If economic determinism wouldn't animate Western Marxists in the style of post-1843 Marx, cultural polarization would.

And so Soviet Communist Party Politburo member Karl Radek met with top Bolshevik colleagues under the Marx-Engels Institute roof to develop strategy and plans. With a globalism of their own, the Bolsheviks knew no national boundaries. From behind thick round glasses, the frizzy-haired Radek, a native of Poland, liked to experiment with different styles of outlandish sideburns, beards, and mustaches, posing for pictures with a long-stemmed pipe drooping from a strange, toothy smirk. Radek was the Bolsheviks' chief propagandist and Comintern secretary.

Hungarian revolutionary Georg Lukács joined him. For years, Lukács had networked among European artists and intellectuals. To judge him by his appearances would be to miss his genocidal intent. Lush black hair and a sagging mustache sandwiched a huge nose on which perched a pair of frail, wire-rimmed spectacles. He looked comical, but there was nothing funny about him. Lukács had been the education and cultural commissar of the short-lived Bolshevik regime of Béla Kun in Hungary and a theoretical architect of the regime's Red Terror, during which hundreds of political opponents were murdered. He smiled a lot. Perhaps too much. He expanded his theoretical architecture to what he called "abolition of culture," the wholesale destruction of history, belief, and values, right down to the tearing apart of family life and the sexualization of small children to dehumanize the next generation. Back in Moscow, after the Hungarian experiment's collapse, Lukács would become a founding father of modern Western Marxism, cultural Marxism, and critical theory. He ended up as one of the last of the senior Bolsheviks, active almost to his death in 1971.

A third member of the group, the ingenious thirty-year-old Prussian Communist Willi Münzenberg, busily organized the Comintern's elaborate network of international front groups. Fronts were organizations that outwardly acted independent and sometimes as non-Communist, but always remained under Soviet regime control. With endless authority, imagination, and cheerful charm, the lantern-jawed Münzenberg built the system from radical cadres and coopted organizations to wage indirect warfare abroad. He was a brilliant propagandist who could barely write. This committed Communist would amass a personal fortune for himself in the process, shaking down American and European socialites, heiresses, and everyday do-gooders for as long as his comrades allowed him to live. He rode to his meetings with Lenin in his own limousine.[10]

A fourth member of the group, Cheka commissar Feliks Dzerzhinsky, wielded the ultimate authority. He represented Lenin. Tall, gaunt, and humorless, with sunken cheeks and a long goatee that curled inward from constant stroking, Dzerzhinsky, now in his early forties, determined life or death as head of the Bolshevik secret police. He maintained an air of the lesser Polish aristocracy into which he was born, but tried to project himself as a *narodnik*, a man of the people, in a plain revolutionary uniform. It was a fashion that Mao Tse-tung and Fidel Castro would later mimic. Like Stalin, at one point Dzerzhinsky was interested in becoming a seminarian and studying to save souls, before declaring *Non serviam* and turning to Communism. His Western intellectual admirers saw him as the great dispenser of social justice. Those who knew him said he radiated a cold hate. Dzerzhinsky supported the institute idea as a means of expanding Chekist espionage and influence networks globally by penetrating the elites of Europe, Asia, and the Americas.

The Cheka commissar had a lot on his mind at the time. Russia's post-revolutionary civil war raged savagely. Dzerzhinsky was running Operation Trust, a spectacular five-year deception plot to attract anti-Bolshevik forces from exile, fund them and arm them, build up their leaders, unite them to the extent possible, and do everything necessary to recruit and mobilize supporters across the old Russian Empire—even though it meant getting loyal Bolsheviks killed in the process. Dzerzhinsky's cold logic was that his enemies would never suspect that their resistance movement depended on the Cheka, and everything they did would enable the Chekists to identify and liquidate them all.[11]

Memo from Hell

Cheka cadres were instructed to be all smiles and pleasantries as they went about their work before taking people away to be shot. An internal Cheka staff memo set the rules with sickly sweet banality: "Always be correct, polite, modest, resourceful. Do not shout. Be soft, but know where to exercise hardness. Before you speak, you must think. In your searches be prudent, skillfully warn of misfortune, be polite, accurate, and punctual." Then Iron Feliks set the example: When officers find suspects, "do not sound the alarm, as this will spoil the matter. It would be commendable if you cover them red-handed and then pillory them in front of everyone. Keep the orders given by you as the apple of your eye." Signed, F. Dzerzhinsky.[12]

Revolutionary and counter-counterrevolutionary art required a certain soft sophistication. Shortly before the meeting at the Marx-Engels Institute, Dzerzhinsky had reorganized the Cheka from an emergency commissariat into the more institutionalized State Political Directorate. Known as GPU, it was, as its lineage and name suggested, a domestic political intelligence service with police powers.

From arrest and interrogation to summary execution, the Cheka-GPU enforced Communist Party policy as codified into Soviet state law. Or whatever it deemed suitable as the party's sword and shield. Dzerzhinsky expanded the GPU to run an international intelligence network for espionage and influence operations. This required a global network of dedicated, organized, trained, and disciplined revolutionaries; their willful collaborators, known as fellow travelers; and their unwitting dupes, or useful idiots. To make that all possible in a short time would require a constellation of disciplined Communist parties under control of the Comintern.

Those controlled parties would assess, vet, and recruit Kremlin loyalists as spies and—more importantly—emplace them abroad as agents of influence and recruiters. An agent in place, embedded in a foreign university or government where he could influence perceptions, opinions, and decisions and bring others into the service, generally would yield far greater value to the Cheka-GPU than a mere thief of secret information. Separately, the military general staff, under Military and Naval Affairs commissar Leon Trotsky, ran its own Main Intelligence Directorate known then, as now, as GRU.

Permanent Revolution

With Europe as the first target, the group at the Marx-Engels Institute included other top European Communist figures, including Austrian Communist Party founder Ruth Fischer. They designed the mechanism for a worldwide campaign and system that differed from doctrinaire Marxism-Leninism. The mechanism ruthlessly criticized every aspect of Western civilization to tear it down from within. It was perfectly Marxist, and it fit well with Trotsky's idea of "permanent revolution."

Germany under its catastrophic Weimar Republic made the perfect place to start. Berlin had become the most decadent city on the continent. Monarchist, Catholic, Lutheran, Socialist, National Socialist, International Socialist or Communist, and Anarchist factions battled for control. Germany remained a modern, industrialized country, with its working-class proletariat in no mood to wage a violent overthrow.

A German teardown required a whole new approach from what the Bolsheviks had done in Russia. The revolutions in the Western democracies and republics would emerge through a corrupted ruling class. Through constant criticism of all parts of Germany's anxious, humiliated society, the revolutionaries would spread decay among the self-confidence of the people in those institutions and weaken their will to hang on. The existence of a German state or nation-state wasn't the issue. What blocked a real revolution was Western civilization and its deep Old and New Testament culture passed from one generation to the other by family and church or synagogue.[13] Those cultural anchors had to be corroded away.

We know about Dzerzhinsky's personal participation in this Marx-Engels Institute meeting from attendee Ruth Fischer, a high-value Soviet agent who led the German Communist Party after founding its Austrian counterpart. Fischer knew Radek, whom she had visited as a revolutionary in prison, and Lukács, Münzenberg, and Dzerzhinsky. She worked directly with most of the Bolshevik leaders, including Stalin, whom she supported but would later oppose.

Münzenberg shuttled between Moscow and Berlin to coordinate Comintern assets to collapse Germany's first federal republic in Lenin's direction. He and Lukács saw a fertile climate for chaos in cosmopolitan Berlin's drunken, drugged, and sexed-up rejection of tradition. That mess could either turn all of Germany into a fraternal and obedient Communist state, or simply wreck it to nothing—*nihil* in Latin. Nihilism would suffice as an easier destruction engine where the more challenging, doctrinaire Communism would not. Münzenberg's instruments would be less Bolshevik-style violent terrorism and more quiet and patient subversion of the population through motion pictures, theater, the new medium of radio, the news media, and Germany's fine educational system.

Such a revolution needed mechanics built within an architecture set upon a theoretical base to govern perception, reasoning, logic, organization, and action. That theoretical foundation existed piecemeal among German intellectuals alienated from society and its traditions. It appealed especially to German intelligentsia from religious, Yiddish-speaking, Jewish families who rebelled both against their pious elders and Germanic society. Those alienated intellectuals envisioned human progress as never before, a progressivism that would catapult humanity forward by cutting off the past. Münzenberg joined them. He became head of the German Communist Party and helped build the project under the umbrella of an unsuspecting prestigious academic institution. The host became Goethe University in the Prussian river metropolis of Frankfurt am Main.

Journalist and historian Ralph de Toledano, a wartime OSS man who later interviewed several of Münzenberg's European co-conspirators, recounted that the Lenin-approved plan was "to finance the creation in Germany of an organization which would succeed beyond his wildest dreams—the Institute for Social Research—in the context of Marx's earlier destructionism, putting aside concepts of immediate world revolution. It was Lenin's canniest move."[14] It marked the conception of a force that would migrate to the United States in due time. The institute set up shop informally in Frankfurt am Main in 1923.

The Institute for Social Research attracted glamorous and edgy artists and literati before long, dominating much of trendy cultural life in Weimar Germany and beyond. It even reached out to British academic and intellectual circles at Oxford and Cambridge, and associates in the British secret services, popularly known as MI6, which the Soviets were busily penetrating.[15]

Münzenberg and the Frankfurt School's newly arrived intellectuals would exhume the early Karl Marx ravings of 1843, with their critical theories to destroy culture and all of human society through "purely scientific" Marxism, the enduring kind of science that people could trust, not the "party-political" kind that changed with the prevailing Kremlin winds.

As an added twist, the Frankfurt School alloyed cultural Marxism with the fast-growing "science" of psychology, itself infused with a neo-Freudian theory of sexual assault on traditional values. Breaking all sexual taboos, especially with alcohol and drugs in a permissive society, would add to the fun and pleasure of an un-violent, sophisticated revolution. Frankfurt School revival of the much-forgotten cultural revolutionary side of Marx, merged with neo-Freudianism, would come to America and take root.

The Frankfurt School was only one of Münzenberg's countless projects. The Soviet agent from Prussia shuttled by steamship from Europe to America, organizing people and front organizations, charming wealthy donors and bilking the common people of donations large and small for Soviet famine relief. He found that engaging people in "solidarity" activities led not only to more money, but to more idealistic volunteers energized for activism. He pioneered networks of what he derisively called "Innocents' Clubs" to dupe supporters. The Comintern man aimed high. He co-opted American cultural elites as his agents or fellow travelers: the greatest of the great writers Upton Sinclair, Sinclair Lewis and his perky journalist wife Dorothy Thompson, John Dos Passos, Ernest Hemingway, playwright Lillian Hellman, and others in popular literature and entertainment.[16]

J. Edgar Hoover and Wild Bill Donovan would have to deal with the fallout from this Marx-Engels Institute meeting directly, but they would do it in very different, irreconcilable ways.

Chapter 7

"A secret police system may become a menace to free government and free institutions because it carries with it the possibility of abuses of power which are not always quickly comprehended or understood."

—Attorney General Harlan Fiske Stone, 1924[1]

G-Men versus Gangsters

Woodrow Wilson's three Republican successors during the Roaring Twenties—presidents Warren G. Harding, Calvin Coolidge, and Herbert Hoover—showed considerable conservatism, but the idealistic coercion of progressivism would increase the appeal and power of central government in time for the Great Depression's ushering in of Franklin D. Roosevelt and his New Deal.

The constitutional amendment to ban alcoholic beverages fueled an underground economy in the 1920s among states and from smugglers abroad, and spurred the dawn of interstate organized crime. Prohibition marked the rise of the gangsters. Bank robberies, drug trafficking, kidnapping, and more overwhelmed state and local police, and criminals escaped over state lines.

During his short administration that began in 1921, President Harding used the Bureau of Investigation to hunt his mainstream political opponents. Even the FBI's official history concedes, "In the early twenties, the agency was no model of efficiency. It had a growing reputation for politicized investigations."[2]

Harding died suddenly in 1923 and was succeeded by his vice president, Calvin Coolidge. That year, with the exposure of the Harding-era Teapot Dome oil scandal, word of the late president's corruption and his political abuse of the bureau became known. An FBI history recalls, "the nation learned that Department of Justice officials had sent Bureau agents to spy on members of Congress who had opposed its policies."[3]

America then bustled with inward-looking optimism. In New York, the charismatic and aggressive Bill Donovan worked upper-crust financial and legal circuits and became involved in Republican politics. Coolidge named him U.S. attorney for the state's Western District, where he earned a reputation as a relentless prosecutor. Donovan, who enjoyed whiskey, lost old friends and made new ones during his vigorous enforcement of Prohibition. For Donovan, the law was the law.

Facing not only the criminal gangster empires of Al Capone and the Mafia but also high-level corruption in the government he had inherited, Coolidge sacked his Harding-appointed attorney general and set out to clean up a filthy, corrupt Justice Department. He brought in a new attorney general, Harlan Fiske Stone, who found the Bureau of Investigation "in exceedingly bad odor," a unit "filled with men with bad records" with "many convicted of crimes," a "lawless" entity whose "agents engaged in many practices which are brutal and tyrannical in the extreme."[4]

Stone recruited Donovan from New York to run the Justice Department's Criminal Division. Within that division, Stone promoted twenty-nine-year-old Hoover to head the Bureau of Investigation.

Donovan kept Hoover on a short leash. Stone wasn't sure about Hoover, either.

With his mandate from Coolidge and Stone, Hoover purged the bureau of what he called "political hacks." He professionalized its agents and other employees. He ended up slashing nearly a quarter of the bureau's special agents, from 441 to 339.[5] More federal laws to "fix" problems called for a larger federal apparatus to enforce those laws. This duty fell to the people fighting the Communists controlled by the Cheka-GPU and the Comintern, the anarchists, the militant socialists of the kind that shared the Communist-anarchist endgame of overthrowing the government, the recently revived Ku Klux Klan, and other subversives. Stone kept Hoover as the bureau's director.

But the attorney general had a stern warning: "The Bureau of Investigation is not concerned with political or other opinions of individuals. It is only concerned with their conduct and then only with such conduct as is forbidden by the laws of the United States. When a police system passes beyond these limits, it is dangerous to the proper administration of justice and to human liberty, which should be our first concern to cherish. Within them it should rightly be a terror to the wrongdoer."[6] Hoover, hunter of subversives, was now a lawman.

As would become his trademark, Hoover had a dossier on Donovan before Donovan ever arrived in town. The two shared little in common and didn't hit it off. Rather short in stature, with eyes set wide apart, Hoover was neat and tidy, physically fit, a fastidious record-keeper, considered introverted, and with a small social circle despite his lifetime in Washington. Government jobs didn't pay much then. Hoover had remained in the family's Capitol Hill row house to care for his widowed mother, his father having died in 1921.

The tall, dashing, sociable, and outgoing Donovan, twelve years Hoover's senior and with a glamorous and wealthy wife, was Hoover's almost exact opposite. Their only common traits seemed to be a shared birthday on January 1, Republican Party sympathies, and snappy suits.

Hoover saw his boss as a shoddy lawyer and administrator, a social climber married to money. Donovan found Hoover a detail-oriented but dull and visionless bureaucrat who had no life and lived with his mother. He became too interested in the bureau to Hoover's liking and vetoed some of Hoover's decisions. Hostility between the two would last until Donovan's death in 1959, with Hoover always expanding his Donovan file.[7]

On the Georgetown social circuit with Ruth, Donovan became friends with Commerce secretary Herbert Hoover, no relation to J. Edgar. He joined the secretary's 1928 presidential campaign team. Candidate Hoover had promised Donovan the post of attorney general. But once president, Herbert Hoover would pick someone else. The Klan, influential with powerful Southern lawmakers and more, and intimidating wherever they went, demanded that no Catholic ever run the Justice Department.

That would be another point in common for Donovan and the FBI chief: total opposition to the KKK at a time when many in Washington found it advantageous to listen to the Klansmen, or at least look the other way.

Denied the attorney general post, Donovan returned to New York to expand his law business on the crest of the Roaring Twenties economic boom begun under Coolidge.

J. Edgar Hoover stayed at the bureau to take on the gangsters. Few federal laws applied, and even then, violations of Prohibition were the legal responsibility of the Bureau of Prohibition to enforce. The FBI assisted state and local police. Hoover modernized the bureau's standards, recruitment, screening, training, and techniques. In 1924 he built a world-class fingerprint index, first by consolidating more than 810,000 records from the National Bureau of Criminal Identification and the federal prison at Leavenworth.[8] He bootstrapped to build a scientific crime laboratory, first housed in 1932 in a single room at the

Old Southern Railway building by the Justice Department.[9] Federal law did not permit bureau agents to make arrests or even carry weapons, but that would change. The bureau was expanding from domestic intelligence with police powers to become more of a law enforcement agency. Hoover built an image-making machine to match.

The Harding and Coolidge administrations, and bipartisan majorities in both houses of Congress, inherently understood what was happening with the Communist onslaught from the Soviet Union. Edgar Hoover was America's top official in charge of collecting and synthesizing intelligence on these subversive networks, and regularly briefed Congress and the Justice Department.

The stock market crash of 1929 drove the country into the Great Depression, with economic desperation and the desire for prohibited goods breeding more crime of an organized character. The FBI took on the crime waves and assisted state and local police. It helped with the arrest of Chicago gangster Al Capone. Most organized crime, though, did not violate federal law. Murder, then as now, was a state matter. Pennsylvania authorities arrested Capone in 1929 on state weapons charges. Capone served nine months in jail, then spent another six months in jail for contempt of court for not complying with a grand jury subpoena. The Treasury Department finally got him on federal tax evasion, and he pled guilty to Prohibition violations.

The FBI's role in curbing organized crime remained minimal until 1932, when the interstate kidnapping of the infant son of aviation hero Charles Lindbergh brought the bureau into the case, and later when criminals like celebrity bank robber John Dillinger went interstate.

The nation soon repealed Prohibition with the Twenty-first Amendment to the Constitution. Then the criminal gangs, many having become household names, started going down by arrest or gunfight: Machine Gun Kelly in Tennessee; Bonnie and Clyde in Texas; then Dillinger in Chicago; Pretty Boy Floyd on a farm in Ohio; Baby Face

Nelson, who killed three FBI agents outside Chicago and died in his final shooting; and Doc Barker and the more notorious Ma Barker in Florida. The bureau concedes its "small supporting role" in helping Texas track down Bonnie and Clyde and aiding local police in Floyd's takedown, but still claims full credit for the rest.

By this time, mass media and entertainment generated intense public interest in the fight against gangsters. As Lukács and Münzenberg had discovered in Europe, technological advances in news and entertainment created a new battlespace. The exploits of the G-Men under J. Edgar Hoover enraptured the American public. The Communists were steadily infiltrating Hollywood, but Hoover nevertheless made his own friends in Tinseltown to dramatize the bureau's reputation as America's invincible lawmen and build the brand that today's FBI still enjoys.

The School at Frankfurt

The optimistic American spirit burst forward in the excitement of the 1920s. Automobiles replaced the horse and buggy. Detroit blossomed as a beautiful city of the future. Walter Chrysler built his elegant, stainless steel Art Deco skyscraper in Manhattan, the tallest structure in the world for a very short while until, competitively, the Empire State Building went up a few blocks away. Aviation captured popular imagination. Radio and recorded music played in millions of homes.

Americans wanted nothing to do with the Old World's problems that they had just sacrificed to solve. And since the Great War, they wanted even less to do with anything German. The United States had no foreign intelligence service to watch a political pandemic unfold in Europe, a pandemic that had already infected American society.

The Land of Opportunity that had beckoned immigrants who sought a better life had not eclipsed Germany as the Soviets' first target.

Though not all in full agreement, the Institute for Social Research intellectuals would combine neo-Marxist cultural destruction with a neo-Freudian theory of sexual assault on traditional values, making their form of revolution a more exciting adventure. Dzerzhinsky didn't live long enough to see the operation take root, but the institute's Frankfurt School of thought and its intellectual appeal would turn the enterprise into a magnet for a sweeping high-society, global espionage and influence network that likely would have exceeded the Cheka founder's greatest dreams.

Sitting in a modern, squat, almost cubic blockhouse, the Institute for Social Research in Frankfurt became a hive of intimate worker bees. It buzzed with creativity, artistic expression, and glamor. A run through some of the cast of characters reveals the tight-knit and occasionally incestuous, often squabbling atmosphere of the Frankfurt School. The intellectual giants included T. W. Adorno, Erich Fromm, Max Horkheimer, and Herbert Marcuse, some of the fathers of cultural Marxism and critical theory, and the progenitors of political correctness and twenty-first-century wokeness.

These intellectuals provided cover for operationally minded influencers. They show the early nexus of conjoined radical theorists and Soviet agents and their globalist teamwork. Hede Thune Eisler, an Austrian actress, operated there as a controlled Soviet agent and recruiter for Stalin's GRU military intelligence service. Her first husband, Gerhart Eisler, directed Comintern underground operations in the United States and became a future Communist Party USA senior functionary. British intelligence suspected that Gerhart Eisler was the Soviets' covert control agent who actually ran the CPUSA.

Gerhart's brother Hanns, a musical composer with the institute, would later write the score for a CPUSA pageant at Madison Square Garden in New York, get a Hollywood contract, and, after World War II, write the East German national anthem. Gerhart's and

Hanns's prolific sister, Ruth Eisler Fischer, had cofounded the Austrian Communist Party, chaired the German Communist Party, and was elected to the Weimar Reichstag. She had been part of the 1922 meeting in Moscow with Lukács, Münzenberg, Dzerzhinsky, and the other Bolsheviks to set up the institute and Frankfurt School.[10]

All along, the Comintern used the Frankfurt School to solidify ties among intellectuals in the United States.

Hede left Gerhart Eisler and shacked up with New York City–born Julian Gumperz, whom we'll see again in a moment.[11] The cuckolded Gerhart would later move in with his ex-wife and Gumperz, and impregnate Hede's teenage sister Elli. Hede's recollection of those times reflects the practice of the Frankfurt School's theoretical approach toward family that would break out in ensuing decades. Her ex-husband would play the role of father figure to her and her pregnant sister, with nothing said about his child. In Hede's words, "Gerhart assumed the father role for Elli and me, and Julian was my husband. The world was fine."[12]

Gumperz got his doctorate in economics at the institute. Hede left Gumperz to cohabitate with Paul Massing, a German sociologist and Communist Party member who handled "illegal" or underground agents for Moscow. Another Frankfurt School personality, Richard Sorge, had recruited Hede as a GRU agent. Hede and Sorge had been friends since 1923, when they met at the Marxist Workweek which formed the groundwork for the Institute for Social Research. Paul Massing would also become a Soviet spy. An intellectual cornerstone of the early institute faculty was Herbert Marcuse, who would become a powerful philosopher-practitioner of cultural Marxism and critical theory, and an icon of the American New Left.[13] But we are getting ahead of things.

Within a few years, Weimar Germany started eating itself alive—with Moscow stoking the furnace and pumping the bellows. The Communists made no inroads as political revolutionaries despite the cultural advances at the Frankfurt School. The Comintern in 1928 declared a new "third period" of revolution that, according to Dartmouth University professor Mark Bray, "required a strategy of heightened antagonism toward socialists in order to clarify their alleged role in safeguarding capitalism."

The idea was to polarize German society to the breaking point. To rip apart and collapse the middle ground. Socialists across Europe were now to be branded "social fascists" and treated accordingly.[14]

Everyone a Fascist: The Comintern's Antifa

Everybody knew that the only German fascists were in Hitler's National Socialist German Workers' Party, and that the fascist label on others was phony. "In fact, a significant reason for the 'social fascist' turn was Stalin's need to fend off [Comintern chairman Grigory] Zinoviev and Trotsky to his right in the ongoing struggle for power in the USSR," writes Bray. "Moscow politics often influenced continental anti-fascist strategy more than Italian or German realities."[15]

That meant creating a militant "anti-fascist" shock force to fight everyone else in the streets, because everybody else, in the Stalin party line, was obviously a fascist. Deadly riots rocked radical Berlin. In a three-way spate of violence, the city's socialist police chief had to crush the Communist uprising while Nazi stormtroopers provoked leftists in the most left-wing sections of the city.[16]

The socialists had their own paramilitary group, the Iron Front, that fought both the Nazis and the Communists. "The popularity of the Iron Front prompted the KPD [German Communist Party] to form *Antifaschistische Aktion* . . . as a network of factory cells, neighborhood groups, apartment blocks, and other geographical associations," according to Bray. The network's "local executive boards consisted of representatives of the KPD, the RFB [*Rotfrontkämpferbund*, or

Alliance of Red Front Fighters], communist sports leagues and earlier communist anti-fascist platforms."[17]

Little of the Communist violence was indigenous. Moscow directed everything and brought the wayward into line. Antifascist Action, as Bray portrayed it, was a Soviet creation based on the needs of internal Soviet power struggles. The KPD kept splintering for reasons personal and tactical. Like military units, groups needed logos, colors, flags, and hand signals to mark their presence and distinguish themselves from one another. Antifascist Action sported a circular logo of black and red banners on a field of white. Another splinter, the RFB, signaled with a raised, jabbing, clenched-fist salute.

Hitler and his Nazi gangs would respond with their own more dramatic and classical hand signal: an extended salute of the right arm, palm facing down and fingers fully extended. The Nazis cribbed it from Mussolini's fascists, who had appropriated it from ancient Rome.

Years later, some of these emblems and hand signals would emerge as symbols of extremist factions in the United States.

Playing the Long Game

The Frankfurt School remained above the violence sweeping Germany. Its environment remained one of education, art, literature, music, culture, science, sex, and high society. With the Nazi storm-troopers, the Iron Front, Antifascist Action, and others fighting in the streets and retreating to beer halls, Frankfurt Schoolers preferred to develop their criticisms and theories in salons, classrooms, cinemas, performance theaters, and drug dens.

A little planned provocation now and again helped steer events. Münzenberg empowered his agents and their organizations to create the desired social and political vacuum. His strategy was to tear out the fragile society's mainstream traditional and socialist political parties, cultural identities and symbolism, private enterprise, and the church, then fill the vacuum.

Comintern shock troops attacked just about everyone else, because the new Soviet line was to condemn everyone else as Nazis. Antifascist Action fought the conservative monarchist aristocracy. It fought the Catholics and Lutherans. It fought private businesses, both Christian and Jewish. It fought the liberals. It fought the socialists. Sometimes it fought Nazis.

Raucous as it was, Antifascist Action remained an obedient agent of Münzenberg and Stalin. Like its Comintern parent, it had a catchy abbreviation: Antifa.

Antifa's job was not to fight the Nazis first. It was to fight them last.[18]

Moscow's polarization strategy backfired and arguably helped the Nazis take power by destroying potential coalition allies from the left. The Soviet agents and fellow travelers, inadvertently, one suspects, helped Hitler gut the broad center of German society. That misstep allowed the Nazis, not the Communists, to fill the vacuum.

The fun of cultural Marxism in Weimar Germany came to an end once Adolf Hitler became chancellor in 1933. The critical theorists from the Frankfurt School, disproportionately atheist Jews, would migrate to safer and more welcoming environments in Switzerland, France, and the United Kingdom. Those free countries would shelter them as refugees.

So would the United States, which would import most of the Frankfurt School and allow it to take root.

Chapter 8

A Communist in a Fascist Prison

Similar ferment consumed Italy, with a new strain of revolutionary thought ripening in a fascist prison, a different kind of cultural Marxism that would spread through Europe and insinuate its way into American popular culture.

A young socialist named Benito Mussolini hybridized Marxism to forge something new. He revived the ancient symbol of classical Roman authority, a neat cluster of wooden rods tied together with a battle axe blade protruding from one side, known as a *fasces*, and applied that to the name of his movement.

Once in power in 1922, Mussolini sidelined and repressed rival extremists. In 1926 an Italian court sentenced a prominent Comintern man, Italian Communist Party figure Antonio Gramsci, to prison. The strategically minded, brilliant Gramsci had already bonded with Frankfurt School figures who shared his long-held idea of penetrating and taking over existing institutions for a long-term, gradualist revolution. In prison, Gramsci used his solitude, with authorities' permission, to write three thousand pages of notebooks to reshape Marxism in a way very different from Mussolini or even Stalin.

The fascist regime proved rather benign toward Gramsci. Sensing no imminent danger, it allowed him to develop his theories and plans. Gramsci favored a grassroots cultural socialism but publicly remained loyal to Stalin, while quietly refining a safer, more gradualist approach toward the same endgame. Gramsci went beyond taking control of government or the means of production to destroying Western civilization itself.

Gramsci had mastered the art of strategic psychological warfare. Bolshevism and Stalinism would fail as organic globalist movements. Gramsci favored working generally within the system and the law to avoid repression. He sought patient coalitions with socialists and fellow travelers, not as mere tactical allies as the Comintern was doing, but to capture the culture and conquer existing institutions. Maneuvering through legal rules and procedures, he argued, would permit freedom of action.

Gramsci developed a method to rewrite history to create new perceptions of reality. He borrowed heavily from Niccolò Machiavelli in designing practical approaches to subvert the public mind to manufacture consent. That artificial consent would allow the election of the proper political leaders, appointments of bureaucrats and judges, and so forth. Some argue that Gramsci took some inspiration from Mussolini's own gradualism.

Gramsci differed with Stalin's 1928 tactical return to insurrectionism abroad that had been intended to shape the collapse of the doomed Weimar Germany. He envisioned a broad movement that he called "an organism; a complex, collective element of society which has already begun to crystallize as a collective will that has become conscious of itself through action." This movement or party would be "the organizer and the active expression of moral and intellectual reform . . . that cannot be tied to an economic program."[1]

Like the freewheeling Frankfurt School, Gramsci refined from his prison cell a Marxism without the dialectical materialism nonsense. Gramsci imagined a society that stripped itself of religious belief and Western traditions and values, turbocharged by a Marxist-Machiavellian notion that "reduces all to politics, to the art of governing men, of assuring their permanent consensus."[2] It was all about control.

Cultural hegemony, as Gramsci saw it, was supposed to ease its way into the public consciousness. It would convince through repetition, making people uncomfortable but certainly not to the point of total alienation. Gramsci envisioned winning without giving cause for reaction. The population would willingly, if grudgingly, adapt to and absorb his hegemony.

"Socialism is precisely the religion that must overwhelm Christianity," Gramsci had written in 1915, early in his revolutionary career. "In the new order, Socialism will triumph by first capturing the culture via infiltration of schools, universities, churches, and the media by transforming the consciousness of society."[3] He built upon that idea years later in his cell.

Mussolini's authorities released the physically ill Gramsci from prison for humanitarian reasons, with his notebooks, while keeping him under a sort of house arrest. Gramsci outwardly went along with Stalin until the end, but, thanks to the fascists, left a legacy in his unfinished *Prison Notebooks* as a philosophical and practical guide for cultural Marxism and critical theory.

Almost nobody in the United States followed these developments at the time. But they would within a generation, upon publication of English translations of the *Prison Notebooks* in the 1960s. Gramsci's captive thoughts, with parallel theories from the Frankfurt School intellectuals, would sit among the founding principles of a "post-Marxist," culturally Marxist, critically theoretical school of thought less than a generation later.[4]

Once these imported German Marxist intellectuals implanted their Central European ideas to transform American culture—especially in the university humanities and law schools that incubated new leaders—they would, in time, create a spillover effect that would transform the cultures of the FBI and CIA.

Stalin's Fellow Travelers—and a Future FBI Director Yet to Be Born

Without the fellow travelers, the Comintern's Institute for Social Research and its Frankfurt School would not get far. American intellectuals gravitated to Germany to meet their Frankfurt School counterparts. Some went for an audience with Paul Tillich, a widely published Protestant theologian who pioneered a Marxist-Christian hybrid—an important development, since other left-wing Christian scholars had found the two incompatible. Tillich was a socialist, not a Communist Party member but part of the Comintern united front. Separately, in the spirit of Dzerzhinsky and Stalin, the Comintern was running agents to study at seminaries to infiltrate mainline churches as Catholic priests and Protestant clergy in Europe and America, just as Stalin was doing among the Christian Orthodox.[5] Tillich's German-language tomes captivated left-wing American speakers of German, some of whom traveled across the Atlantic to meet him.

Tillich's best-known American fan was Reinhold Niebuhr, cofounder of the Fellowship of Socialist Christians in New York. The Frankfurt School of thought appealed to Niebuhr in many ways, as did Tillich's writings. The Great Depression had set in, and people were looking for answers. Niebuhr steamed to Germany to meet Tillich in 1930.

At the time, German was the most commonly spoken language in the United States after English. Niebuhr grew up speaking German at home. Tillich's 1925 book, *The Religious Situation*, captivated Niebuhr so much that he translated it into English in 1931. During his visit that year, Niebuhr and Tillich began an enduring friendship.

Private individuals and organizations on their own helped countless German intellectuals escape the impending Nazi revolution. Niebuhr arranged for Union Theological Seminary faculty to donate a portion of their salaries to fund Tillich's relocation from Germany to New York, where he would teach at the seminary. The Niebuhr-Tillich team would influence a large political-spiritual movement in the United States and attract devoted followers, including some of the nation's most powerful figures.

The Institute of International Education (IIE) relocated hundreds of European academic refugees to positions as professors at colleges across the country. It resettled top Frankfurt School figures like Herbert Marcuse, who would dedicate his influential book, *Reason and Revolution*, to Max Horkheimer and the Institute for Social Research.[6]

The IIE was not a Comintern operation. It was a prestigious academic-exchange organization. Nobel laureate and former secretary of state Elihu Root, City College of New York professor Stephen Duggan, and others founded it after World War I to promote ideas and internationalism. Duggan directed the Council on Foreign Relations from 1921 to 1950. His son, Laurence, worked in the State Department. Laurence led a secret life as a Soviet NKVD agent.[7]

After his experience in Germany, Niebuhr became an early supporter of the American League Against War and Fascism in 1933, one of countless Comintern operations in New York. Its original founders included the Women's International League for Peace and Freedom, which would remain a steadfast Soviet active measures instrument until the death of the USSR; the socialist League for Industrial Democracy; and the Communist Party USA. CPUSA chief Earl Browder gave a speech at the league's founding. Union Theological Seminary professor Harry F. Ward became league chairman. And so began liberal American Protestant collusion with the Kremlin.

Through the 1930s, Niebuhr became active in American politics, running several times as a Socialist Party candidate for public office. He and Tillich continued their collaboration. He translated another Tillich book into English, opening up new Central European ideas to American clergy and other influencers. The two debated issues at the seminary and the larger intellectual scene. Their work dovetailed with Tillich's Frankfurt School comrades, now ensconced nearby at Columbia University. Marxist theory heavily influenced Niebuhr's intellectual development in the 1930s.

Tillich's "theological and broader cultural work deeply influenced Niebuhr's thought, despite the fact that there are few textual references in Niebuhr's works to attest to such influence," a sympathetic biographer noted.[8] By then, Niebuhr had become one of the most influential Protestant theologians, and one of the heaviest-hitting American philosophers of any kind, of his day.

The Hitler-Stalin pact of August 1939 suddenly made objection to fascism problematic for party members, so the league changed its name to the American League for Peace and Democracy, but dissolved later that year. Niebuhr, who was anti-Stalinist but not anti-Communist, supported American intervention in Europe. His national fame, his networks of devoted students and followers, and his political connections gave him significant influence in the American government, especially the State Department and its Office of Policy Planning, run by a welcoming Alger Hiss.

Niebuhr had profound prominence in academia, theology, politics, and policy. He popularized, but is wrongly credited with authoring, the beloved "Serenity" prayer that goes:

> God, grant me the serenity to accept
> the things I cannot change,
> Courage to change the things I can,
> And wisdom to know the difference.

The prayer had been around a decade before he made it famous during World War II, but it stuck with Niebuhr's legacy. Prayer or no prayer, the philosopher had affiliated with so many Communist causes and Soviet front organizations that the FBI became concerned that he and other newcomers from Germany could be agents of, or at least transmission belts for, Kremlin disinformation and propaganda.

The FBI's Niebuhr file would ultimately number more than six hundred pages. The bureau would start monitoring the Frankfurt School's Marcuse during the middle of World War II and would continue until 1976.

A future FBI director yet to be born would also take intense interest in Niebuhr, but for a very different reason than Hoover.

Chapter 9

"We will make America stink."

—Willi Münzenberg, Comintern propaganda chief[1]

FDR Empowers a New FBI

During his first presidential campaign in 1932, Franklin Delano Roosevelt had promised all Americans a "New Deal" to pull the country out of the Depression. His strategy called for the massive expansion and centralization of the federal government. He consolidated various federal detective offices into the bureau and elevated the force to the semi-autonomous Federal Bureau of Investigation. FDR appointed Hoover to lead the FBI.

All those years, Hoover and his FBI rode high in public esteem as true national heroes. Although some of the name-brand gangsters were in prison or dead, more remained at large. The New Deal called for newer and bigger bureaucracies and more federal laws to grant them power and authority. More federal laws meant more need for central investigation and enforcement, which led to a growing FBI.

Hoover's mindfulness of image expanded his ties with Hollywood and the nation's largest news organizations. Image mattered.

Roosevelt added more national security burdens on the FBI when he extended diplomatic recognition of the Soviet Union during the first year of his presidency. Previous presidents going back to Wilson had not recognized the Communist regime in the Kremlin because of its stated commitment to subverting and overthrowing the United States government. Roosevelt extended diplomatic recognition to Stalin without conditions.

Even without diplomatic ties, the Comintern and Soviet intelligence services had operated with substantial freedom in the United States. A new Soviet embassy in Washington and consulates from New York to San Francisco eased the Kremlin's ability to intensify espionage and influence operations across the country, with the added benefit of diplomatic immunity.

FDR and Congress gave the FBI a larger mandate and a larger budget. As diligent as the bureau was, federal laws constrained its activity against foreign agents and spies. Soviet covert cadres aggressively advanced. The Comintern had penetrated and even taken over key American labor unions and teachers' organizations. FDR's New Deal provided Stalin's secret services ample opportunity to find jobs in America's expanding central government. New Deal programs like the Federal Writers' Project of the Works Progress Administration paradoxically subsidized Soviet spying and influence operations by providing employment to otherwise unemployable Comintern operators, Communist Party agitator-propagandists like Frank Marshall Davis, and fellow travelers.

The FBI also confronted a new threat: the militarist Tojo regime in Japan and Hitler's Third Reich in Germany, whose agents fanned across the country. The FBI learned counterintelligence on its own, with help from Army and Navy intelligence that had already detected the enemy networks.[2]

The hardships of the Great Depression caused some Americans, especially those of German ancestry, to develop a soft spot for the man and movement seeking to revive Germany and oppose Stalin. Communism had already become a popular cause, especially among European immigrants like those who greeted Trotsky in 1917, or the Frankfurt School migrants who imported their Old World extremism to America. The Communist Party USA and "other like-minded organizations" attracted more than one million members.

Roosevelt tasked the FBI with investigating American Nazis in 1934 for links to foreign agents. Two years later, he and his secretary of state assigned the FBI to collect "intelligence" on "fascist and communist groups" as threats to national security, according to the bureau's current official history.[3]

Roosevelt personally instructed the FBI to surveil, research, and otherwise investigate "fascism and Communism" around the country. Hoover had learned his lessons from the Palmer Raids and, with more laws at his disposal, paid more attention to civil liberties. "He cultivated relationships with ACLU and NAACP leaders and pledged fealty to their civil rights concerns," professor Jack Goldsmith noted in *The Atlantic*.[4]

Hoover had become a New Deal insider, a character whom Beverly Gage, in her meticulous, eight-hundred-page biography of the FBI leader, called "a darling of the New Deal establishment, known as a protector of civil liberties and a vanquisher of Nazis, saboteurs, and race-baiters."[5] Goldsmith added that Hoover "opposed the West Coast internment of Japanese Americans and investigated white southern lynchers. He arrested few political dissidents."[6]

"We Will Take Over the Intellectuals"

After the Frankfurt School tried brief experiments in Paris and London, its permanent home became New York City.

Julian Gumperz, the New York City native in Europe who by now was married to Soviet GRU agent Hede Eisler, led the negotiations for the Institute for Social Research to reside at Columbia University in New York.[7]

Again, trust fund money and its do-gooder equivalents would fund the operation. A Rockefeller Foundation grant underwrote the migrant Communist activist-academics—they were not refugees, as they had left Germany before Hitler's persecution and were living safely in free parts of Europe at the time—in their relocation to New York. They had sufficient operating funds from Frankfurt to set up shop right away. In the months before the move, Münzenberg had become involved in the turmoil of Stalin's purges and refused to return to the USSR for fear of his life. The Comintern stripped him of his duties in 1937. Continuing his activities in Paris, Münzenberg saw his Frankfurt School comrades off as they set out to the great city in 1938.

New York was awash in the discharge of Communist Party members and fellow travelers, many of them native speakers of German and Yiddish and Russian who had given Trotsky his warm welcome two decades earlier. The Frankfurt Schoolers found an enthusiastic host, a philosopher named John Dewey, a revered fixture at the Columbia University Teachers College. That college taught a substantial percentage of teachers who would go on to populate schools across the United States.

Though not a Communist Party member, Dewey was a socialist who made himself a willing Comintern fellow traveler. He had criticized Stalin but, after a well-timed tour of the USSR, wrote a six-part series in the *New Republic* gushing with admiration for the Communist system, and particularly the Stalinist education system.[8]

At the time, Dewey was experimenting with education methods on American children as head of the National Education Association (NEA) teachers' union. He believed that teaching children to become individual achievers was a capitalist plot to keep the ruling bourgeoisie in power. His methods would gradually detach children from their families and shape them for what he called a collective "social purpose." He would do this, he said, by "controlling methods of teaching and discipline and materials of study" to create "education for a new social order." That new order would be socialism.[9]

The National Education Association would never stray far from the intellectual base of the Frankfurt School. American public education then was a matter for state and local governments. Public school teachers were generally poorly paid and needed access to the best teaching methods. The NEA would act as a collective bargainer for those teachers, who would fund the organization by paying regular dues. As Dewey had envisioned, the NEA would use its unsuspecting, dues-paying members as agents of change to push critical theory and cultural Marxism to generations of American schoolchildren, avoiding such terms in front of its own rank and file. FBI director Hoover and others warned for years about subversion of American schools as everything unfolded, but most people, including teachers, didn't think it could happen to them.

Few proponents of Frankfurt School ideas consciously understood or embraced critical theory as a Marxist product; they didn't even realize what was going on. They just carried on with what they were trained to teach, with what seemed modern or fashionable, or what sounded like good and innovative ideas to help children.

"We will take over the intellectuals," Münzenberg told Ruth Fischer. "We will make America stink."[10]

Common Template

The FBI saw it coming. When not fighting crime, Hoover and the FBI monitored Soviet subversion in nerve centers like New York and mapped the networks. The Big Apple was, as the *New York Times* would headline many years later, "the capital of American Communism."[11]

Communist parties everywhere created a seemingly infinite galaxy of front organizations. They excelled at taking over other, non-Communist organizations. Infiltrating and controlling existing organizations had the advantage of allowing the party to manage or influence branded entities that people already knew and accepted.

The formula varied, but a common variation went like this: The Communists ran a command structure of vertical networks of controlled cadres from Moscow center to the streets of any given country or city. The cadres worked in covert groups called cells. From the cells they built horizontal networks across sectors: labor, education, the arts and trades, culture, politics, and even business and religion. Not all those in the horizontal networks were under control of the vertical hierarchy, but they worked together with them and would usually, but not necessarily, submit to the control of the center through its designees. The Communists exploited every opportunity they could.

The vertical command structure would assign people in the horizontal networks to join or penetrate certain organizations, sometimes in their own country and sometimes abroad, building new cells in each. Those in the horizontal networks would advise the command structure of talents or capabilities. The ones under party discipline would move where needed as instructed. Those not under control, but acting willfully as "allies," would go where they chose or thought they were needed.

From the horizontal networks at the low levels, a cadre would join an organization as recruits or volunteers "from below," the grassroots, and would build alliances with people in the middle and upper levels, setting up controlled cells along the way. Some would join, or even be imposed "from above," at the leadership level. They might be recognized for their prestige, skill, or leadership. Prestige had a value of its own because it commanded immediate respect and attracted a broader force of people.

Cell members in the middle would elevate favored loyalists from below and pressure non-Communists at the top, when possible with help from those already working "from above." This is how small numbers would take over existing and trusted organizations. Defectors revealed that the party needed very few people to take control of an entire organization once they seized a few levers of power. Thus the party's small formal membership in the United States was no impediment to furthering strategic goals. Subversion trumped electoral numbers.

The Comintern agents and fellow travelers under the vertical command structure in those networks would recognize one another as allies and align and organize particular political messaging and activism horizontally, among other organizations, to create a broad movement with a united message.

This formula became more refined over the years, developing into a non-ideological political technology or template that would far outlive the organizers, and even the Soviet Union and its international fronts. Some of these structures would become networks for economic change. Some would pressure for political, educational, cultural, or social change. The methodology, once understood, is easy to recognize.

Hoover Keeps Tabs on Communist Networks

Hoover had a straightforward reason for monitoring Communist Party members and their networks: By taking membership in the party, an American immigrant or citizen pledged to become a Soviet agent, when called, to subvert, spy on, and ultimately overthrow his own constitutional government. By working or organizing with party members, others became part of that organized criminal conspiracy.

Every party member took the oath, identical or similar to this official version from 1935:

> I pledge myself to rally the masses to defend the Soviet Union, the land of victorious Socialism. I pledge myself to remain at all times a vigilant and firm defender of the Leninist line of the Party, the only line that insures the triumph of Soviet Power in the United States.[12]

Obviously, taking such a pledge would place one crosswise with federal law. It was the duty of the FBI, as a law enforcement organization, to monitor such people and their networks, because they were willfully part of a foreign-sponsored organized criminal conspiracy, what would become known as Soviet active measures, to overthrow the Constitution. When Communist Party members and fellow travelers got into trouble, they had a reliable bank of free lawyers to help. The ACLU, founded in response to the Palmer Raids, proved the first resource, but it was not known to be under party control. The ACLU defended Communist networks from an extreme interpretation of the First Amendment that disregarded the Founding Fathers' profound concerns about foreign influence and subversion, of which George Washington had warned in his Farewell Address.

A separate group, the National Lawyers Guild (NLG), founded in 1937, acted as the legal arm of the CPUSA and Soviet espionage networks. It gained acceptance because it welcomed people of all races at a time when the American Bar Association remained racially segregated. The NLG functioned as the "legal bulwark of the Communist Party, its front organizations, and controlled unions."[13]

The situation became so serious after the Molotov-Ribbentrop pact of August 23, 1939, that President Roosevelt directed the FBI six weeks later "to take charge of investigative work in matters relating to espionage, sabotage, and violations of the neutrality regulations." He requested "all police officers, sheriffs, and all other law enforcement officers in the United States promptly to turn over to the nearest representative of the Federal Bureau of Investigation any information obtained by them relating to espionage, counterespionage, sabotage, subversive activities and violations of the neutrality laws."[14]

As the threat of war loomed under the nonaggression pact between Hitler and Stalin, Hoover gave speeches around the country to warn the public about how Soviet-sponsored subversion worked. Through their proxies, the Soviets exploited every vulnerability and tension in the United States to drive deeper rifts and pit Americans against one another. CPUSA leader Earl Browder wrote a book denouncing Britain's defense against the Nazis as "The Second Imperialist War" and promoting peace movements to discourage resistance to Hitler.[15]

"Communists recognize that they cannot infiltrate and undermine American society unless they first turn the people against established authority," Hoover told a women's group in 1940, while the Nazis and Soviets were joined in their pact and CPUSA loyalists stopped opposing Hitler. "In particular, communists strive to arouse Negro hostility toward policemen as a means of fomenting racial strife."[16] Agitprop agents like Frank Marshall Davis in the Chicago party machine busily worked toward this goal.

Hoover warned in an American Legion speech that Communists and their allies "are the very first ones who would introduce un-American, violent, murderous types of spy systems into our country. They desire to break down true law enforcement in every part of America under the guise of the protection of alleged civil liberties so that they may, in turn, destroy the very things that they pretend to revere."[17]

Hoover understood what cultural Marxism, propelled with its logic chain of critical theory, would do to attack American society by working legally within the system. "Herein lies the greatest threat of the foreign isms," he told the American Legion. "Wily, cunning masters of perversion that they are, with no regard for truth, they poison and pollute the very atmosphere of freedom with venomous attacks upon everything which we hold dear—our flag, our country, our churches, our homes, our institutions and our traditions. It is the object of these schemers to raise doubt in the minds of our misinformed citizens, who too frequently follow the leader for the mere purpose of gaining some recognition."[18]

And then there was the deliberate misuse and distortion of language. Hoover got it. He tried to help the public understand it. "The strictest loyalty to communist ideas is combined with the ability to make all necessary compromises, zigzags, and retreats. Aesopian language or double talk is a prominent deceptive advice used by communists to fool noncommunists," Hoover said in a 1940 college commencement address. "Communist Aesopian language always has two sides—the deceptive line for public consumption and the real Party line to advance communism. Hence the words and terms uttered by communists, such as democracy and peaceful coexistence, have a meaning vastly different from accepted usage."[19]

Hung Up on His Own Success

Münzenberg is a case study of how top Comintern agents went back and forth from Europe to the United States to run Kremlin political influence operations.

Throughout the 1920s, when he wasn't operating newspapers in Germany or leading the German Communist Party, Münzenberg ran ops in the United States. The Comintern man organized protests for Nicola Sacco and Bartolomeo Vanzetti, two Italian-born anarchists arrested for murder. Their six-year prosecution had been a cause célèbre for socialists and Communists on the grounds that Sacco and

Vanzetti had received unfair treatment because they were extremists and, for good measure, because the prosecution was racist against Italian immigrants. Even Mussolini attempted to intervene. The state of Massachusetts thought otherwise and executed them by electric chair.

Münzenberg raised large sums from American liberals and Communists in Hollywood. He covertly published the fashionable *PM*, a New York newspaper launched with seed money from wealthy Americans who wanted to be trendy. The paper's offices were a Plaza Hotel suite on Fifth Avenue under the direction of playwright Lillian Hellman and screeenwriter-novelist Dashiell Hammett. Münzenberg recruited or paid journalists, entertainment figures, and political figures and is considered one of the most important Soviet agents of influence in history.[20]

In the process, he made a fortune for himself, raising money from well-meaning people for nonexistent or corrupted charities and doing some legitimate business.[21]

During the Great Purge, the Prussian Comintern figure began to question Stalin's policies. The Kremlin had Münzenberg recalled to Moscow for consultations with the central Comintern leadership. He survived the meeting and left for France to coordinate Comintern aid to the anarchist and Communist factions in the Spanish Civil War. Stalin had him pushed out of the Comintern by 1937, but Münzenberg remained a good Communist and saw his old Frankfurt School friends in Paris as they left for Columbia University. He opposed Stalin's non-aggression pact with Hitler in 1939, whereupon the Communist Party expelled him as an enemy.

Hoover's FBI never caught up with Münzenberg.

But Stalin's NKVD did. In 1940, Soviet agents tracked down the Comintern's most ingenious leader in a forest in Cagnet in south-western France. Some say that Münzenberg killed himself. Others say the NKVD did it. Either way, the rotting corpse of the Frankfurt

School cofounder was discovered under the hanging tree, a wire garrote wrapped around his neck.[22]

Part II

Three-Way War

"I'd put Stalin on the OSS payroll if I thought it would help us defeat Hitler."

—General William "Wild Bill" Donovan, director, OSS[1]

Chapter 10

Donovan and Hoover: Rivals for Foreign Intelligence

World War II was a three-way war for the planet and mankind. A two-way war joined the United States and free Europe and their worldwide empires, free China, and other countries as allies with Stalin's Soviet Union to defeat the Axis powers led by Nazi Germany, fascist Italy, and Imperial Japan. The Allies versus the Axis. Very simple. And very simplistic.

The third way, a world-war-within-a-world-war, pitted the Soviet Union and its Comintern agents against the rest of the Allies while they were allies against the Axis.

Once the United States actively poured its forces into the Pacific and Europe, defeating Hitler was only a matter of time. The Kremlin had no quarrel with Tojo's Japan until opportunistically grabbing Japanese territory in the final days of the war. By 1943, it was clear to the Soviet leadership that the Nazis would be destroyed. For Stalin and his team, the real war was for how Europe and the rest of the world would look after the Allied victory. Moscow sought an ultimate defeat of the British and French empires and of America's new power.

British prime minister Winston Churchill also recognized this three-way war and how Stalin was planning to re-order the post-Axis world under the red banner.

Faced with the near-term task of defeating the immediate enemy and worrying about the rest later, the Roosevelt administration showed little concern about Moscow's long-term war aims, despite Churchill's warnings. A bipartisan consensus in America remained that the Soviets did indeed present a long-term threat to the integrity of the United States government and institutions, but President Roosevelt and his very large team of liberal progressives didn't necessarily share that view.

Stalin and his loyal Comintern cadres welcomed FDR's benign, indulgent, no-questions-asked approach.

In Washington, J. Edgar Hoover stood almost alone in the federal government as an exception. He was no geostrategist except for a profound understanding of global subversive systems and how they operated. He would squeeze Nazi and Soviet spy and influence agent networks as a national security imperative to expose them, divide them, peel away defectors, and shut them down as the nation's flimsy laws allowed.

Yet he was far from isolated in the Roosevelt administration. Philosophically, Hoover and Roosevelt were near opposites. Personally and officially, they enjoyed one another's confidence and company. The president assigned the FBI director to monitor political rivals. Roosevelt trusted Hoover, and Hoover served the president as he had all the others.

Roosevelt's top aide, Harry Hopkins, privately asked Hoover to have the FBI spy on his own wife. We don't know the exact reason;

Hopkins was friendly to the Soviets and may have been running his own counterintelligence against the FBI to see what it knew about his activity, or he may have been trying to make sure his wife wasn't informing on him, but this is speculation.

During the middle of World War II, Hoover investigated messy administration scandals and covered some of them up. Hoover saw the cover-ups as necessary to maintain the president's image as a wartime leader. Eleanor Roosevelt foamed when the FBI did a background check of her social secretary, writing a cross letter to Hoover: "This type of investigation seems to me to smack too much of the Gestapo methods."[1] Privately, Hoover viewed Eleanor as a Communist sympathizer,[2] which indeed she was.

The United States fought foreign subversion at home with the FBI; it had no standing foreign intelligence service. As the threat of war grew before Pearl Harbor, Washington had few means of collecting and synthesizing intelligence of its own. Its ability to insert secret agents into hostile territory, or even into contested areas to resist an enemy advance, was zero. Uncle Sam had almost no experienced civilian intelligence professionals, no reserves, no retirees, no experienced veterans. It had no place to train new recruits, and no office to recruit them in the first place.

President Roosevelt needed a foreign intelligence service, and he needed it fast. It was the spring of 1941, before Hitler attacked his non-aggression partner Stalin, and well before the Japanese attacked the U.S. Navy in Hawaii.

Hoover came up with a plan. The FBI would become America's worldwide intelligence organization. His plan was bold and well-conceived. Roosevelt seemed to like the idea. But as a political leader, the president preferred teams of rivals—he fancied himself a "juggler" of people and policies—and he wanted an alternative.

Birth of the OSS

As Democratic governor of New York in the late 1920s and early '30s, Roosevelt knew Wild Bill Donovan as an honest and capable leader of rival Republicans in state politics. When FDR vacated the governorship to run for president in 1932, Donovan ran unsuccessfully to succeed him.

Donovan continued to travel the world. He visited Ethiopia in the mid-1930s to watch Mussolini's forces battle for control of that ancient Christian empire. President Roosevelt quietly tapped Donovan, still in his private law practice, to visit London in 1940 and learn what he could about Britain's will to resist the Nazis. Donovan met with Churchill, who opened military and intelligence services to him. He toured British sites across the Mediterranean. He visited the Balkans. The Brits liked him.

London's embassy in Washington handled Donovan almost like an asset. Its top military attaché, an admiral, and its Secret Intelligence Service station chief, William Stephenson, met with Roosevelt to suggest he set up an American spy service with Donovan as its chief. Stephenson would be immortalized by his code name: Intrepid.

FDR asked Donovan to devise plans for a new intelligence service. Weeks after Hitler turned against Stalin in Operation Barbarossa, FDR created a Coordinator of Information (COI). It was the summer of 1941. The president asked Donovan to run it. He re-commissioned Donovan as an Army officer with the rank of brigadier general. None of this sat well with naval intelligence, the Army's G-2 intelligence, the military top brass, or the FBI.

But the general's star put Donovan near the military leadership, from which he could cherry-pick the best of the best.

Hoover had proposed the FBI as a complete international espionage service. Donovan didn't plan COI that way. He envisioned COI as supporting the military in the field with top-quality research and sound, actionable analysis for civilian decision-makers and uniformed war-planners. He also saw COI as running propaganda and unconventional warfare operations to augment regular combat forces. But not espionage, otherwise known as spying. And not counterintelligence, which was to detect, disrupt, and defend against foreign spies and agents.

Time was the enemy before the Axis made war on the United States. Donovan, true to his nature, winged it. The COI started as a seat-of-the-pants, pop-up enterprise. Donovan reached into his personal networks to build a team of skillful, learned scholars and operators.

The quality-conscious Donovan sought an army of industrious self-starters. Referring once to recruiting burglars for tough jobs, he said, "You can hire a second-story man and make him a better second-story man. But if you hire a lawyer or an investment banker or a professor, you'll have something else besides."[3] A sophisticated kind of hardness.

Donovan began to see the need for a real espionage service with human agents, clandestine communications, and all that went with it. He split the COI in two: one for overt communication abroad and the other for foreign propaganda, collection and analysis of foreign intelligence, and for running intelligence operations abroad.

The energetic New York Irishman, constantly enthusing with new ideas, thought big. He would head the second entity with an appropriate name, the Office of Strategic Services. OSS would be funded quietly out of a secret presidential budget.

The larger-than-life personalities of Donovan and Hoover could not have been more different in approaching the challenge. Both men still disliked, perhaps hated, each other. Wartime emergency didn't preclude personal rivalry. Hoover called Donovan a Communist sympathizer. Donovan called Hoover a closet homosexual.[4]

With his intense energy wrapped in an easy style, Donovan built an irregular intelligence service of amateurs from conscripted soldiers and sailors, enlisted men and officers; bankers and international lawyers; journalists and broadcasters; and faculty from what were then the nation's most prestigious universities. Civilians received military ranks and enlisted men dressed as civilians to work with senior officers peer-to-peer. Donovan got help from wherever he could get it—anybody with the skills, necessary ethnic or cultural background, language fluency, contact networks, physical constitution, self-discipline, mental strength, and motivation to defeat the enemy.

Donovan's improvised OSS depended on crucial training, planning, and other support from the British, who had centuries of cloak-and-dagger experience behind them and a deliciously subversive leader, Prime Minister Churchill.

Churchill took what could be called a Keep Great Britain Great approach to statesmanship. The prime minister didn't help build the OSS to help the Americans. He did it to save the British Empire.

A foreign country's intelligence service would breed and deliver America's first worldwide intelligence service. Hoover saw danger.

Countermoves: Moscow's Frankfurt School Man in Tokyo

In the six months between Barbarossa and Pearl Harbor in 1941, as Donovan scoured the country for OSS talent, Stalin desperately focused all his efforts on fighting Germany and avoiding a two-front war with Japan. GRU military intelligence coordinated influence operations in Tokyo to ensure that Imperial Japan, already occupying a large swath of China, would not invade the Soviet Far East and doom the USSR.

The Japanese military was divided. Already occupying Chinese Manchuria, the army preferred Soviet possessions in Vladivostok and the Soviet Far East, while the navy aimed to take British, French, or Dutch possessions in the Pacific.

Richard Sorge, the GRU spy with the Frankfurt School, had gone to Tokyo under cover as a German journalist with strong Nazi connections. His job was to interview Japanese officials and confirm to them the futility of attacking Soviet territory. His Japanese facilitator, Hotsumi Ozaki, was also a Communist Party member and Soviet agent.

Sorge wrote in his memoir that he advised the Japanese leaders he interviewed that Moscow had no intention of fighting Japan or competing in the Pacific. He said he offered friendly advice that Tojo should move beyond China to points south instead of north, those "southern" points interpreted as British-ruled Burma, sovereign Thailand, French Indochina, Korea, Dutch-ruled Indonesia, and American interests in the Philippines, Guam, and even Hawaii.[5] Such a move would expand Japan's reach while pinning down Germany's enemies, perhaps even neutralizing the United States.

In Washington, the Roosevelt administration sat divided over an Asia strategy. Americans sympathized strongly with nationalist China, horrified at Japanese atrocities there. Squeezing Imperial Japan too hard could provoke it to attack American interests in Asia, or indeed American territories across the Pacific. President Roosevelt and his military leadership leaned toward a truce with Japan.

Others pushed back. They included FDR's assistant Lauchlin Currie, responsible for China policy; Treasury Department official Harry Dexter White, who pushed hard for powerful sanctions on Japan; and Johns Hopkins University professor Owen Lattimore of the Institute of Pacific Relations.

Lattimore was also an FDR-picked advisor in Chungking to nationalist Chinese president Chiang Kai-shek. The Soviet-backed Communist armies of Mao Tse-tung hid in the mountains, waiting for the Japanese invaders to grind down Chiang's forces and China's civilian population. In a cable from China, Lattimore pleaded for tightening the noose on Japan. That cable persuaded Secretary of State Cordell Hull to opt to prepare for war. Hull proposed an ultimatum to Tokyo. White, who had been briefed on the party line months earlier by Soviet intelligence officer Vitaly Pavlov, helped the secretary of state write the ultimatum. (Pavlov would later defect to the United States.)

Stalin's Eastern Influence Operation

While Sorge persuaded Japan whom to attack and whom to leave alone, Moscow ran covert influence operations in Washington to pressure Roosevelt to dispense with the truce idea and to choke Japan's oil supplies with economic warfare. The United States had its own interests in containing Japan and was debating its options quite apart from Kremlin intrigue. Moscow's agents worked to steer those internal policy discussions. The ideal American approach would prevent Tokyo from joining Hitler's war against Stalin and allow Moscow to concentrate its forces on its western front in Europe.[6]

Everything was made to sound like the United States was standing with Chiang's heroic Chinese government that was resisting both Imperial Japan and Chairman Mao's Chinese Communist Party. "Thus did policies promoted in official U.S. circles by White, Currie, and Lattimore dovetail with those advanced by the Sorge-Ozaki network in Japan," write historians Herbert Romerstein and M. Stanton Evans, "all converging toward the result that there would be no American-Japanese rapprochement and, even more to the point, no Japanese attack on Russia."[7]

FBI work, congressional investigations, defector accounts, and decrypted Soviet communications would later reveal that Currie was a Soviet asset, White a Soviet intelligence agent, and Lattimore a Soviet agent of influence[8] and a designee of Currie. All would ultimately turn American policy against Chiang Kai-shek in favor of Mao.[9]

While no persuasive evidence indicates that the Soviet agents in Tokyo and Washington provoked the attack on Pearl Harbor, ample evidence shows that Sorge and the actions of Currie, White, and Lattimore influenced Japan not to attack north into Russia, but to strike somewhere else.

Tojo ultimately chose to attack the American Pacific Fleet, hoping to destroy it in Hawaii. If successful, it would be the ultimate bonanza for Stalin: a Japanese military completely focused on China and the Pacific, and a declaration of war by Hitler that would bog down the Nazis—not the Soviets—in a two-front war for survival.

The Soviets would honor the Frankfurt School's Sorge as one of their greatest spies of all time.

Chapter 11

A Poisoned Start for the OSS

London and Moscow needed the United States, and, if it was to win the war in Europe and Japan, the United States needed them. Everyone took whatever allies they could get.

The military and OSS needed people with direct knowledge of everything about enemy territory. They turned to immigrant scholars who had lived under Hitler's rule and in Nazi-occupied areas. There were two general types: immigrants who were genuinely pro-American, anti-fascist, and anti-Communist; and immigrants principally loyal to the Kremlin who wanted American troops to liberate Europe and China on Stalin's terms and ultimately to overthrow the United States Constitution.

Britain gave the OSS a running start. MI6 maintained a substantial influence network in the United States. It knew the obsolescence of the American military and its non-existent foreign intelligence capabilities.

The British had confidence in Donovan as the right partner. Intrepid, the MI6 man, had built and was operating the Crown's covert American networks in an intelligence unit called British Security Coordination.[1] He worked well with Donovan.

Hoover sensed danger but couldn't put his finger on it. He still had no real counterintelligence capabilities. The experienced British hand steadying and guiding Donovan in creating the OSS, and, as some argue, the power behind the throne of American intelligence, was Intrepid's deputy, Charles "Dickie" Ellis. Ellis enthusiastically channeled Donovan to the right people and helped channel the right people to Donovan.

What neither Intrepid nor Donovan knew was that Ellis was a double agent loyal to Stalin.[2] Ellis's victories in Washington had little to do with passing American secrets to his Soviet GRU military intelligence handlers. The Soviet spy's real achievement was influencing the creation of American foreign intelligence.

Wild Bill's Myopia

Donovan seemed blind to the fact that Communists and foreign assets recruited into the OSS would not have American interests first in mind.

Highly recommended American soldiers were brought into the OSS, only to be weeded out because, in the words of Ralph de Toledano, who was one of them and a socialist at the time, they were "too anti-Communist." In the China-Burma theater, under General "Vinegar Joe" Stilwell, "the careers and sometimes the fate of OSS personnel frequently depended on whether they were reliably anti-Chiang Kai-shek and pro-Mao."[3] Many of the pro-Mao personnel would flourish in American intelligence and the State Department after the war.

Donovan knew that intelligence to advise the president and his military leaders required extraordinarily well-informed linguists and experts to do deep-dive research and analysis. With space in Hoover's old Library of Congress stomping ground, Donovan built the OSS Research and Analysis section, known as R&A, from scratch. He recruited brilliant students and professors from American universities, famously from the Ivy League but also from anywhere he could get sharp and disciplined minds.

"Never before and probably never since has such a unique group of scholars been assembled—historians, economists, political scientists, geographers, cartographers, and others, many of them leaders in their fields," recalled John D. Wilson. A Harvard economics instructor who joined the OSS shortly after Pearl Harbor and became a top aide to Donovan, Wilson said that R&A "numbered over 900 in all at the peak."[4]

The United States was home to a huge immigrant population with the languages, human networks, and on-the-ground knowledge that the OSS needed. That meant hiring a very diverse cadre of native-level linguists who spoke everything from Arabic and Japanese to German and Serbian. Many top recruits had their own personal networks of European immigrant families, often with trusted connections back home behind enemy lines. Some of the most important were intellectuals who had fled the Nazis.

Donovan was no Communist sympathizer, no softie, and no fool. He had seen Soviet cruelty up close during the Russian Civil War, and was among the first Americans to collect against the Comintern. Roosevelt's New Deal, Donovan thought, was a "racketeering attempt" that attacked family values and, in the words of biographer Douglas Waller, "bordered on communistic."[5] Before the war, he viewed Stalin as no better than Hitler.

But talent was talent, and OSS needed it in spades.

Crawling with Communists

Donovan found Communists valuable in the OSS because they were internationalists with worldwide networks and showed particular excellence in pinpointing Nazi agents and assets. Many of the immigrant intellectuals had been Communist Party members in their countries of origin, unabashed devotees of Stalin and part of his Comintern machinery. Many Communist immigrants knew the party networks back in Europe, even those in the organized underground.

Donovan knew, as did most Americans at the time, that the Communist Party USA was a slavish tool of Stalin and an instrument of Soviet intelligence, and that it would stop opposing Hitler as soon as it got the word, as had happened between August 1939 and June 1941.[6]

In general, though, Donovan had no idea of the scope of Soviet penetration of his organization. Journalist John Scott left *Time* magazine to join the OSS. He was openly pro-Stalin in his reporting, and, like a number of American journalists in major publications, a recruited agent of the NKVD. A future CIA contract analyst, Nellie H. Orr, would write warmly of Scott as an "observer" of the "excitement" of the Stalin period.[7]

From London, with the help of MI6, which had its own Soviet infiltration problems through the Cambridge Five network of Kim Philby, the OSS recruited exiled German Communists to execute spy missions in late 1944 during the German penetration campaign. Some collected successful military intelligence. Some died under mysterious circumstances. Philby and others in the ring had direct involvement with the OSS. One researcher found from East German archives that some of the recruits betrayed OSS sources and methods to Soviet military intelligence.[8]

Had it been permitted greater duties, the OSS might also have broken up Nazi rings in the American hemisphere. In the pre-OSS wrangling, Hoover had secured Latin America and the Caribbean as the FBI's foreign intelligence turf to combat Nazi activity. The FBI ran up a string of successes as some of the bureau's unsung historical accomplishments.[9]

Hoover's bureaucratic fighting was vindicated for another reason. OSS Latin American Division chief Maurice Halperin, it turned out, was another Soviet spy.[10]

Soviets' American Networks Grow and Grow

The FBI faced immense challenges against both Nazi and Soviet networks in the United States. New York City sat as the epicenter. Hede Thune Eisler Massing, the actress and Austrian Communist Party leader who had moved with the Frankfurt School to New York, now worked for Amtorg, the Soviet trading company. Amtorg's cofounder was Soviet agent Armand Hammer, whose father, Julius, had helped fund the Bolshevik Revolution.

Outside of Amtorg, Hede worked at the Institute for Social Research at Columbia University, the Frankfurt School's new physical home. Richard Sorge had recruited her into the GRU. Hoover turned the screws on Hede and other Frankfurt School figures. They formed the core of Moscow's newer imported networks in America. FBI agents questioned Hede about her first husband, Gerhart Eisler, the Comintern agent running operations in the United States.

Hede's most recent husband, Paul Massing, was a German Communist Party member and GRU spy who handled Stalin's American networks of "illegals," or deep-cover agents. While the FBI rooted out Soviet agents to shut them down, the OSS was recruiting them. The U.S. Army Signal Corps, under its super-secret, brilliant Venona program, intercepted and decrypted a message in which Paul Massing had informed his GRU handlers that the OSS had just enlisted one of his trusted friends.[11]

The Army Signal Corps, whose leaders recognized the three-way nature of the war, quietly broke the codes of 5,000 pages of wartime communications cables of Soviet military intelligence in its Venona operation. It unmasked some 350 Soviet spies in the United States government and private industry. Venona alone found that at least 15 Soviet agents had penetrated the OSS. It certainly would have found more had it been able to decrypt everything it intercepted.[12]

Hoover knew about Venona and the contents of many of the decrypts. He needed to protect the secret that the United States had broken the Soviet code. He made sure that nobody outside his trusted circle knew—not even Donovan, who was blind to the problem, or the president, who had brought some of those agents and fellow travelers into his inner circle.

With Hoover protecting one of America's most vital secrets while passing on knowledge of the threat, the FBI warned how the Soviets and their proxies had been penetrating the American educational system for a generation. Hoover appeared to be concerned in part about the Frankfurt School, with its new teach-the-teachers program at Columbia University's Teachers College, though the Communists had targeted schools before the Frankfurt comrades' arrival.

"Over the years, the American Communists have developed a propaganda machine and a nefarious and elaborate school system of their own," Hoover said in 1944, at the height of the war against Hitler and the Axis. "Their officials in secret and public meetings urge that the propaganda phase of their work must be accelerated. Brazenly, they have urged the development of courses, lectures, and assemblies as media to espouse the ideologies of Marxism and to establish Marxism as a school of thought in the United States."[13]

1943: Moscow Finds a "Main Enemy" beyond Hitler

The Kremlin initially recoiled from the idea of U.S., British, or other Allied intelligence services actually collaborating with its own assets within its global network of Communist parties. That access, the Soviet leadership feared, would allow the Americans and others to exploit the occasion to infiltrate and disrupt Communist parties and the Comintern itself. Through its outpost in New York, Moscow instructed its American agents to stand down.

Some American Communists, unaware of such a secret order, still joined the OSS as individuals.[14] As the war advanced, however, the Comintern began to support this, even instructing its operatives to join the OSS to infiltrate American intelligence.

From its start, OSS inadvertently made itself a magnet for Communist operatives and Soviet agents.

Infiltration of a foreign intelligence service, especially at its center, is generally difficult and time-consuming. But the OSS, because of the necessary wartime haste in standing it up, the urgent need for foreign-born talent, and the uniqueness of the war, presented an exception.[15]

OSS proved an easy target for Stalin's GRU military intelligence and the Chekists of OGPU/OKGB/NKVD, the name-changing precursors of the KGB. For all his experience and beliefs, Donovan took a naïve view about Stalin. The younger men building and running the OSS had little experience and almost no understanding of Moscow's long-term strategic goals. The FBI had no real counterintelligence capability yet. Naval intelligence and G-2, by contrast, posed hard targets against penetration.

For the United States, the goal was to defeat the Axis. By 1943, with the Nazis repulsed from Soviet territory, Stalin was focusing on the United Kingdom and the United States, his most vital allies, as his "main enemy."

Dickie Ellis, One of Stalin's Men in MI6—and OSS

This is when controlled Soviet agents flooded into the OSS, quite apart from other Communists and Soviet assets who had already joined on their own. Frankfurt School faculty and graduates joined among them to advance Stalin's postwar agenda. Their inherent knowledge and abilities naturally gravitated toward the OSS's Research & Analysis division, the unit that interpreted the information that was collected and converted it into intelligence for President Roosevelt and other decision-makers. Three of those Frankfurt School men, Franz Neumann, Otto Kirchheimer, and Herbert Marcuse, became top members of the division's Central European Section.

According to a CIA summary of a 2013 book, Neumann "had been vetted by the FBI." For the Frankfurt School group, as with the controlled Soviet agents in the OSS, the immediate job was to defeat Hitler, but the second and more important job was to revive their 1920s work to shape postwar Germany in their image.[16] To accomplish that strategic objective, they would steer the OSS to ignore, undermine, and discredit the anti-Communist German resistance to Hitler.

The ever-helpful Dickie Ellis, deputy head of MI6 at the British embassy in Washington, recruited powerful talent to help Donovan build the OSS.

From start-up, Donovan had his astonishing team convert everything from rural New Deal make-work encampments to the Bethesda Country Club as OSS training camps. He had his eyes and ears, his researchers and analysts, his linguists and cultural warriors, his clandestine operators. But he needed people with irregular warfare experience. With no commando school to train recruits and no commando veterans to do the training, Donovan got British help to train OSS guerrilla fighters and saboteurs at a secret school in Canada, called Camp X. He welcomed any anti-Nazi he could find. He needed experienced guerrilla fighters who knew and trusted one another in combat. The United States didn't have any.

That is, except for former members of the Abraham Lincoln Brigade. Those young men had fought a few years earlier as a volunteer guerrilla force in the Spanish Civil War. Donovan reached out personally to Milt Wolff, the twenty-six-year-old commander of the Veterans of the Abraham Lincoln Brigade.

One in Seven Are Spies

There was a problem. The Abraham Lincoln Brigade had fought under Soviet control in Spain. Its veterans' group was a Communist Party front. Wolff was a controlled Soviet asset. Just months before Donovan met him, prior to Hitler's breaking his pact with Stalin, Wolff and the Veterans of the Abraham Lincoln Brigade had militantly opposed any American resistance to the Nazis.

President Roosevelt, Wolff said, was a fascist and a racist. In a Chicago speech, Wolff excoriated FDR as a "red-baiting, union-busting, alien-hunting, anti-Negro, anti-Semitic" leader bent on a "jingoistic road to fascism in America." Spanish Civil War veterans who supported Roosevelt, Wolff said, were "deserters."[17]

That was all in accordance with the Comintern line set after the Hitler-Stalin pact of 1939. But after Operation Barbarossa, Stalin needed Wolff and his veteran guerrillas to take a different tack. The Comintern directed all Communist parties to make war on Hitler. Wolff followed the latest Soviet line and met with Donovan.[18]

So did others. The OSS needed natives of the multilingual, multiethnic Balkans to aid the resistance in Yugoslavia. Thomas Babin, an immigrant from Croatia, joined the OSS. Babin escaped all scrutiny. The United States had deported him as a Communist in 1925, but Babin returned to the United States illegally, organized extremists in New York, and fought on the Communist side in the Spanish Civil War. In the OSS he continued to spy for Soviet military intelligence. He selected trainees for anti-Nazi partisan operations in Yugoslavia as loyal contacts for the GRU.[19] Babin also ran a Soviet operation in

New York Harbor to spy on American shipping, using Communist longshoremen and sailors.[20]

Neither the OSS nor the FBI doubled Communist agents to American control. Scholars Harvey Klehr and John Earl Haynes identified at least fifteen agents in the Venona intercepts, with the actual number estimated higher. Those historians concede that their estimate may be low because Venona was unable to decipher many of the KGB messages and most of the GRU cables. They concluded, "Since the total number of Communists in the OSS was at least fifty and perhaps as high as a hundred, at least one in seven and perhaps as many as one in three Communists in the OSS were spies."[21]

Those who were not actual spies served as Soviet agents or assets of influence.

Communist agent Philip Keeney, after being fired by the University of Montana for radical activity, got a job in Washington at the Library of Congress in 1940. When the war broke out, he became a librarian at OSS, which had significant staff housed at the library. The Venona papers show that he and his wife, Mary Jane, who worked at the Board of Economic Warfare once the war broke out, had been recruited by Soviet military intelligence in 1940. Both joined Communist Party front groups in the nation's capital and networked with actual and alleged Soviet spies. Moscow transferred them from GRU to NKVD control in 1944 or 1945. After the war, Mary Jane moved to Europe on a job with the Allied Staff on Reparations, while Philip shipped off to Tokyo to work on the staff of General Douglas MacArthur.[22]

Hoover Torpedoes Liaison with the Kremlin

Donovan reached out to the Kremlin for a wartime intelligence liaison proposal to smash the Nazis. The idea had value as long as it was at least mutually beneficial in practice. Back in Washington, Hoover led opposition to Donovan's liaison terms with Stalin's intelligence service, then called NKGB but still known as NKVD. Donovan and his Soviet counterparts hammered out a deal in Moscow that would permit the OSS to station agents in the Soviet Union.

Hoover's concern was that the deal would also permit the Soviets to station more spies inside the United States. He told President Roosevelt so to his face.

The liaison issue became a political problem for Roosevelt, running for his fourth term in 1944. Attorney General Francis Biddle, who got along well with Hoover, "worried that in an election year the political fallout would be toxic if conservative Republicans discovered the administration had allowed communist espionage agents to enter the United States," according to Donovan biographer Douglas Waller.[23]

Roosevelt's closest confidant and war policy advisor in the White House, Harry Hopkins, agreed with Biddle. It was an unusual move for Hopkins, but made sense politically, as FDR had dumped his pro-Soviet vice president, Henry Wallace, in favor of Senator Harry S. Truman as his running mate. Hopkins sympathized with Stalin and eagerly accommodated Moscow's demands while meekly insisting on no reciprocity. Some researchers and former Soviet intelligence officers allege that Hopkins was either a fully recruited or unwitting Kremlin agent. Others, having scoured all available evidence, find no indication that he was under Soviet control and no proof that he was not, but acknowledge that he gave Stalin whatever he wanted.[24] Regardless of whether or not Hopkins was a Soviet agent, the fact remains that he was most benignly an unwitting Soviet asset, a fellow traveler if not a useful idiot whose views fit a pattern in the Roosevelt administration of affinity toward the Kremlin.

"Donovan could barely contain his outrage over what he considered baseless paranoia," Waller recounts. The OSS chief did not know about Soviet penetration of the Anglo-American Manhattan Project and probably was unaware of the atom bomb project at all. But he did know that FDR wanted to treat Stalin as an ally, and he knew that senior administration officials, including Hopkins, had passed secrets to the Soviets.

The OSS chief fired off angry memos saying that the Soviets already had undercover agents in America, and that the presence of a few known ones would do the nation no harm. He argued that it was as important for the United States "to know how your allies conduct their subversive work as to know how your enemy does it." Roosevelt's decision to veto Donovan's liaison with the NKGB was motivated by domestic politics, he said, arguing that working closely with the Soviets "in the fields of intelligence and subversion is as essential as collaborating in other types of military and naval operations against the enemy." The American military, Donovan said, "would be the only loser."[25]

Roosevelt nixed the project anyway.

Hoover knew more than he let on. He had access to some of the Army Signal Corps's Venona decrypts of intercepted Soviet intelligence traffic between its American agents and Moscow. Donovan and Roosevelt knew nothing about them, and they never would.

Chapter 12

Men among Men: Donovan's Heroes

Wild Bill Donovan's greatest contributions to the war effort were of the paramilitary type, supplying commandos and other unconventional forces to fight the Nazis and their allies behind the lines. Donovan wanted movers and innovators. His blind spot for Stalinists was his weakness, and he had a personal animus against the prime man who called them out. His great strength rested in his endless energy and his search for those committed to the mission. Those OSS men, with commitments to no bureaucracy, performed some of the most remarkable feats of the war. Several of Donovan's world-class picks of amateurs would become some of the most legendary heroes in American intelligence.

One of them was thirty-year-old Navy officer Richard Helms, a German-speaking former journalist with United Press in Berlin who had once sat down for a private interview with Adolf Hitler.

A Suite of OSS Super Spies

♠ **Allen Dulles.** Both an uncle and a grandfather of Dulles had been secretary of state, and his brother, John Foster Dulles, would go on to hold the same position. Allen Dulles went to Princeton, learned German, and did his World War I duty in the Foreign Service in Switzerland and Vienna. He blew off meeting a Russian revolutionary so he could go on a date. The revolutionary was Vladimir Lenin. That misplaced priority became a valuable lesson for him. Dulles became a lawyer at the big New York law firm Sullivan & Cromwell. He got the firm to shut down its Berlin branch in 1935 after the Nazis took power. Widely traveled, Dulles met European leaders including Mussolini and Hitler. He ran for Congress in 1938. Donovan picked him to run the COI's New York office in late 1941. Dulles worked with a British mentor, William Stephenson (Intrepid) of British Security Coordination. He collected intelligence from businessmen, journalists, and refugees. He ran OSS operations from Switzerland during the war and arranged the surrender of German forces in Italy through SS general Karl Wolff in Operation Sunrise.

♥ **James Angleton.** Drafted into the Army out of Yale Law School, twenty-five-year-old James Jesus Angleton grew up in Idaho and was educated in England. His father, an American cavalry officer like Donovan, met his mother, of Mexican ancestry, during the Mexican Revolution. Angleton learned Spanish from his mother and studied the Italian language and culture abroad. The OSS recruited him for his Italian knowledge and assigned him to X-2, the counterintelligence branch in Washington. The hardworking Angleton soon asked to be stationed in Europe and made such an impression that the X-2 chief dispatched him to London. War needs returned Angleton to Washington. Late in 1944, the OSS sent him to liberated Rome and had him run all X-2 operations in Italy. Angleton found a way to use British-decrypted German Ultra intelligence for U.S. Army counterintelligence. Three years after the war, Angleton played a vital role in countering Soviet covert action for a Communist Party electoral takeover of Italy in 1948. Angleton ran an operation that saved Italy from falling to the Communists and shaped the Cold War history of all of Southern Europe and the Mediterranean. Angleton then worked in the new state of Israel with the Mossad and Shin Bet before returning to Washington and becoming head of CIA counterintelligence. He was known by his enemies and took strong positions that remain controversial to this day. The CIA still praises Angleton as "a model of an innovative, activist counterintelligence officer whose contributions exceeded his job description."[1]

♦ **William Colby.** A young Army lieutenant, Colby had lived in Georgia, Vermont, Panama, and China. He attended Princeton and Columbia. During the war in 1943, he saw that the OSS needed French-speaking soldiers and signed up. He cheated on an eye exam to qualify as a paratrooper. Colby led OSS Jedburgh parachute teams to support Allied forces from behind enemy lines. He blew up railroads and bridges and supplied local guerrilla resistance forces, first in France. His team rescued the right flank of Lieutenant General George S. Patton's Third Army as it advanced on the Wehrmacht. Colby, promoted to major, then led a team in Norway.

Operation Rype supplied Norwegian resistance fighters to help them blow a railroad vital to the Wehrmacht in the north of the country, where the Nazis were sending troops southward to Europe and ran a tritium plant crucial for their atomic bomb development. The British refused to loan their own aircraft for Norwegian pilots to fly the operation, so the OSS reverted to U.S. B-24 Liberators with novice pilots to parachute Colby and his team on skis into the Arctic Circle wilderness. Colby succeeded against all odds, despite the crashes of two planes that killed members of the team and lost precious supplies. Colby almost certainly did not know at the time that his effort was in support of the British operation to sabotage the Norwegian tritium plant and stop Nazi development of an atomic bomb.[2]

♣ **William J. Casey.** Bill Casey was a Jesuit-educated lawyer from Queens who invented the tax shelter to help entrepreneurs legally avoid President Franklin Roosevelt's New Deal confiscations of wealth.

Donovan recruited him from the Navy to become OSS chief of intelligence for the European theater. After the D-Day invasion led by General Dwight Eisenhower, Donovan assigned Casey the audacious task of infiltrating behind enemy lines in Germany to support the Allied push from Normandy to cross the Rhine toward Berlin. The British thought the plan impossible but had no plan of their own. Casey, dressed in civilian clothes to conceal his junior officer rank and thus allow him to speak plainly to senior American and Allied officers, insisted that it could be done. In London, he jotted down objectives and selected agents from among the Belgian, Czech, Dutch, German Polish, and Russian exiles there.

Despite foul weather and a shortage of aircraft, Casey was able to parachute thirty teams operating to support the Allied invasion, including a team of thirty Berlin natives, to a point near the German capital. The OSS teams would operate ahead of the invasion forces, collect information on the enemy, and send back constant intelligence via OSS networks. Germany was all but impenetrable to the Allies until Bill Casey's too-crazy-to-be-true operation. In all, Casey devised a means to infiltrate Nazi Germany to collect on key targets to be bombed ahead of the Allied ground offensive. He assembled and dispatched fifty-eight secret agent teams into Germany in a matter of weeks to prepare for the American, British, and free French occupation of West Berlin, defying the much more seasoned British allies' expectations.[3]

Helms had valuable personal insights into the Nazi leadership.[4] Another, forty-eight-year-old former diplomat and international lawyer Allen Dulles, who had met Hitler and Mussolini and thus had as good a firsthand view of the enemy leadership as any American, would run the OSS station in neutral Switzerland.[5]

Donovan had gotten to know Allen and his brother, John Foster Dulles, during their legal careers. He recruited a British-educated, twenty-five-year-old Mexican-American Army conscript from Idaho named James Jesus Angleton, fluent in the Italian language and with graceful cultural skills. He brought aboard one young Army lieutenant, an adventurous, audacious, reverently Christian paratrooper named Bill Colby, who had once had a youthful flirtation with joining the international brigades in Spain but thought better of it.[6] Another Donovan recruit, a shrewd twenty-nine-year-old business-lawyer-turned-naval-officer named William J. Casey, had cleverly invented the tax shelter to help entrepreneurs avoid FDR's New Deal confiscations of wealth.[7] All had innovative streaks and a fearless knack for making things happen.

Triumphs of Wild Bill

Donovan knew the value of leveraging networks of people. His recruits, many with their own trusted personal networks, jump-started the reach and capabilities of the OSS. Donovan even got the archbishop of New York, Francis Cardinal Spellman, to cast his net worldwide through the Catholic Church to collect intelligence for the Office of Strategic Services.

The OSS teemed with talented people whom Donovan would hire but never know. A future television chef named Julia Child. A scrappy young Army private, Ralph de Toledano, a Morocco-born Sephardic Jew whose father came from Italy. Like Angleton, de Toledano was one of the speakers of Italian in the OSS with the requisite talents who wasn't a fascist sympathizer or a Communist. Although a committed socialist at the time, he was deemed "too anti-Communist" for deployment to Italy.

After the war, de Toledano would become a prominent journalist and author. He worked for the Washington bureau of *Newsweek* while the magazine was owned by Vincent Astor and provided cover for the FBI. He joined William F. Buckley as a founder of *National Review*. He befriended J. Edgar Hoover and Whittaker Chambers. He got to know many other defectors from the Communist Party underground and exposed Soviet clandestine networks in the United States. He knew all about the Frankfurt School as it developed in New York, and he exposed its Comintern history because he knew and interviewed some of the key players involved with Radek, Lukács, Münzenberg, and Dzerzhinsky.[8] He mentored young people for generations.

And then there were OSS people like "Jim," whose histories went unwritten, who would talent-scout for new amateurs decades later, when their old friend Bill Casey ran the CIA, to finish off the Soviet Union and end the Cold War.

Rot among the Bounty

For all its extraordinary innovation and heroism, the OSS was rotten through and through. The organization would succeed as long as its mission suited Soviet interests. For it to survive after the defeat of mutual enemies, American intelligence would have to be abolished and reconstituted.

Although OSS X-2 counterintelligence was effective in rooting out Nazi and fascist spies in Europe, Donovan's approach was so lax that the "OSS had a dismal security reputation," according to an official CIA history. "Established agencies like the FBI and G-2 [military intelligence] believed that Donovan's oddball outfit, built as it was from scratch with not a few corners cut in the hiring of its staff, had to be riddled with subversives and spies."[9] However, the CIA says that "this rap was not wholly fair; OSS headquarters was not in fact penetrated by Axis agents, and its field security (at least in Europe) was adequate."

Note the caveat: the CIA carefully specified Axis agents. It lied by omission, acknowledging that OSS had been heavily infiltrated from top to bottom with non-Axis, Soviet agents. Many of these penetrations had been known for decades when the CIA wrote that history. That history raises questions about still-classified CIA analysis. How much more was doctored or whitewashed? By whom? And why? Which subordinates did they protect and promote, and where are those subordinates now? The National Security Agency began releasing the Venona papers in 1995, filling in many of the missing pieces.

Donovan's own confidential assistant, Lieutenant Colonel Duncan Lee, was a traitor. Like the FBI's official histories, the official CIA history downplays Soviet intelligence penetrations. The present CIA history says that Lee was not a Communist, but it does refer to him, in throwaway fashion, as having "passed information to Moscow." In fact, Lee was both a fully recruited NKVD spy who passed Moscow OSS secrets, including counterintelligence on U.S. detection of Soviet assets inside the OSS, and an agent of influence to shape Donovan's perceptions and policies. Lee would be identified in the Venona decrypts with the cryptonym "Koch."

"OSS operations in China," the CIA history conceded, "were badly penetrated by Communist agents working as clerical and housekeeping staff, or training in OSS camps for operational missions."[10] The CIA history does not say that Lee ran the China unit of the OSS Secret Intelligence Branch. Lee's wife was a Communist Party member who knew of his spy work, and he was having an affair with another Soviet agent.

This posed a problem for everybody, including the OSS, but Donovan appointed Lee in 1944 to run the Japan unit of a secret OSS department. A Soviet intelligence cable intercepted and decrypted under Venona reported that Lee "advises that his section has man working with a little group of Japanese Communist Party members in Communist territory on the problems of dispatching people to Japan."[11]

"Donovan was unaware that a number of these Communists were spying on the OSS for the NKVD. His aim was to protect the image of his organization and of the Roosevelt administration, and his lies to Congress about Communist infiltration of his agency were based on that, not on any sympathy for the Communist cause," Venona researchers Romerstein and Breindel wrote. "This myopic view nevertheless allowed the Soviets to penetrate and spy on American intelligence and endanger the missions and the lives of OSS officers and agents."[12]

Lee's NKVD courier, Elizabeth Bentley, would defect to the FBI in 1945.[13] The public learned the truth after Bentley's public revelations in 1948. Nevertheless, the following year, in 1949, after Mao Tse-tung took full control of mainland China, the CIA hired Lee through a front company to protect a fleet of Nationalist Chinese–owned aircraft in Hong Kong.

A certain soft-on-Communist mentality would permeate the American intelligence and counterintelligence communities, prompting people to ask, "Who lost China?" That mentality persists to the present day. But there are always exceptions.

No Mercy for a Traitor

Former State Department official Noel Haviland Field, operating in France, guided the OSS into Germany. Allen Dulles had known Field since World War I at State. Field had been a senior Europe expert at the State Department and a known Soviet sympathizer. He counted Frankfurt School figures in Europe among his friends and operational contacts. Such contacts are important from an intelligence perspective, but Field hoped that those individuals and their networks would build post-Nazi Europe in Stalin's image.

The FBI had a file on Field as a known Soviet agent. Back in 1935, Alger Hiss had helped convince Field to betray his country and become an agent of the NKVD. Field was named a U.S. representative at the League of Nations in Geneva the following year.

During World War II, Field worked with American Quaker and Unitarian relief and rescue missions for Jewish refugees from

Nazi-occupied territory. The relief work might have been purely humanitarian, but Field's involvement suggests Comintern, GRU, or NKVD work to bring out Soviet loyalists and agents. (Some of those Quaker and Unitarian relief groups became elements of Soviet active measures campaigns throughout the Cold War.) Field built on underground Communist networks, including pro-Stalin resistance forces in southern France. The top OSS man in Switzerland, Allen Dulles, green-lighted Field's work. Dulles used Field as OSS liaison with the Communist elements of the French underground. Even without access to the FBI files, the wily Dulles knew what he was doing. He used Field to discern Stalin's goals for Western Europe after the impending Nazi defeat.[14]

Field's continued employment by the OSS is not a black mark on the OSS record. It was instead clever manipulation of someone who Dulles suspected was a traitor. Dulles would make it right in due time.

Chapter 13

The OSS Chief's Big Lie

As the war approached its end, some policymakers grew worried about what postwar Europe would look like. In March 1945, a congressional committee called Donovan to testify about four Communist OSS officers serving in Italy. The four had fought as members of the International Brigade on the Communist side during the Spanish Civil War. Donovan told the House Committee on Military Affairs that he had investigated the allegations and "did not find that they were Communists." Indeed, he said, "I found that they were not." In fact, as historians Klehr and Haynes found, all four OSS officers had been Communist Party members.[1]

Some of the best biographies of Donovan miss the Comintern problem completely. They portray Donovan as diligently purging Communists from the service.[2] The OSS chief did fire some, more out of concern for political exposure and the organization's public image than for securing American national interests. A sympathetic biographer conceded, "Donovan could be ruthless in getting rid of them, particularly when they were outed by Hoover or congressional witch hunts"[3]—the last two words erroneously implying, as most revisionist history does, that Congress was hunting imaginary witches.

Such firings caused the OSS collateral damage during the war. Even Communists and fellow travelers could be respected for intellect and talent, especially if some found their treason excusable for the greater good of the war effort. And even subversives have friends. When Donovan sacked two allegedly Communist staff writers, forty-two of their colleagues signed a protest letter. Donovan threatened to fire them too. They relented.[4]

Donovan insisted to Congress that all OSS personnel had been screened. "I try to determine whether a man is or is not a Fascist or a Communist—I have never taken a man of whom I had any doubt," he testified. A congressman asked if the OSS had ever recruited a former Communist or even a contributor to "some Communist magazine," because of certain special talents or assets he could contribute to the war effort. It was a softball question. Donovan had leeway to qualify his answer, but instead stated categorically, "I should say right here no such case has ever happened."[5]

"Would you take a person into your organization who you knew had been a Communist?" asked a lawmaker. "I have never done so," Donovan replied, adding, "No man has been taken in with my knowledge who was a Communist." He defended Veterans of the Abraham Lincoln Brigade leader Milt Wolff by name.[6]

"Donovan," write historians Klehr and Haynes, "lied to the Congress. From the origins of his agency in mid-1941 he recruited dozens of persons he knew to be Communists." Donovan could have tried to explain at least some of it, even justify it, by citing wartime needs for certain skills, knowledge, and networks, but he lied.

So did others. "After World War II some former senior OSS officers kept up Donovan's deception that the OSS had never recruited Communists and that only a handful had ever succeeded in joining the organization," Klehr and Haynes recount.

Some former OSS officials were honest. They explained the logical reasons for hiring qualified Communists, under OSS control, to fight the Nazis and fascists, and said that Donovan had expelled some for placing their Communist loyalties ahead of the OSS mission.[7] Privately, Donovan had told a member of his staff, "I'd put Stalin on the OSS payroll if I thought it would help us defeat Hitler."

And that made perfect sense—as long as putting Stalin on the payroll meant a net benefit to the United States and not the other way around. "There is no exact count of the number of Communists who worked for the OSS," Klehr and Haynes concluded, "but the total was easily more than fifty and probably closer to a hundred or even more."[8]

Agents of Influence Shape Postwar Europe

Allen Dulles's on-the-ground knowledge enabled the OSS to limit Soviet agent Noel Haviland Field's influence to the American objective of defeating Hitler without letting him advance Stalin's objective for the future of West Germany.

But witting and unwitting OSS reliance on Communist agents and underground networks ended up sidelining anti-Communist future leaders of postwar Europe. The Soviets had a strategic vision for Europe; the United States did not. Ralph de Toledano recalled from his years of meetings with former members of the Field and early Frankfurt School networks that U.S. intelligence in Europe "ignored anti-Communist Germans and worked mainly with the *Rote Kapelle*, the Soviet Union's chief underground and espionage organization in Germany."[9]

As a journalist, de Toledano conversed with and interviewed many of those involved at the time and in subsequent decades, writing about them for the next fifty years.[10] "Individuals lived or died as a result of OSS political bias, but diplomatic, political, and national policy depended on the work of the OSS Research & Analysis branch," he wrote in his last work, published in 2006. "And it was particularly and emphatically in the Central European desk that the Frankfurt School attempted, and almost succeeded in making the American, British, and French Zones copies of what became the Deutsche Demokratische Republik"—East Germany, ruled under the grip of the party and the Stasi.[11]

Congress heard testimony identifying a Soviet spy at the top of OSS who betrayed American assets in Europe as anti-Soviet troublemakers who would complicate a Stalinist occupation after the war.[12]

Postwar Yugoslavia went Communist largely because the Allies together had favored the Communist factions of the resistance. Babin, the Croat in the OSS, was one of several cases of known Communists who helped Stalin take the long view toward a post-Nazi Europe by selecting Kremlin loyalists from among OSS assets.

On the other hand, Donovan made a brilliant strategic decision that jump-started American foreign counterintelligence against the Kremlin. His one-sided experience with the Soviets, along with their penetration of the OSS, dashed his hopes of a productive relationship. He now worried about the Kremlin's behavior once the war was won. American intelligence on Moscow was practically blind.

With the Nazis facing imminent destruction and surrender to the Americans, Donovan decided to protect General Reinhard Gehlen, a top German intelligence officer on the Eastern Front against the Soviets. Donovan kept Gehlen, his people, and his archives safely in OSS hands.[13] Gehlen's organization had a network inside the USSR. The Soviets wanted to wrap it up. Gehlen and his men had never harmed the United States. Thanks to Donovan's quick action, the Gehlen Organization became critical to American efforts to contain the Soviets during the Cold War.

After the Nazi defeat, State Department official Alger Hiss secretly warned his NKVD brother Noel Haviland Field not to return home to America. Field remained in Soviet-occupied Czechoslovakia. Back in Moscow, NKVD chief Lavrenty Beria worried that the Communists in neighboring Hungary were too liberal and independent. He dispatched the NKVD's surrogate StB service in Prague to arrest Field. The StB transferred him to Hungary for incarceration and torture as part of a show trial for a Hungarian Communist Party purge. In Budapest, prosecutors accused the unfailingly loyal NKVD agent Field of spying for the Americans whom he had betrayed. Field suffered harsh treatment in a Hungarian prison.

Dulles, soon to become CIA director, showed no sympathy or concern for his former State Department and OSS colleague. This was an intelligence war, not a law enforcement matter. An American who betrays his country as a Communist would receive no mercy. Field was an enemy agent. Dulles refused the impassioned pleas from Field's sister for help.[14] Field would never see America again.

Like Dulles in Germany, James Angleton in Italy was wise to the Communist underground and political network against Mussolini. Angleton remained astutely anti-Communist and anti-fascist. He had his own plans for how the United States should protect postwar Italy from a Soviet subversive or electoral takeover. Once approved in Washington, he would score one of America's lowest-cost, highest-impact strategic covert postwar victories by working the Italian elections of 1948 to keep the Communists from power and Stalin out of the Mediterranean, and building up the center-right Christian Democratic Party as a check against the socialists.

That vital operation, and others like it abroad, provided precedent and skills for the CIA to become a covert political player against Communist expansion worldwide.

Part III

Cold War Defense, Double-Dealing, Success, and Malaise

"We want no Gestapo or Secret Police. FBI is tending in that direction."

—President Harry S. Truman, 1945[1]

Chapter 14

American Intelligence after the War

President Roosevelt had understood the OSS, strongly supported its mission, and trusted Donovan. He backed the idea of a peacetime intelligence agency after the war. With the defeat of Germany in sight by September 1944, Donovan had his staff draw up plans for a civilian central intelligence service. Roosevelt formally asked Donovan to keep working on how the service should serve the national interests.

Some government agencies supported such a service, but the Department of War didn't like it. Neither did the Department of the Navy. Vice President Truman neither knew nor understood much about the OSS and never got a briefing until after becoming president.

When Roosevelt died in April 1945, but before the Germans went down in defeat weeks later, Secretary of War Henry L. Stimson, with approval from the Navy, State, and Justice Departments, threw ice on Donovan's idea. They found a very receptive Truman.

Armed with his own plan for postwar intelligence, refined from the one FDR had rejected at the dawn of World War II, Hoover went on the offensive for the FBI to take the lead. He had little trouble persuading the new president that a Cold War defense against the Soviets would never survive with an intelligence community full of Communists and Soviet agents. He took the fight to the public and to Congress. Different interests leaked information to the media designed to sway public opinion and influence legislation in Congress about peacetime foreign intelligence.

And then there were the inevitable rumors. Allegations swirled that the OSS failed to account for funds—true, because it operated on an emergency wartime basis from a secret presidential budget and paid out usually in cash—and there were complaints of too many banking and business figures at the top. Something reeked, the stories went. Donovan had trouble defending the OSS because all its activity had been clandestine within wars around the globe.

After the Japanese surrender in August 1945, top OSS staff urged Donovan to inform the public about what the service had done to help with the victory. The public had no idea. The OSS leader sat down with journalists and generated positive press. Articles appeared nationwide, captivating the public mind with headlines like "If OSS Didn't Exist, It Would Have to Be Invented" in the *Chicago Daily News*, "4,000 Stranded Flyers, Rescued by OSS Underground Railway" in the *Washington Post*, and "U.S. 'Cloak and Dagger' Exploits and Secret Blows in China Bared," in the *New York Times*.

The articles boosted OSS morale. But they didn't move Truman or his budget chief.

President Truman broke up the OSS by fiat in September 1945. Nobody even consulted Donovan.[1]

Counterintelligence

Counterintelligence (CI) is the art of detecting, disrupting, and disempowering foreign intelligence operatives and operations. CI is more than just stopping spies who steal secrets, which is counterespionage. Counterintelligence, done properly, counters any intelligence activity, including subversion.

Widespread Soviet penetration of the OSS ranked high in public attention by the end of the war. Soviet intelligence had already penetrated American academia, journalism, entertainment and culture, politics, and the federal government itself. Government targets included the Treasury Department, State Department, War Department/Defense Department, the Justice Department, the Commerce Department, the intelligence community, the White House, the courts, Congress, and more.

The Cold War with the Soviets demanded full investigations. The clandestine nature of Communist Party activity confused and frightened the public. And it confused non-Communist friends and colleagues of those living secret double lives.

Not all these agents were spies, that is, controlled operatives whose job was to steal secrets and pass them to Moscow. Many had more influential work. Their task was not to spy in the popular sense of the word, but to manipulate the perceptions, policies, and actions of others to benefit the Kremlin. Some served as couriers, administrators, and logisticians. These agents maintained or ran their own networks of cooperative non-Communists, the knowing "fellow travelers" being the Soviets' kind term for them.

At the bottom of the pecking order sat the "dupes," those gullible people whom the Communists charitably called "innocents" or, less charitably, "useful idiots." Very intelligent, some with advanced degrees or impressive credentials, but useful idiots just the same. Fellow travelers, dupes, innocents, and useful idiots defended their Communist friends and causes. Many themselves acted as a clandestine Communist agent would act, so that narrow fringe of American society came under suspicion and scrutiny.

Hoover had to use Venona intelligence to pursue infiltrators by other means, but he also had to protect the existence of the Army Signal Corps codebreaking program at all costs throughout the Cold War. Venona was aimed at Soviet secret communications, not American citizens. The FBI used the decrypts as leads to investigate with probable cause, building evidence when it could for prosecution without exposing the decryption secret to anyone. So Hoover provided sanitized reports to the president, the press, and Congress. And he ran his own secret ops.

Some Communists Self-Destruct

OSS security had been so sloppy that Congress held hearings in the middle of the war. Leonard Emil Mins worked for the OSS Soviet section in 1942 and 1943 to survey strategic energy and mineral reserves in the Soviet Union and Asia. Historians Klehr and Haynes called Mins "the most blatant GRU agent" imaginable. "That he could ever have been in a position to provide classified information to the Soviet Union testified to the ease with which the American government could be infiltrated," they wrote in *Venona*.[2]

A congressional committee hauled in Mins, whose NKVD cryptonym was "Smit," to testify. Mins denied being a Communist but admitted to writing for various Communist-controlled publications, membership in two CPUSA front groups, and to living in Moscow for two years before the war. It took two months after the hearing for the OSS to fire him.

In reality, Mins had been a Communist Party member since 1919. He served the top levels of the Comintern as a translator; worked for Communists in Germany and then in the United States, where he operated in the CPUSA Agitprop (Agitation and Propaganda) Department;[3] then "transferred his party membership to the Communist Party of the Soviet Union."[4]

Mins was such an open Communist that even some in the OSS—including fellow Soviet infiltrators—feared to be seen with him. Soviet agent Elizabeth Bentley complained to her handler that Mins was too obvious to be a useful spy.[5]

According to Klehr and Haynes, Venona intercepts show that, while at OSS, Mins reported to the GRU "on the training of American military intelligence officers to break Soviet codes, and [was] trying to obtain a highly secret OSS report on discussions between President Roosevelt and Prime Minister Churchill concerning the USSR." Mins was "a talent-spotter for other potential Soviet sources" to spy on the American Department of War and, according to a decrypted GRU cable from New York station, "for general military and political information."

The decrypts show that, in July 1943, Mins told his GRU handlers that John Morrison, deputy head of the OSS Russia section, had learned that a group of American military officers were "promoting the idea of war with the Soviet Union" and that a university in the United States provided eighty-one Army officers in Russian-language training for service in a special codebreaking unit.[6]

Already disillusioned with the Soviet Union, Hede Massing would defect to the FBI, break with Communism, and, after coming to terms with everything, publicly expose the networks.[7] So would her friend and former sister-in-law, Ruth Eisler Fischer, who had been with Lukács, Münzenberg, and Dzerzhinsky at the founding of what would become the Frankfurt School. Whittaker Chambers, who had been a Communist agent and editor of *Time* magazine, had set the example when he defected earlier.

By coming forward, these and others who left the dark side would illuminate Soviet networks across the country. Most would pay a terrible personal cost, suffering vicious attacks from journalists, progressive groups, and allied politicians.

The McCarthy Problem

For years, both houses of Congress held hearings about Marxist and Communist Party subversion. Such investigations began as generally bipartisan matters. A leading star and Hoover favorite was a young congressman from California named Richard M. Nixon, who sat on the House Committee on Un-American Activities. In the Senate, Joseph McCarthy of Wisconsin emerged as a leader, especially after becoming chairman of the Permanent Subcommittee on Investigations.

The FBI provided both lawmakers, and any member of the House and Senate committees who wanted it, with huge amounts of information. Nixon built his political career on his investigations. But McCarthy became problematic for the new Eisenhower administration, as well as for the FBI. Hoover cut him off. Allen Dulles, now CIA director, wanted nothing to do with him. McCarthy had become careless, demagogic, and politically isolated. Much to the delight of the Communists and their allies, and with no small amount of help, McCarthy self-destructed. His colleagues censured him. He died at age forty-eight and became blacklisted by history.[8]

Over the years, the results of McCarthy's well-meaning recklessness, along with vicious attacks from Communist and fellow-traveler networks, made it politically and professionally painful, sometimes impossible, to track and expose the Communist Party networks and their New Left successors as they marched through America's institutions. Even the sincerest questions fell under the fatal label of "McCarthyism."

Chapter 15

". . . an apparently bastard organization with an unpredictable life expectancy."

—CIA director Richard Helms, about the OSS[1]

Early Cold War Reset

The United States reorganized its defense and national security strategy and structure after World War II. President Truman dissolved the OSS. In early 1946, George F. Kennan, a distinguished diplomat at the American embassy in Moscow, wrote a historic classified "Long Telegram" about understanding the sources of Soviet behavior, followed by a public article, which proved extremely influential, in the establishment *Foreign Affairs* journal under the pseudonym "Mr. X."

From his Moscow perch, Kennan knew the Soviet leadership better than most Americans. He was a staunchly anti-Communist liberal. During the war, pro-Soviet elements in Washington, led by Alger Hiss, pointedly prevented Kennan from directly advising Presidents Roosevelt and Truman about shaping the postwar world. Even when Roosevelt met Churchill and Stalin in the Soviet city of Yalta to plan the aftermath of the war, Kennan was frozen out.

Now, with FDR having given Stalin most of what he had wanted, it took the United States a couple of years to decide its new postwar victor's role and face the fact that the Soviet Union would remain an unrelenting foe. Development of atomic weapons, and missile systems to deliver them, changed the dynamics of military and international political power to threaten the very existence of the United States, with the old Comintern subversive network still burrowing in to undermine America and its allies from within. The Communists would never relent. This is when Kennan came forward with his classified "Long Telegram" and his public article as Mr. X.

Hoover's Commandments

The FBI held the ground in fighting Soviet and residual fascist subversion internally, as well as the Ku Klux Klan. Hoover wrote guidelines for the public in a 1947 *Newsweek* article called "How to Fight Communism."[2] He remained evenhanded and nonpartisan:

> Don't label anyone as a Communist unless you have the facts.
>
> Don't confuse Liberals or Progressives with Communists.
>
> Don't take the law into your own hands. If Communists violate the law, report such facts to your law enforcement agency.
>
> Don't be a party to the violation of the civil rights of anyone. When this is done, you are playing directly into the hands of the Communists.
>
> Don't let up on the fight against real Fascists, the KKK, and other dangerous groups.
>
> Don't let Communists in your organizations or Labor Union out-work, out-vote, or out-number you.

Don't be hoodwinked by Communist propaganda that says one thing but means destruction of the "American Way of Life."

Expose it with the truth.

Don't give aid and comfort to the Communist cause by joining front organizations, contributing to their campaign chests or by championing their cause in any shape or form.

Don't let Communists infiltrate into our schools, churches, and moulders [shapers] of public opinion, the press, radio and screen.

Don't fail to make democracy work with equal opportunity and the fullest enjoyment of every American's right to life, liberty, and the pursuit of happiness.

Saving America from Communist Imperialism

American public opinion on the best foreign policy strategy divided three ways: isolation from the problems of the rest of the world, rolling back Communism to destroy Stalin and Mao and preserve Western civilization, and maintaining a permanent status quo in a strategy called containment.

Pure isolationism was politically popular but held little practical appeal, as the United States was now the most powerful country in the world beset by a relentless foe.

Rollback or *liberation*, an offensive strategy popularized by James Burnham and embraced mainly by Republicans who wanted to help Soviet-occupied people liberate themselves, lost out because Americans had tired of their second war for other countries, and the idea had little support in the Stalin-friendly foreign policy establishment. In fairness, Republicans like General Dwight Eisenhower, who led the American war effort in Europe, wanted no more offensive action abroad, at least not overtly.

That left *containment*, put forward by Kennan and embraced strongly by Democrats, in which the United States and its anti-Communist allies in Europe and Asia would build permanent military alliances to "contain" the expansion of Communism worldwide.

Everything would be reset. Under Truman, containment quickly became the bipartisan compromise and grand strategy that would govern the United States' role as a superpower for the next four decades. The containment strategy resulted in merging the War Department with the Navy to create the Department of Defense as we know it today. It established the NATO alliance and other alliances. It spawned the CIA and most of the rest of the intelligence community, and various other federal agencies, front organizations, non-governmental organizations, think tanks, and a military-industrial complex to enforce a permanent defensive war footing.

Containment also guided the expansion of transnational organizations and the creation of a constellation of new ones in diplomatic, political, economic, cultural, and other forums, ostensibly to treat all countries as equals. Because the Communist threat was global, so would be containment. As the Korean War showed, containment would result in indecisive conflicts and return American-led victories back to the Soviets in the name of world order.

Stalin had his own form of globalism. Now the new American foreign policy establishment had a globalist *raison d'être* of its own. This would drive the course of the CIA and affect the counterintelligence work of the FBI.

The services would only be as good as the people running and staffing them. This would change as American education and culture transformed.

To implement the grand strategy of containment, battling the Soviets and the appeal of Marxist ideology on all fronts around the world, required immense effort and the education and credentialing of new elites to implement for a long-haul Cold War with no apparent end. Attempting to create and maintain international coalitions of unity with common causes that transcended national interests energized the old progressive, globalist elites who had predated the war, and with them socialist or big-government ideologues who saw large-scale state intervention in societies as the key to battling Stalinism.

With the unceremonious abolition of the OSS, Wild Bill Donovan retired from public life and had almost no influence in the creation of the Central Intelligence Agency, which took off in fits and starts. Some of the OSS men who had served under Donovan, men like Allen Dulles, Richard Helms, William Colby, and James Angleton, would build the new CIA in the following years and decades. These were honorable men operating in a gray world but with honorable intentions.

President Eisenhower generally took an America First approach upon inheriting the Korean War debacle. The international institutions the United States had created were supposed to be dominated and used as instruments of containment. Ike kept Hoover as a steady hand running the FBI, with no significant controversies, though Hoover enjoyed none of the inner-circle status that he had had under Roosevelt. Eisenhower ordered CIA covert operations to beat back the Soviets, preserving American access to vital resources and trade for the nation's postwar recovery without involving American troops. Soviet subversion was now seeking to control democratic elections abroad.

When left-wing Mohammad Mosaddegh won election as president of Iran with Stalin's blessing, Eisenhower deftly deployed the CIA to remove the Soviet proxy and restore the Iranian monarchy for twenty-five years of stability. He had the can-do men of the CIA mount a creative operation in 1954 to prevent the Soviets from securing a foothold in Guatemala. Former OSS man Angleton, whose quick covert work had saved Italy from voting itself into becoming a virtual Italian Soviet Republic in 1948, helped the new state of Israel stand up its internal Shin Bet and Mossad intelligence services and weed out the NKVD agents among immigrating Soviet Jews. Stalin's USSR had been the first government to recognize Israel, which he envisioned as a tool against French and British interests in the Middle East. The Israelis built a statue to honor Angleton.

To counter the Soviets' lock on information in areas under Communist control, the CIA beamed radio and other messages to populations inside the Soviet Union through surrogate Radio Liberty, and to Soviet-occupied Europe via Radio Free Europe, two covert operations that were stunning successes and later made independent as overt U.S.-funded media.

These and other covert operations were low-cost, high-impact strategic triumphs under the circumstances. Under Eisenhower, the CIA planned the overthrow of the Soviet-backed regime of Fidel Castro in 1960, which the warrior-president's successor, John F. Kennedy, botched at Cuba's Bay of Pigs the following year. Kennedy's failure of leadership enabled the Soviets to place nuclear missiles in Cuba, provoking America's first immediate existential threat, the Cuban Missile Crisis of 1962, and enabled Castro and a larger movement to inspire the emerging New Left generation with an alternative to former Stalin loyalists.

As gratifying and necessary as it is to re-examine many of the CIA's Cold War covert operations as brilliant successes to celebrate, instead of scandals for which we have been conditioned to be ashamed, we return now to the attacks on American intelligence on the inside. The CIA's main shortcomings were not so much in covert operations—though some severely misguided ops, ranging from drug and mind-control experiments to assassinations, would emerge, most of the latter under the personal direction of President Kennedy—but in intelligence analysis. This is boring stuff but is the meat and potatoes of foreign intelligence.

The CIA's primary job was, and is, to collect information around the world, analyze it, and provide it to the president and his designees as intelligence to keep them informed so they can make the best national-security and diplomatic-planning decisions possible. Intelligence analysis has little of the exciting, sexy flair of covert operations (most of which are themselves disappointingly mundane), which is probably why failures in analysis, even where they led to poor or catastrophic presidential strategies and decisions, have failed to attract sustained public interest.

Here is where the cultural Marxists of the Frankfurt School and their critical theory really matter. Their united efforts began as a Soviet covert operation. Largely weeded out of American intelligence after World War II, some bore into the new CIA's Directorate of Intelligence, the rough analogue to the OSS Research and Analysis, that produced the intelligence products. Others returned with a vengeance, not through a direct or sudden assault, but through years of patient work in education, culture, politics, and law—what proponents would dub, in a hat-tip to Chairman Mao, as "the long march through the institutions."

What If Intelligence Analysts Stopped Believing in Founding Principles?

Intelligence analysis and policy are only as good as the analysts and policymakers themselves. Proper intelligence analysis never seeks to drive policy. Intelligence analysts, like everyone else, are generally products of their personal upbringing and K–12 education, the universities where they studied, and the intellectuals who underpin the curriculum and methods that they are taught. When intelligence agencies recruit analysts who lack academic integrity and rigor, or are short on personal courage, they build unreliable, weak, lazy, or even dishonest teams subject to groupthink. This leads to a lack of diversity of life experience and professional assessment, which leads to politicization. An honest CIA defender will acknowledge that agency analysis traditionally has leaned very liberal yet remained nonpartisan, that is, objective for any president to the extent that the collective mindset allowed.

Once intelligence analysis reflects a lack of confidence in, say, American founding principles or the Western moral tradition, let alone hostility to them, intelligence products become stunted and destructive. The same goes when the service wrongly gets involved in domestic affairs.

With the exception of Soviet infiltration, civil servants, diplomats, and intelligence professionals were Democrat or Republican but never Marxist. All loyal Americans were anti-Marxist. All but the infiltrators opposed Communism; the chief difference among loyal Americans was their opinion on the degree of intensity or the means with which to enforce containment. Some preferred smashing Communism head-on, while others sought to turn its methods into weapons to subvert and divide it from the left.

The anti-Marxist OSS men who populated the early CIA, men like Allen Dulles, Richard Helms, Bill Colby, and James Angleton, would keep their moral compasses, even if their long careers in intelligence would provide plenty of opportunities to make mistakes while waging covert wars that successive presidents demanded of them. In general after Eisenhower, the CIA preferred to enforce containment from the left, that is, to support center-left parties and movements abroad to deny the Soviets and their allies from building broad fronts and coalitions. Part of this was out of a more liberal worldview, but part was practical, as the Soviets viewed anti-Communist leftists as far more dangerous than right-wingers.

The FBI under Hoover, whose strongman kind of leadership gave the bureau a discernible and upright character of its own in defense against all things Marxist, remained apolitical in the sense of not going rogue, but it was often very political in the service of any president who wanted to abuse its powers. Hoover himself never belonged to a political party but was considered Republican. His worst political abuses were on the instructions of Democrats Roosevelt, Kennedy, and Johnson. FBI insularity and rigidity retarded the institutional and operational changes that the country demanded. Lack of checks and balances for decades—weak internal oversight, literally no practical congressional oversight, and a cultish cloak of secrecy—permitted cultures of excess and failure that often broke the law. Remediation would come too little, too late.

Meanwhile, the soft-on-Soviet—and thus soft-on-Marxist—academic and intellectual establishments allowed products and byproducts of the Frankfurt School and their ilk inside the tent. Those intellectual origins form the next part of the story. They trace the ideological chain of custody—the red thread—through the broad anti-Communist optimism and political stability of the 1950s, the rise of the New Left and revival of aging Comintern veterans during the civil rights and cultural and Vietnam upheaval of the 1960s, senior FBI officials' collusion with journalists to oust a sitting president that ripped apart the intelligence community in the 1970s, and the critical Marxists' takeover of much of academia and recruitment into the FBI and CIA.

Chapter 16

"Who Was to Save Us from Western Civilization?"

With Nazism and fascism vanquished and the Cold War raging, the apostles of the Frankfurt School and their disciples could turn their full attention to the main enemy: the Western democracies with Judeo-Christian traditions. This was more than Soviet geopolitics. What the Cheka had fertilized now grew on its own to address Frankfurt School cofounder Georg Lukács's World War I–era question, "Who was to save us from Western civilization?"[1]

Over time, that meant destructively criticizing every aspect of that culture, pushing identity politics into every sphere of life, and attacking, mocking, and delegitimizing all resistance. It meant creation of mechanisms to take over political parties, bureaucracies, universities, philanthropic foundations, and levers of power. It meant canceling other points of view and the people who held them. The fight would be a gradual, relentless war of attrition, refining itself as new generations of writers and operators progressed beyond the old, changing with the times and with technologies but always focusing on withering the roots and leaves of Western civilization and the values on which it was built.

Enforcement of these endless progressions at each step required, as Angelo Codevilla put it, "political correctness as we know it."[2]

"The imposition of P.C.," Codevilla said, "has no logical end because feeling better about one's self by confessing other people's sins, humiliating and hurting them, is an addictive pleasure the appetite for which grows with each satisfaction. The more fault I find in thee, the holier (or, at least, the trendier) I am than thou. The worse you are, the better I am and the more power I should have over you. America's ruling class seems to have adopted the view that the rest of America should be treated as inmates in reeducation camps."[3]

The FBI Resists the Hegemon

President Truman's team redesigned the American defense and national security communities to fight the Cold War abroad, containing Soviet expansionism and amassing an invincible military force with overseas bases and nuclear weapons. Diplomat George Kennan, author of the 1946 "Long Telegram" that inspired the containment strategy, recognized the subversive side of the fight worldwide.[4] J. Edgar Hoover anticipated the subversive side of the fight at home. Both called for education of the American people about the dangers, strategy, and tactics of Communism. This wasn't about the FBI enforcing American law. It was about preserving American culture based on the founding principles on which the law is based.

The FBI director warned Methodist ministers in 1947 of an accelerated Marxist war on religion. "The danger of Communism in America lies not only in the fact that it is a political philosophy but in the awesome fact that it is a materialistic religion, inflaming in its adherents a destructive fanaticism. Communism is secularism on the march. It is a mortal foe of Christianity. Either it will survive or Christianity will triumph because in this land of ours the two cannot live side by side."[5]

In a 1954 article titled "The Communists Are After Our Minds," Hoover wrote, "Being good tacticians, the Communists realize that one concealed Party member in education may be worth a dozen in less strategic fields, and some of their more successful propagandists in this area have influenced, and are influencing, the ideas of thousands of impressionable young people."[6] He outlined ways for average citizens to recognize and counter the Marxist attack in their own schools and communities.

The public understood the threat. Hoover's already high popularity skyrocketed even further. A Gallup poll that year found that 78 percent of the public had a favorable opinion of the FBI director, with only 2 percent unfavorable.[7]

No FBI director has spoken that way, or enjoyed such public confidence, ever since.

Herbert Marcuse: The Comintern Man Who Shaped the New Left

Most of his original Frankfurt School colleagues returned to postwar West Germany to shape its future to look more like the East, but Herbert Marcuse remained in the United States to train the next generations of American activists, organizers, and leaders. He visited Germany to see his old Comintern comrades at the University of Frankfurt. He resumed his academic writing, focusing on critical sex theory, and developed ways to apply critical theory at large to replace the toiling masses with identity groups to wreck society and overturn the American system. In the United States, he remained under the FBI's watchful eye.

The new proletariat, Marcuse said, would be a "coalition of minorities," what he called "the substratum of the outcasts and outsiders, the exploited and persecuted of other races and other colors."[8] This immediately resonated with the more creative elements of the Old Left and the theoreticians of the New.

Marcuse elaborated on this in "Repressive Tolerance," his contribution to the 1965 book *A Critique of Pure Tolerance*, in which he argues that tolerance of traditional ideas and values was repressive of "correct" ones and that such tolerance could not be tolerated. By contrast, "liberating tolerance" would welcome anything from the left while properly imposing intolerance on everything else. In Marcuse's words, "Liberating tolerance, then, would mean intolerance against movements from the Right, and tolerance of movements from the Left."[9] Only the ideas and demands of the "substratum of the outcasts and outsiders" had value and needed to be tolerated. The concerns of others not only had to be ignored but physically repressed. Marcuse called for "the withdrawal of civil rights" from outside his revolutionary substratum, "suppression" of those people.

Repressive tolerance became the basis of college speech codes of the 1980s, the political correctness of the 1990s and early 2000s, and the cancel culture and wokeness of the second and third decades of the twenty-first century. Marcuse laid out the approach: "Withdrawal of tolerance from regressive movements before they can become active; intolerance even toward thought, opinion, and word, and finally, intolerance in the opposite direction, that is, toward the self-styled conservatives, to the political right—these anti-democratic notions respond to the actual development of the democratic society, which has destroyed the basis for universal tolerance." But the time wasn't right in 1968. "The conditions," he wrote, "still have to be created." Even the extremists, what Marcuse called the "forces of emancipation" against America's "repressive society," were still "hopelessly dispersed throughout the society, and the fighting minorities and isolated groups are often in opposition to their own leadership."[10] That would take a generation.

Four years later, in 1972, Marcuse explained in clear terms, without crediting his old comrades from the Comintern, the idea of Marxist cultural revolution. "*Cultural Revolution*: The phrase, in the West, first suggests that ideological developments are ahead of developments at the *base* of society; cultural revolution but *not* (yet) political and economic revolution," he wrote, the italics his own.[11]

Cultural Marxism's Long March through the Institutions

J. Edgar Hoover died the year Marcuse published those words. "Americans were positive about Hoover right to the end," the Gallup polling organization wrote in a history of the FBI chief's popularity, "with about three-quarters in 1971 rating the job he had done as excellent (41%) or good (33%), another 10% calling it fair, and just 7% poor."[12] *The Atlantic*, fifty years after Hoover's death, would acknowledge: "Hoover worked hard—and successfully for many decades—to construct a bureau that was widely seen to embody nonpartisan vigilance. It's an achievement that the modern, embattled FBI might envy."[13]

The FBI kept on tracking Frankfurt School operators like Marcuse. "While, in the arts, in literature and music, in communication, in the mores and fashions, changes have occurred which suggest a new experience, a radical transformation of values, the social structure and its political expressions seem to remain basically unchanged, or at least to lag behind the cultural changes," Marcuse argued.[14]

Thus emerged the groundwork for modern political correctness, intimidation of independent thought, the relentless attacks on religion and the American founding, the extreme politicization of academia and law, and thus government, and politicization in the FBI and CIA. These institutions would not be overthrown; as part of the long march they would be infiltrated, subverted, taken over, and weaponized.

The oppressor was no longer the wealthy bourgeoisie, but the founding principles of the United States and Western civilization itself, along with the straight white men, dead and living, who developed them. The Communists would encourage grievances, the division of society into oppressed and oppressor, and the idea that anyone from the oppressed class (be it ethnic, racial, cultural, gender, or sexual) who worked within the system was indeed working with the oppressor. Objections would have to be ameliorated through personal and professional re-education.

Frankfurt School acolytes further developed critical legal theory, which considered desired social and political outcomes, not law and evidence, as the basis for making legal decisions. With law schools cranking out a surplus of indoctrinated activist-lawyers by the 1970s, those who couldn't flourish in a fact- and reason-based world of private practice found employment in the Department of Justice, the government-funded Legal Services Corporation, and other federal agencies. In time some would become senior managers, prosecutors, and judges. Verdicts in a precedent-based legal system would soon be reached without regard to evidence, legal procedure, law, or even constitutionality.

Identity politics blossomed by the late 1970s in a hybridization with, rather than the immediate overthrow of, constitutional principles. It was easier and safer to weaponize the law to predetermine ideologically motivated outcomes than to act as traditional revolutionaries outside the system. Critical legal theorists in government would then select new appointees to staff and expand their agencies. Over time it would become agenda-driven, a swamp of power relationships. This is what critics called destructionism—the destruction of everything through relentless criticism, the "critic" in "critical theory."

Johns Hopkins University professor Erich Isaac and his wife, Rael Jean Isaac, noted the critical theorists' penetration of American government institutions in their 1983 work *The Coercive Utopians*. "The coercive utopians have found a new use for government bureaucracies—to subvert the constitutional arrangements of the country," they wrote. "While the public continues to assume it has control over policy through electing representatives whose actions can then be endorsed or repudiated at the polls, the new breed of bureaucrats simply disregards the legislative mandates under which government agencies operate to pursue their own goals," the Isaacs observed.[15] This was during the early Reagan administration, when the president himself was leading a national fight to reduce the size and scope of the federal bureaucracies.

Such individuals had been in the bureaucracy since the New Deal, but their numbers ballooned in the late 1970s during the Carter administration, as social justice warrior graduates saw their mission as making change through populating the very government that so many hated. They expanded their presence in the education, welfare, health, labor, environment, national resources, and energy bureaucracies, applying critical theory to their public service. Activists who had spent years agitating to destroy American intelligence capabilities against the Soviets and against New Left extremists at home now took posts in the national security apparatus and the Department of Justice. "What Carter did not realize was that the goals of the utopians were of a very different nature from the traditional consensual goals of Americans," the Isaacs noted.[16]

The government-run Legal Services Corporation, designed to help the poor, became a way to employ unemployable activist lawyers and fund litigation to force radical change. A "very important factor in the subversion of Legal Services has been the massive entry of political radicals into the organization," the Isaacs said, citing a report that "a source of satisfaction some lawyers found in Legal Services was representing political radicals whose actions had symbolic importance both to their supporters and opponents."[17]

The National Lawyers Guild, founded under Stalin as a legal auxiliary for the Communist Party and Comintern fronts in the United States, "according to its own report had 1,000 members in 1979 working in Legal Services programs. This meant that approximately one out of six lawyers working on LSC programs belonged to the Guild." At the time, the Guild was "the major, until recently the only, U.S. affiliate of the International Association of Democratic Lawyers, described in a 1978 CIA study as 'one of the most useful Communist front organizations at the service of the Soviet Communist Party.'"[18]

Identity politics blossomed by the late 1970s as its adherents sought a dominant merger with, instead of an immediate overthrow of, constitutional principles insofar as they could be weaponized.[19] Proponents of cultural Marxism determined 1989 as the year that critical legal theory became prevalent in the federal government—the same year that the *New York Times* declared that, as the Soviet empire was collapsing, Marxists had finally dominated American college campuses.

"As Karl Marx's ideological heirs in Communist nations struggle to transform his political legacy," the *Times* said, "his intellectual heirs on American campuses have virtually completed their own transformation from brash, beleaguered outsiders to assimilated academic insiders. It could be considered a success story for the students of class struggle, who were once regarded as subversives."[20]

Exploiting the Secret Speech

Critics joked, and some seriously alleged, that the Communist Party's biggest funder was the FBI itself because it had so many dues-paying infiltrators. Hoover had kept a purposeful continued focus on the CPUSA. The party still functioned as a controlled Kremlin asset for active measures and espionage.

A brilliant intelligence operation, combined with a State Department and CIA publicity effort abroad, ripped the international Communist movement apart three years after the death of Stalin. Soviet premier Nikita Khrushchev was still consolidating power. Stalin remained a revered cult figure to party loyalists. Khrushchev was as complicit in Stalin's crimes as any of his rivals. To create an image of a shining Soviet Communist Party to lead the world in the new age of national self-determination on earth and Sputnik in space, Khrushchev delivered a historic speech to the Twentieth Soviet Party Congress, a meeting of Communist Party leaders from around the world.

The public record of the Twentieth Party Congress shows that Khrushchev's "criticism" of Stalin was "voiced timidly and with great restraint." He left the impression that "the main villain was not Stalin, whose name he mentioned very casually only twice, but the 'imperialist agent' Beria," the Chekist political police chief whom Khrushchev had had executed.

However, the "Secret Speech" was another thing entirely. Never meant for public consumption, Khrushchev's four-hour address to the Party Congress closed session, from which the foreign party leaders were banned, named Stalin and Stalin alone. In dramatically denouncing Stalin as he did, the Soviet leader was whitewashing his own involvement in Stalin's crimes, along with those of his allies, in a factional struggle for total control. The bloody slate was wiped clean. The Soviet Communist Party and everyone in it were blameless.

U.S. intelligence obtained a copy of Khrushchev's Secret Speech. The new Israeli intelligence service purloined one of its own and provided it to the CIA. The Secret Speech could not remain secret. Its explosive contents were of enormous political value to drive wedges through the international Communist movement.

The Eisenhower administration handled the speech deftly. CIA director Allen Dulles did not leak it to the press. He suggested that his brother, Secretary of State John Foster Dulles, leak news about the speech to the *New York Times*. That worked perfectly. The State Department then published the entire text and distributed it worldwide. To protect Washington's penetration of the international Communist apparatus, the United States allowed rumors to credit the Israelis alone.

For decades, the international labor movement had been a battlespace between the toiling masses of Communists and anti-Communist workers and their political bosses. The American Federation of Labor, staunchly opposed to Communism, battled and ultimately took over the Communist-dominated Congress of Industrial Organizations, the merger creating the AFL-CIO. The Eisenhower administration, which worked closely with the AFL-CIO, provided a copy of Khrushchev's speech in English, which the union summarized. Cooperation between the CIA and AFL-CIO became standard fare for most of the Cold War against Soviet interests worldwide.

A Senate subcommittee published the text and the AFL-CIO summary for public distribution. That document described the steps of the Kremlin's post-Stalin approach to the world: 1) ideological warfare to strengthen Soviet funding of Communist movements around the world and to draw in others from the left, including Social Democrats; 2) revolutionary violence; 3) supporting any and all nationalist movements, even anti-Communist ones, as long as they could be made useful to Soviet purposes; 4) economic and technological assistance abroad to gain at least the neutrality of emerging countries; and 5) diplomatic and propaganda initiatives.[21]

Note the care taken to inform the public and the world about the Secret Speech and avoid politicization: an accurate CIA translation provided to journalists from the diplomatic part of government, not the spy agency, through the nation's largest labor union, which at the time was anti-Communist and operated against Soviet interests abroad; and publication by a bipartisan Senate committee for domestic distribution. No employment of journalists through privileged access or, the secretary of state's use of the *New York Times* notwithstanding, leaks to manipulate public opinion. Everything was straightforward.

Publicity of Khrushchev's Secret Speech provoked crises in ruling Communist parties around the world and within the American left. It split the Communist Party USA in two, one part breaking with Moscow and all its deceptions for which the members had slaved so hard, and the other remaining obedient to the Kremlin as always. The latter part took control of the CPUSA machinery under a Minnesota-born steelworker, a former head of the Ohio State Communist Party and a resolute Stalin loyalist who had done time in prison. Trained at the Lenin School in Moscow, this Midwesterner freely admitted his goals during a 1959 trial in an American court:

> Q: And you are willing to fight and overthrow this government?
> A: Absolutely.
> Q: And you are willing to take up arms and overthrow the constituted authorities?
> A: When the time comes, yes.

J. Edgar Hoover described this public enemy as "a powerful, dynamic, and resolute leader." That leader's name was Gus Hall.[22]

Meanwhile in North Bergen, New Jersey, a four-year-old boy lived blissfully as any American toddler. This particular boy would grow up to vote for Gus Hall as president of the United States. Three short years after casting his ballot for a Soviet agent to run his country, he would enlist in the CIA. In due course, he would become CIA director. And, whether he realized it or not, he would complete the Comintern's legacy work by imposing Frankfurt School cultural Marxism on American intelligence from top to bottom.

Chapter 17

FBI, CIA, the Old Left, and the New Left

Hoover was the primary figure in the United States government who consistently kept the public educated and informed about the nature of Communist subversion. At the time, most American politicians were vocally anti-Communist, including President John F. Kennedy and his brother, Attorney General Robert F. Kennedy, in 1961.

The FBI director remained one of the most popular public figures of his time. He personified the decades-long fight against gangsters, Nazis, and Communists. Despite political differences, Hoover and President Franklin D. Roosevelt forged a close professional and personal relationship. Though disliked by presidents Truman, Eisenhower, and Kennedy, Hoover served as a detached lawman and, for Kennedy, a domestic intelligence overlord, but not a political insider.

He was an excellent communicator with the public, giving speeches and publishing extensively. His bestselling *Masters of Deceit: The Story of Communism in America and How to Fight It*, ghosted by his staff, appeared in 1958.[1] In 1962, Hoover authored *A Study of Communism*, which, in simple language, explained the history and nature of the ideological movement, Soviet control and funding, and its evolving strategies and tactics.[2] This was just as Kennan had recommended in developing the containment strategy.

Hoover wasn't afraid as a government official to remind the public of the Judeo-Christian roots of American government and culture. Once he quipped about subversives who refused to testify about party membership in court: "They always take refuge behind the Fifth Amendment. Our moral atmosphere would be better if they knew as much about the Ten Commandments as they do about the Fifth Amendment."[3]

Third-World Killers Become Cool

The rise of younger Soviet-sponsored revolutionaries, from Ho Chi Minh to Fidel Castro and Che Guevara to the less famous Frantz Fanon of the Algerian and Pan-African cause, inspired younger people with a cleaner and fresher rebellious appeal. Castro would build an intelligence service modeled after the Soviet KGB and East German Stasi, serving as a surrogate to attract, assess, recruit, and train some New Left leaders and racial and ethnic identity extremists through international events and the sugar cane–cutting Venceremos Brigades.

Hoover saw it coming. As if anticipating the New Left with its new Third World heroes, Hoover penned a 1959 pamphlet warning that the Communist "campaign of psychological pressure can be expected to increase substantially in both variety and intensity in the years to come."[4]

"The noncommunist world," he wrote, "is pictured as seething with political instability, economic exploitation, and social upheaval. By identifying the communist world as the hero and the Free World as the villain in the drama of historical progress, communist propaganda represents the triumph of communism, not only as an inevitability, but also the victory of good over evil."[5]

The Frankfurt School intellectuals and agitators had become deeply ensconced at Columbia University and its college to teach the teachers. Frankfurt School professors and instructors found camaraderie among other faculty. Where the parents had been party members, their adult children, the red diaper babies, looked for a more fulfilling and exciting cause.

Columbia professor C. Wright Mills, an anti-Christian sociologist who evaded service in World War II, is credited with coining the term "New Left" for the emerging generation of cultural Marxists who had broken with, or developed independently from, Moscow. Influenced by Marx, among others, and viewing the world along Marxist class-conflict lines as a conflict theorist, Mills specialized in what he called "the power elite." Mills traveled to Cuba and befriended Fidel Castro. He influenced Tom Hayden, a future New Left leader. He acted as a nexus between American street radicals and respectable academia, and helped the extremists mature their minds to think strategically about how to take control of the institutions they presently hated.

Castro supporters, Black nationalists, and a Students for a Democratic Society offshoot called the Weather Underground (renamed from the original Weathermen when it went underground because of connotations of sexism) began a decade-long campaign of murder, kidnapping, bombing, robbery, and cop-killing, all in the midst of the 1963 assassination of President Kennedy and the 1968 assassinations of Martin Luther King and presidential candidate Robert Kennedy. Meanwhile, other agitators in contact with foreign governments would turn the anti-war and anti-draft movement into a solidarity movement for Ho Chi Minh and his regime in North Vietnam, an American fifth column for the country's wartime enemy.

The party didn't want an end to poverty, racial upheaval, and social strife. It wanted to polarize people on these issues.

During this period, Gus Hall reshaped the Communist Party away from the ugliness of Stalinism and terror, working to make it more relevant to 1960s America. The party would seek to establish Communism in the United States through nonviolent means by manipulating rules, laws, and constitutional loopholes that radicalized civil liberties lawyers were constantly expanding. The word "socialism" would replace the "C" word, which invited unwelcome attention.

By the late 1960s, courts nullified most federal laws against Communists, freeing up the party to work out in the open. A 1951 Supreme Court decision had forced the party underground. Now the party no longer required paid membership cards. It became decentralized. Its internal discipline changed with the times, though it still didn't welcome homosexuals and frowned on drug use. It became less rigidly doctrinaire. "The Party's post-Stalinist format is to create conditions which, sooner or later, will bring about a communist transformation of our capitalist-democratic society," Hoover wrote.

The party's popularity had waned, and its numbers shrank, especially among young adults who saw it as a bureaucratic relic of the past. The New Left would emerge. But the New Leftists' rejection of disciplined command and control, systematic organization, and planned cadre-building would force them to look back to the Old Left after a decade of chaos and violence.

COINTELPRO and What It Did Right

Some commonsense approaches can get out of control if not properly supervised, and even well-run operations can get discredited once the information war ratchets up. A good example is the FBI's Counterintelligence Program, known as COINTELPRO. It was started officially under President Eisenhower in 1956, after Khrushchev's Secret Speech, to wreck the Soviets' primary covert operation against the United States: the Communist Party USA. COINTELPRO ran as a unitary FBI program—not an investigation but an operation—for fifteen years.

Most of what we hear about COINTELPRO is terrible denunciation of the trampling of American civil liberties and rights. That is a simplistic view. As John F. Kennedy had warned for years as a senator and as president, Soviet-sponsored subversion against the United States at home, and its interests worldwide, was very real and arguably more dangerous than nuclear weapons because it impacted almost every citizen almost every day.

Over its long existence, COINTELPRO implemented 2,370 proposals, 56 percent of which were against the CPUSA.[6] Any operation against the Communist Party USA was rightly a counterintelligence effort because the CPUSA was a foreign active measures operation. The purpose of COINTELPRO in 1956 was to infiltrate, penetrate, disorganize, and disrupt the CPUSA, according to Herman O. Bly, the special agent who ran COINTELPRO for the first five years. It was never intended as a law enforcement operation.[7] After Bly was forced out in a bureaucratic battle, the ambitious William C. Sullivan, the initiator of COINTELPRO who had his eye on succeeding Hoover as director, broadened the program beyond its counterintelligence mission and outside the law.

There were seven COINTELPRO operations. The main one, begun under Eisenhower and with no special name, was the largest. It was aimed solely at the Communist Party USA. The FBI's brilliant spy duo of Jack and Morris Childs infiltrated the Soviet government and CPUSA under the code name SOLO until the 1970s.[8] Among others, COINTELPRO targeted Stanley Levison of the New School in New York City, a lawyer and CPUSA money man who aided the defense of convicted Soviet atom bomb spies Julius and Ethel Rosenberg.[9] Childs identified Levison, a businessman, as a Soviet bagman for the CPUSA at least as early as the 1950s. COINTELPRO also targeted Jack Hunter Pitts O'Dell, for two generations a Soviet asset within the CPUSA who would remain a fixture in active measures campaigns into the 1980s. Another longtime FBI target was CPUSA operative David Carr, who had had direct ties to Soviet intelligence since the 1930s, when he was with the *Daily Worker.*

President Kennedy and his attorney general brother recognized that the Soviets were exploiting America's internal tensions and attempting to radicalize the civil rights movement led by Rev. Martin Luther King Jr., whom they supported. The Kennedys continued COINTELPRO to monitor and disrupt the Communist Party's infiltration of the movement. This was a proper use of counterintelligence if aimed at suspected foreign agents and assets. Part of taking down a hostile covert operation is to exploit divisions within its cadres, as with exposing Khrushchev's Secret Speech, and to cause the factions to fight one another and even to break away and help the FBI. These are necessary and ordinary measures to break apart foreign active measures in one's own country.

But they are not law enforcement. As CPUSA operatives expanded operational work with a new generation of non-party members in the late 1950s and early '60s, the line began to blur. This was good for the enemy but difficult for the FBI. In the early years of the Cold War, the CPUSA resumed exploiting American racial tensions to channel certain civil rights activists and stoke racial tensions in ways that would not seek reconciliation or solutions but would provoke further polarization and chaos.

King had at least three known Communist Party agents in his inner circle who had been on the FBI radar for years: Levison, O'Dell, and Carr. That operation, which Sullivan personally ran, got out of hand. King said he would cut ties with Levison but did not. Wiretapping King became a full-time operation to spy on the civil rights leader's private life and threaten him.[10] Sullivan himself is held responsible for a letter encouraging King to kill himself. Exposure of these abuses discredited talk of foreign exploitation of American racial tension.

The second operation was COINTELPRO-WHITE HATE, begun under President Lyndon Johnson's instruction to destroy the Ku Klux Klan. The FBI launched it in September 1964. Hoover had been reluctant to go after the Klan because it was violating no federal laws under FBI purview, and because he sought to avoid the risk of having FBI assets within the Klan become responsible for racist violence.

Johnson directed the FBI to move against the Klan as part of his recent epiphany on civil rights. "Now I don't want these Klansmen to open their mouths without your knowing what they're sayin'," former segregationist Johnson told Hoover. "I think you oughta have the best intelligence system, better than you got on the communists."[11]

Hoover complied. COINTELPRO moved hard against the Klan, splintering it for good as a cohesive, influential, national organization. The FBI had infiltrated the Klan so deeply that between 6 and 20 percent of all Klansmen in 1965 were FBI informants.[12] But it did not infiltrate the Klan leadership to any significant degree. Operation WHITE HATE ran for seven years until the KKK was broken. By that time, new federal civil rights legislation had given the FBI more legal mandates and tools.

The FBI did not consider the KKK to be an instrument of hostile foreign intelligence services. No evidence suggested that it was. Therefore, the COINTELPRO approach to defeating the Klan and some of the other extremists was improper in the counterintelligence sense. The bureau had crossed the line from legitimate counterintelligence work into law enforcement work, or, more properly, work in a gray area where few federal laws gave clear mandate. This paved the way for future abuses decades after COINTELPRO was made public.

"These were internal security cases, not criminal investigations," Weiner notes in his exhaustive history of the FBI. "They depended on the infiltration, surveillance, and sabotage of the members of the Klan and their murderous leaders. . . . The gung-ho mood of the FBI agents who ran WHITE HATE was remarkable, given the fact that their colleagues were fighting Communist infiltration of the civil rights movement with equal intensity."[13]

A third operation, COINTELPRO-BLACK HATE, was run against militant Black Power networks that opposed the mainstream civil rights movement that King led. Instead, the Black Power movement embraced, threatened, or committed political violence, including murder, terrorism, and guerrilla warfare. FBI targets included the Black Liberation Army and the Nation of Islam. Because of foreign influence or possible control from Algeria, Cuba, or the USSR, a counterintelligence operation would have been proper.

Separate COINTELPRO operations were run against Cuban-backed Puerto Rican terrorists or violent extremists; the Socialist Workers Party, a small but effective Trotskyist extremist group which had foreign ties and sought the overthrow of the United States Constitution; and elements of the New Left, particularly as they were being courted or run by Cuba's revolutionary regime and its Soviet-surrogate intelligence services, or were tied to the North Vietnamese regime and its Vietcong proxies that were fighting American and allied forces. Johnson saw the FBI as essential to defend against the foreign-sponsored Communist threat domestically. This included the New Left's waves of violence, which it characterized as "bringing the war home" and which the North Vietnamese called their "third current of revolution."[14] This fact, plus the foreign origins of the New Left's progenitors and ideologues, made the New Left a legitimate target of COINTELPRO.

The FBI agents in COINTELPRO understood the Frankfurt School's promotion of cultural Marxism and critical race theory. It knew more than anyone how the Soviets were exploiting other fissures in American society, including radical feminism, Puerto Rican socialist independence, and secession movements in the Deep South to establish a segregated black socialist regime.

Separately, investigation of Puerto Rican extremist groups was normal. Not only were the Soviets and later their Cuban proxy exploiting them, but just a few years earlier, in 1954, a group of Puerto Rican extremists invaded the U.S. Capitol with firearms, shot up the House of Representatives, and wounded four congressmen. Shortly before, members of the same movement tried to assassinate President Truman and killed one of his guards.

While COINTELPRO was heavily underway, Hoover still ranked as one of the most popular and trusted figures in America. He shut down COINTELPRO in 1971 after militants burglarized an FBI field office in Pennsylvania and revealed the program's existence.

There was reason for concern about abuses under COINTELPRO. Following the Watergate scandal and Nixon resignation, a deep and broad Senate investigation of intelligence, led by Senator Frank Church (D-ID), reached this conclusion:

> The Committee finds that the domestic activities of the intelligence community at times violated specific statutory prohibitions and infringed the constitutional rights of American citizens. The legal questions involved in intelligence programs were often not considered. On other occasions, they were intentionally disregarded in the belief that because the programs served the "national security" the law did not apply. While intelligence offices on occasion failed to disclose to their superiors programs which were illegal or of questionable legality, the Committee finds that the most serious breaches of duty were those of senior officials, who

> were responsible for controlling intelligence activities and generally failed to assure compliance with the law. Many of the techniques used would be intolerable in a democratic society even if all of the targets had been involved in violent activity [*sic*], but COINTELPRO went far beyond that.[15]

The Church Committee continued: "The Bureau conducted a sophisticated vigilante operation aimed squarely at preventing the exercise of First Amendment rights of speech and association, on the theory that preventing the growth of dangerous groups and the propagation of dangerous ideas would protect the national security and deter violence."[16]

Whereas COINTELPRO had targeted extremists committed to subversion and violence, the FBI had conducted domestic political spying of one sort or another for decades.

Chapter 18

"I'd rather have Edgar in the tent pissing out, than have him outside the tent pissing in."

—President Lyndon B. Johnson[1]

The Political FBI

Most of the early complaints about FBI politicization—complaints which dominate many histories of the FBI—came from the Communists and their friends. Spying on and operating against subversive groups acting as foreign agents or committed to overthrowing the Constitution is a legitimate FBI national security function. This makes any Marxist or anarchist, by definition, a legitimate target, but only if the law allows. J. Edgar Hoover understood this, and given the circumstances, the FBI acted with restraint. It even acted with too much restraint, because its record for actually busting up these networks was poor.

In the political mainstream, for over half of its history, the bureau has illegally intervened, one way or another, in domestic politics.

Hoover and the FBI flagrantly acted outside the law and the Constitution by systematically spying on, and keeping dossiers about, law-abiding Americans. He weaponized the FBI against ordinary citizens and their elected representatives. Once a security or police service is able to keep files on citizens and the people they voted into office, operating with no effective legislative oversight, able to spy on elected officials and Supreme Court justices, it becomes an entity unto itself, a state within a state. It becomes an extralegal, if not illegal, organization. It becomes a Central European–style secret police, a political police.

FDR loved the FBI because it empowered him politically. He enjoyed J. Edgar's prurient reportage on political adversaries and friends in Congress, and tasked the FBI to monitor any illicit sexual activity of his critics. After the Supreme Court ruled that wiretaps were generally unconstitutional, Roosevelt personally authorized the FBI to conduct warrantless surveillance of "persons suspected of subversive activities against the Government of the United States, including suspected spies," an order that lasted a quarter century.[2]

The FBI kept files on Harry Truman before he became president. On succeeding Roosevelt in 1944, Truman immediately called for his file.[3] The new president feared the FBI would become a Gestapo. His concern indicated he felt that nothing held the FBI back. Ten days after Adolf Hitler committed suicide, Truman scrawled a note to himself: "We want no Gestapo or Secret Police. F.B.I. is tending in that direction. They are dabbling in sex life scandles [*sic*] and plain blackmail when they should be catching criminals. They also have a habit of sneering at local law enforcement officers. This must stop. Cooperation is what we must have."[4] The thought nagged him, as Truman told an aide that he worried Hoover was "building up a Gestapo." Journalist and historian Tim Weiner summarized, "The president time and again returned to that theme."[5]

Yet Truman, similarly to other presidents, viewed the bureau, and Hoover himself, as indispensable in fighting crime and political violence and countering foreign subversion. He fired his attorney general yet kept

Hoover on board, albeit at arm's length, guiding the FBI in its lane as a domestic law enforcement and security service and rejecting Hoover's proposal to make it a central foreign intelligence service as well.

Truman's successor, Dwight Eisenhower, needed the FBI as a Cold War internal defense, but Hoover never became part of Ike's inner circle anywhere near on par with CIA director Allen Dulles. A review of Hoover's most secret files after the director's death showed that Truman and Eisenhower never misused the FBI for political purposes.[6]

President John F. Kennedy had no fondness for Hoover. He knew Hoover had kept a file on him and doubtless mulled over how the information could be misused. He also retained Hoover as director. "You don't fire God," Kennedy quipped.[7] JFK and his thirty-five-year-old brother Bobby needed the popular Hoover to keep eyes on Communist penetration of the civil rights movement, leading to Attorney General RFK's instruction to Hoover to wiretap Rev. Martin Luther King Jr.

The Kennedys had a larger political purpose for keeping Hoover aboard. Journalist Ralph de Toledano, who covered the FBI for *Newsweek* at the time, noted that it "was clear from the start that Robert Kennedy had decided to cut Hoover down to size, to make him an arm of the Democratic Party rather than a nonpolitical director of an investigative agency."[8] The Kennedys waived the mandatory federal retirement age of sixty-eight so that Hoover could stay in place. "From the very start, Robert Kennedy had made it clear that he considered the FBI a kind of private police for the Administration and Hoover a kind of desk sergeant to carry out orders," de Toledano wrote.[9]

No credible evidence shows FBI or CIA involvement in the Kennedy assassination, though many believe either or both agencies were behind the murder to one degree or another. The Warren Commission's flawed investigation and the intelligence community's stubborn refusal to declassify all of its files sixty years after the fact, when the sources and methods of the early 1960s no longer need protection, continue to raise legitimate questions.

President Lyndon B. Johnson, for many years a close neighbor of Hoover who knew him well as a "Washington friend" (as opposed to a real friend), often shared drinks with the FBI director and swapped gossip. "Lyndon Johnson concentrated information and power in the Oval Office better than any president since Franklin Roosevelt. He admired the way Hoover used secret intelligence. He used the FBI as a political weapon in ways no other president had done," Weiner recounted.[10] In his safe, Johnson kept FBI dossiers on congressmen and senators who hired prostitutes, prostitution then being a crime that was actively prosecuted. He wondered aloud to Bobby Kennedy, running for Senate in New York the same year Johnson ran for election in 1964, whether he should selectively leak files on Republicans as Election Day approached.[11]

Shortly before the 1964 election, a top Johnson aide was arrested for sodomy, also then a crime, in a Washington, D.C., men's room. Apparently worried that Republican opponent Barry Goldwater would use it against Johnson, a presidential assistant directed Hoover to dig up homosexual activity among anybody on Goldwater's staff. That directive, which survived in FBI files, came from presidential assistant Bill Moyers, who would go on to become a major TV news figure on CBS.[12] Johnson also used the FBI "to snoop on his friends and enemies in Congress and on the Supreme Court, to keep the lickspittles of the liberal left in check, and to slay the dragons of the far right," according to Weiner.[13]

Johnson also needed Hoover to keep him informed of Soviet, Cuban, North Vietnamese, and other penetration of the social and political protest movements that were tearing the country apart. In popular culture, the bureau remained a steadfast enforcer of law and order, with Efrem Zimbalist Jr. starring in the weekly action show *The F.B.I.* (with Hoover in the credits).

There was also the practical matter of keeping rivals close so that one could exert control over them. Johnson, according to de Toledano, "knew that a Hoover replaced would cause far more problems than a Hoover in office." What might a replacement do with Hoover's cache of files? Those files, "built up over the years, would be a delayed-action charge with anyone less dedicated to the preservation of their inviolability than Hoover."[14]

Former federal judge Laurence Silberman confirmed the nature of the files. "Hoover had indeed tasked his agents with reporting privately to him any bits of dirt on figures such as Martin Luther King, or their families. Hoover sometimes used that information for subtle blackmail to ensure his and the bureau's power," recalled Silberman, who had the job of poring through the details of those files and testifying on their contents to Congress.

Johnson instructed the FBI to surveil Maryland governor Spiro Agnew, whom Richard Nixon chose as his 1968 running mate. Agnew had taken bribes while in office, but this particular operation "was not for law-enforcement purposes." Johnson even had the FBI watch his own appointees to make sure they were not "too close to Robert Kennedy" after the attorney general left the administration to run for Senate.[15]

Poring through those files was "the single worst experience of my long governmental service," Silberman wrote thirty years later. He never revealed their details and made good on his promise to "take to my grave nasty bits of information on various political figures—some still active."[16]

Then came President Richard M. Nixon in 1969. Hoover had placed his bets on him in the early 1950s, when Nixon was a young congressman from California on the House Committee on Un-American Activities and later Eisenhower's vice president. As president, the ethically fluid Nixon knew Hoover had become a liability to both the FBI and the country. Hoover was an anachronism, a Luddite, a relic holding things back.

Like Roosevelt, Kennedy, and Johnson, Nixon saw the FBI as a useful political tool for himself but didn't completely trust the bureau or his old friend Hoover. That distrust led Nixon to create his own political intelligence network, "the plumbers," who hatched the Watergate break-in and other capers to stop the leaks during his 1972 reelection campaign.[17] Nixon wanted to force Hoover to retire. Then Hoover, who had headed the bureau since 1924, died.

"Hoover was my crony and friend," Nixon told his aides after Watergate became a public scandal. "He was closer to me than Johnson, actually, although Johnson used him more." Nixon lamented that Hoover would have been a big help: "He's got files on everybody, goddamn it."[18]

In comparison to what would come with Crossfire Hurricane, Hoover had used his secret files with restraint, and he served each president regardless of party. Nixon made it clear he wanted an outsider to run the bureau. He named one of his Justice Department appointees, L. Patrick Gray, as acting director. The number two man in the bureau, Deputy Director W. Mark Felt, had ambitions of his own. He had been with the FBI since 1942 and owed his career to Hoover. He ran the FBI as de facto director because of Gray's frequent absences from Washington.

And so Nixon's 1972 reelection committee's skullduggery committed the bush-league break-in at the Watergate hotel. A high-level source, whom the *Washington Post* named "Deep Throat" after a popular pornographic movie, leaked details of the FBI's Watergate investigation. Acting Director Gray and senior administration officials soon suspected Felt. Deep Throat, it turned out, was Deputy Director Mark Felt.

It wasn't about ideology—Felt was a hand-picked Hoover loyalist who had run COINTELPRO in its later stages. And it wasn't about crime, as Felt easily could have taken his Watergate concerns to a grand jury.

It was about raw power.

Decades later, Felt admitted his role but never explained his motivations. Author Max Holland, who made the most careful study of Felt's motivations, argued that Felt became Deep Throat to undermine his boss, Director Gray, and to get Nixon to bestow upon him, Felt, his rightful position as Hoover's true successor.[19]

Felt likely helped take out Gray, who had to step aside because he destroyed incriminating documents. Confronted amid suspicions about his leaks, Felt denied everything, but many suspected it was him by the time he resigned from the FBI. He was later convicted for ordering illegal break-ins in pursuit of bomber suspects while at the FBI, and ultimately received a pardon from President Ronald Reagan.

After Gray, Nixon ultimately tapped Clarence M. Kelley for the permanent job. Kelley was a former FBI special agent in charge who had retired in 1961 to become the chief of police of Kansas City, Missouri. He was a civic-minded figure who served on the national boards of charities like the Boys' Club and the United Fund and various law enforcement auxiliary groups, and he sat on a post-Hoover commission to improve FBI training. He ran the bureau honorably for five years and improved the training of new agents. This took place under the benign and short administration of President Gerald R. Ford, with Kelley serving until the Carter administration, when he asked to retire.

Carter named Judge William H. Webster for a congressionally mandated ten-year fixed term. Webster served for most of President Ronald Reagan's presidency without scandal. Reagan named Judge William S. Sessions to succeed Webster, but Sessions had to resign for ethical lapses under the early Clinton administration. Clinton replaced Sessions with FBI agent Louis Freeh, who resigned in mid-2001 after taking fire for a range of errors and omissions, including grave counterintelligence lapses that allowed special agent Robert P. Hanssen's espionage to go undetected and likely earned Hanssen's common comment that Freeh knew "nothing about CI." President George H. W. Bush designated Robert S. Mueller III as the next FBI director. Mueller served for a full ten years plus a two-year extension, making him the longest-serving director after Hoover.

For the nearly forty years after Deep Throat—a.k.a. FBI deputy director W. Mark Felt Sr.—left the bureau, and despite a range of triumphs, abuses, setbacks, mistakes, and incompetence, FBI politicization was never a real problem. And then, in Mueller's last years under a special extension that Congress granted at the request of the Obama administration—years in which Mueller showed visible cognitive decline—everything changed.

The Church Committee and Beyond

Most of the revelations and exposures of FBI and CIA abuses in the 1970s came from the left, with conservatives generally defending both agencies. But the concerns crossed the political spectrum. A bipartisan Senate report spoke for all in 1976 when it said, "The American people need to be assured that never again will an agency of the government be permitted to conduct a secret war against those citizens it considers threats to the established order."[20]

Still, as under Hoover, Congress took little action to create new laws. The FBI would now follow "guidelines" under Attorney General Edward H. Levi, and the CIA and much of the rest of the intelligence community would now be answerable to special select committees on intelligence established in both houses of Congress.

Meanwhile at the demoralized CIA, Ford named former OSS man and career intelligence officer William Colby as director during the turmoil of the Church Committee hearings in the Senate. Ford replaced Colby with an affable former congressman and ambassador to China, George H. W. Bush, who served for eleven months. President Jimmy Carter cut the CIA's wings even more under Director Stansfield Turner, who had little confidence in human intelligence and sacrificed HUMINT for technological intelligence collection. The 1970s purges of the CIA changed the professional complexion of the agency and gutted its human intelligence and operational capabilities. None of the changes had anything to do with politicization, however.

Reagan attempted to revive the CIA to wage the end of the Cold War against the Soviet Union. He issued Executive Order 12333 as the new guide for intelligence, which remains in force despite amendments by his successors. He named former OSS man William J. Casey, who distinguished himself fighting the Nazis while paving the Allies' way to Berlin after D-Day, to run CIA. Casey served as director from 1981 to 1987 but faced resistance from the generally liberal, careerist bureaucracy as he demanded more rigorous analysis of Soviet strategic intentions, support for terrorism, and active measures. He favored journalists like Claire Sterling; private operatives like Michael Ledeen, who worked with Sterling to prove CIA deficiencies in its terrorism and Soviet analysis; and amateurs who outshone CIA collection and analysis on issues like Soviet support for terrorism and guerrilla warfare. He ran OSS-style covert operations against the Soviets and their proxies that threatened the comfort of careerists. Casey was the last of the OSS veterans at the CIA.

Reagan's vice president and successor, George H. W. Bush, was welcomed at the agency and made no waves.

As liberal as the CIA was, it still was not politicized, let alone politically correct. It did at times interfere in politics, but these were the exceptions to the rule. President Bill Clinton showed little interest in intelligence. When a small private plane crashed into the White House grounds, CIA director R. James Woolsey joked that it was him trying to get Clinton's attention.[21]

The real politicization started under Clinton's second CIA director, George Tenet. Seasoned intelligence professionals of the old school could see the tide turning. Some of the most prescient warnings came not from FBI or CIA insiders but from outsiders. One was a humorous, soft-spoken defector from the Soviet Union, who came forward during the first years of the Reagan administration. He was a trained propagandist, an agent of influence without the supposedly glamorous rank of KGB officer, so few paid attention.

Chapter 19

"So we have religion, we have education, we have social life, we have power structure, and we have labor relations, unions, and finally we have law and order. . . . These are the areas of application of subversion."

—Soviet Communist Party propaganda agent and defector Yuri Bezmenov, 1984

Influence Operations Are the Real Name of the Game

Most foreign intelligence work of the Soviet KGB had little to do with spying, which is to steal secrets. KGB foreign intelligence devoted a large amount of its resources to supporting agents who influenced foreign elites and top-level decision-making, influencing public opinion more broadly and waging long-term, strategic subversion to undermine Western societies from within.

In the 1970s, the FBI and CIA lost their experienced leadership and analysts who readily understood this, and focused instead on the espionage part of intelligence and counterintelligence. A congressional panel revived interest in active measures in 1980, and the new Reagan administration did to a more sustained degree starting in 1982. However, even the Reagan team focused on active measures as relating to diplomacy, proxy wars, and arms control, not subversion of American society from within.

Of the KGB defectors who emerged during this period—even those with operational experience in running active measures—most had worked against allies in Europe or Japan, not internally in the United States. A few Soviet bloc defectors, intelligence officers like Czechoslovak StB major Ladislav Bittman and KGB major Stanislav Levchenko, had the most direct personal experience to share.[1] So did the highest-ranking defector from the bloc, Romanian intelligence chief Ion Mihai Pacepa.[2]

This is the part of KGB intelligence work, influence and subversion, that escaped the attention of most Cold War books and movies, which focused on the espionage component of intelligence, the theft of secrets. With such Cold War focus on the KGB, Soviet defectors who had not been KGB officers went underappreciated.

Yuri Bezmenov Was Right

A Soviet propaganda agent in India named Yuri Bezmenov, who turned himself in to the United States in 1970, was one of those underappreciated defectors. He settled in Canada under the new identity of Tomas David Schuman.[3] Bezmenov was not a KGB staff officer. He did not go to the KGB Higher School or the Andropov School. The son of a senior Soviet military officer, he was a trained foreign propagandist for the Soviet Communist Party. All Soviet propagandists stationed abroad routinely performed tasks for the KGB under some form of direction and control. Bezmenov wrote for the state-controlled Novosti Press Agency, and he was a man with unusual insight into Soviet psychological strategy.

Moscow's strategy, Bezmenov explained in archival video aired in a *New York Times* video series and on a Public Broadcasting Service program, was "to change the perception of reality of every American, to such an extent that, despite the abundance of information, no one is able to come to sensible conclusions in the interest of defending themselves, their families, their community and their country."[4]

"Most of this activity is overt, legitimate, and easily observable if you give yourself time and trouble to observe it," said Bezmenov in a lively set of interviews and presentations recorded in 1983 and 1984. "But according to the law and law enforcement systems of the Western civilization, it's not a crime exactly because of misconception, manipulation of terms."[5] Free societies had trouble reconciling protection of free speech with protection from foreign enemy manipulation.

Many KGB defectors talked about this, and some wrote books about active measures and disinformation, but few spoke as eloquently and openly as Bezmenov about the far deeper strategy of subversion itself. The Soviets built the world's largest strategic nuclear weapons force, but their most effective work against the United States and its allies was subversion.

Active Measures

"Active measures" is the English translation of a Russian intelligence term of tradecraft that Americans call covert operations. On the violent end of the spectrum, KGB active measures included guerrilla warfare, terrorism, and assassinations. On the unviolent end, active measures consisted of running foreign Communist parties and front organizations, infiltrating non-Communist organizations and movements, running agents and assets to influence how people think and how decision-makers decide, and coordinating or at least shaping demonstrations, protests, riots, and mass movements. A narrow subset of active measures is disinformation, again the English translation of a KGB term, *dezinformatsiya*, which is the fabrication and insertion of false or distorted information into Western news organizations, textbooks, entertainment, or any other medium to influence decision-makers or public opinion.

The Subversive Feedback Loop

These goals were what the Dzerzhinsky-Münzenberg team set for the Comintern and what would become the Frankfurt School. Working toward these goals takes extraordinary focus and persistence. The initial perpetrators might not live long enough to see the finished results, and many knew it.

Stage 1: Demoralization. "It takes from fifteen to twenty years to demoralize a nation," even three generations or more, Bezmenov said. That is the time it takes to educate students, "without being challenged or counterbalanced by the basic values of Americanism, American patriotism," and for them to enter positions of influence, authority, and power at all levels of society.

"It includes influencing or by various methods infiltration, propaganda methods, direct contacts," Bezmenov said, "of various areas where public opinion is formulated or shaped. Religion, educational system, social life, administration, law enforcement system, military of course, and labor and employer relations, economy."

That's why students have been a priority target. Indoctrinating and recruiting from the next generation made universities and teaching of the teachers such a core priority. University-based influence operations shaped the worldviews, perceptions, and values of generations of young professionals who had no idea that they had been indoctrinated. J. Edgar Hoover's warnings from decades earlier remained valid.

Bezmenov saw the results of the Frankfurt School and those influenced by Marcuse, Gramsci, and others. Radicalized college graduates from the 1960s, he said, "are now occupying the positions of power in the government, civil service, business, mass media, educational system. You are stuck with them. You cannot get rid of them. They are contaminated. They are programmed to think and react to certain stimuli in a certain pattern. You cannot change their minds."

"To rid society of these people you need another twenty or fifteen years to educate a new generation of patriotically-minded, commonsense people who would be acting in favor and in the interests of the United States society," Bezmenov said. That rearguard action would slow the spread of the demoralization, but would prove insufficient as radicals—imbued with or sympathetic to critical theory or cultural Marxism—by now had been channeling into the institutions.

Longtime KGB chairman Yuri Andropov, who by the time of Bezmenov's interview led the Soviet Union, would have found a remarkable return on investment as the demoralization spread virally and developed like an intellectual pandemic. America's existing problems, from civil rights and poverty to the Vietnam War and political corruption, had their own organic demoralizing effects. Sustained KGB efforts to exploit and channel that demoralization—and efforts of legacy individuals and schools who had nothing to do with the KGB but whose worldviews had been shaped by the institutions the KGB had created or supported—helped make it worse.

Stage 2: Destabilization. "The next stage is destabilization," Bezmenov said. "This time the subverter does not care about your ideas and the patterns of your consumption," as the idea of reasoned debate and normal interpersonal discourse is gone, and much of society sees the world in absolutes. Absent some resiliency, decline can come suddenly and precipitously. "This time it takes only from two to five years to destabilize a nation, what matters is essentials: economy, foreign relations, defense systems. And you can see quite clearly that in some areas, in such sensitive areas as defense and economy, the influence of Marxist-Leninist ideas in the United States is absolutely fantastic. I could never believe it fourteen years ago when I landed in this part of the world that the process would go that fast."

Stage 3: Crisis. "The next stage, of course, is crisis," Bezmenov said of goal three. The crisis would be permanent and usually naturally occurring, sometimes manufactured, always channeled in a desired direction. This stage seeks to plunge a society into a state of permanent crisis, to infuse the public with constant uncertainty and nagging anxiety, punctuated by attacks of panic and breaks in the public's trust in institutions and in each other. It even breaks individuals' own psychological ability to cope with reality. Reason breaks down.

Stage 4: Normalization. "And after crisis, with a violent change of power, structure, and economy, you have the so-called period of normalization. It may last indefinitely. Normalization is a cynical expression borrowed from Soviet propaganda," Bezmenov said. This is the new normal: "You are not living in a time of peace. You are in a state of war and you have precious little time to save yourself."

The saying that it's easier to deceive a person than it is to convince him that he's been deceived held true with the KGB.

For the past century, Europeans and Americans have been a primary target of disinformation and active measures. The Soviets, as with the Communist Chinese and others, invest in very long-term strategies that include the cultivation and management of controlled agents and other human assets for decades and even generations.

Westerners, and Americans in particular, are vulnerable because they don't think this way. They tend to think in the short term, in a matter of months or years, or an election cycle. The Soviets, like the Communist Chinese, thought in the very long term with a defined desired end state. The United States had no such strategic vision. The Dzerzhinsky-Münzenberg team meeting in Moscow in 1922 that would create what became the Frankfurt School shows the hundred-year legacy that took on a life of its own. The Soviet Union would not survive its own creation.

In his recorded lecture and interviews,[6] Bezmenov described four successive goals or stages that the KGB waged against the United States, Canada, Europe, and other adversaries. The first goal was to demoralize entire societies. Once a society is demoralized, it is subject to the second goal, destabilization. Once destabilized, a society becomes vulnerable to the third goal, a naturally occurring or manufactured crisis.

The fourth goal, emerging from the crisis, is collapse or overturning of the existing order.

Every Part of Life Is Up for Grabs

Social or political movements of all kinds are there to be exploited. Religion, education, social life, political life and power structures, the economy—all had been and would remain under sustained attack. "To take advantage of these movements, to capitalize on them, is the main purpose of the originator of subversion," Bezmenov said. "So we have religion, we have education, we have social life, we have power structure, and we have labor relations, unions, and finally we have law and order. . . . These are the areas of application of subversion."

The attack on religion, which Lukács, Dzerzhinsky, and the rest incorporated into the Comintern institute that honed cultural Marxism and critical theory, was at the core. Not to create a *Homo sovieticus*, but simply for the nihilistic purpose of destruction.

"What [it] means exactly in the case of religion," said Bezmenov: "destroy it, ridicule it, replace it with various sects, cults which bring people's attention, faith, whatever it is, naïve, primitive, doesn't really matter. As long as the basically accepted religious dogma is being slowly eroded and taken away from the supreme purpose of religion, to keep people in touch with the supreme being, that serves the purpose."

The KGB's campaign against education in free societies, Bezmenov explained, was to "distract them [the targeted young population] from learning something which is constructive, pragmatic, efficient. Instead of mathematics and physics, foreign languages, chemistry, teach them history of urban warfare . . . home economy, your sexuality, anything as long as it takes you away."

In the target population's social life, Bezmenov said that the KGB strategy was to tear citizens away from natural civic life and to create bureaucratic walls and command structures. In his words, "Replace traditionally established institutions and organizations with fake organizations. Take away the initiative from people. Take away responsibility from naturally established links between individuals, groups of individuals and society at large, and replace them with artificially, bureaucratically controlled bodies. Instead of social life and friendship between neighbors, establish social workers' institutions—people on the payroll of whom? Society? No. Bureaucracy. The main concern of social workers is not your family, not you, not social relations between groups of people."

These artificial social organizations run by activists serving as public officials on the taxpayers' payroll would be engines to infiltrate the power structures and, in time, take over the reins of administration and control.

"Power structure," Bezmenov said, "the natural bodies of administration, which are traditionally either elected by people at large or appointed by elected leaders of society, are being actively substituted by artificial bodies. The bodies of people, groups of people who nobody elected, never—as a matter of fact, most of the people don't like them at all—and yet they exist." These unelected or unaccountable groups would organize horizontally as networks across and among bureaucracies, all promoting common identity themes, grievances, and demands.

After years of organizing, they would build enough critical mass and outside support to pressure weak leadership to provide privileged status within the bureaucracy or promote them prematurely, and often without objective merit, to the highest levels of the civil service or the equivalent and the entry levels of senior executive service. It would then be a matter of time for politically sympathetic leadership to emerge at the top with its own political appointees to finish the job.

This is a simple formula, agonizingly protracted for years. It goes like this: The good professionals inside the bureaucracy become demoralized. Some of the best younger ones will quit early, others will keep their heads down and try to ride it out, more will go along to get along but without much enthusiasm, and those further along in their careers, eyeing retirement, will dejectedly do their jobs until they can end their careers with full benefits. And after retirement? Many hope to move on to lucrative post-retirement careers in government contracting or Big Tech. A few become so disgusted that they cut ties and walk away from what they view as the whole sordid business. Some keep their criticism subdued, restricting it to trusted friends from the community, not wanting to tarnish the brand of their former agency or risk ostracism, hoping beyond hope for a miraculous return to the good old days of upright purpose and fighting crime.

And So It Goes . . . Corruption, Rot, and Collapse

This demoralization, from school boards to universities, private business to defense contractors, consumers of news and entertainment to victims of unjust judicial processes or bureaucratic harassment, sports fans to religious believers and more, will ultimately consume a society.

"The moment you bring a country to the point of almost total demoralization, when nothing works any more, when you are not sure what is right or wrong, good and bad, where there is no division between evil and good, when even the leaders of the church sometimes say, 'Well, violence for the sake of justice, especially justice'"—here, Bezmenov referred to conflicts relating to indigenous rights or anti-imperialism or anti-racism—"And we listen to them and say, 'Yeah, probably it's true.'"

"Is it true? No, it is not true. Violence is not justified, especially for the sake of quote-unquote 'social justice' introduced by Marxist-Leninists," Bezmenov said. "Okay, so we reached that point."

That was more than a generation ago. Practically every teacher, professor, lawyer, judge, bureaucrat, FBI agent, intelligence officer, analyst, and journalist active at that time has retired or died. The national education system shaped their replacements.

Part IV

State of Fear: 9/11 and the Central Apparat

"It was the transition that 9/11 represented in my mind. . . . And understanding that we'd moved from a situation where we perceived something like 9/11 as a terrorist attack versus an act of war had a big impact on how we dealt with the aftermath, what we did in order to prevent future attacks."

—Richard Cheney, 2014[1]

Chapter 20

Big Brother Is Family Now

Two cultural revolutions swept the FBI and CIA after the al Qaeda attacks of September 11, 2001. President George W. Bush fumed that the intelligence community had failed to detect the terrorist conspiracy. He and his team, with near unanimous congressional support, vowed to stop at nothing to prevent such an attack from happening again.

FBI director Robert Mueller had been on the job for a week. A Marine and courageous Vietnam combat vet with an upper-crust demeanor, Mueller had run the Justice Department's Criminal Division under the president's father, former president George H. W. Bush. He was a cautious and careful lawyer. The younger President Bush told him to develop a "wartime mentality."

Vice President Dick Cheney, a former congressman who had been defense secretary under the elder Bush and earlier served as White House chief of staff under President Ford, handled the levers of power decisively. He led the administration's national security team. He would revamp the all-seeing security apparat that he, the president, and just about everyone else in Washington thought the country needed. They issued top-secret instructions to turn the FBI back into a domestic intelligence service with police powers, which inadvertently or otherwise meant returning it to its Hoover roots. The terrorist attacks were not criminal acts to be solved. They were acts of war. Preventing acts of war required aggressive intelligence collection and operation.

Bush, already enthralled by the CIA, kept George Tenet on board as director. At Cheney's tough direction, Tenet turned his near directionless, lower-tech, status quo agency to a focused, more skilled, paramilitarized, super high-tech terrorist-hunting machine. The quick ramp-up for a real technological capability meant hiring a lot of tech-savvy younger people who didn't fit in with traditional CIA culture. They just needed to be the best at their jobs.

Along with that new influx of younger people came an intellectual sea change within the CIA. By 2000, intellectual devolution had become so advanced that the CIA had anointed the Frankfurt School's Herbert Marcuse to the pantheon of OSS Research & Analysis scholars that included leading lights such as Arthur Schlesinger Jr., Walt Rostow, Gordon Craig, and Crane Brinton. The CIA sanitized Marcuse as an American hero. Its internal study of intelligence history, *The Office of Strategic Services: America's First Intelligence Agency*, made no reference to Marcuse being part of the Comintern network, or an extension of Stalin's GRU and NKVD intelligence rings, or a philosopher-architect of the New Left and its nihilistic terrorist bombings and assassinations, or a founding father of American critical theory and cultural Marxism.[1]

The CIA mainstreamed Marcuse as one of its own.

USA PATRIOT Act: The Predatory American Security State Is Born

Congress weighed in with rare unity. Within six weeks of the terrorist strike on 9/11, it rushed passage of the USA PATRIOT Act, which the president immediately signed into law. Because of its unprecedented powers against American citizens and few protections against abuse, the emergency wartime law was to expire in four years.

The complex USA PATRIOT Act established and funded the expansion of a huge domestic security apparat, with legislative language jumping through hoops to avoid offending certain aggrieved or privileged ethnic and religious groups. It beefed up "enhanced surveillance procedures," expanding warrantless wiretapping under the Foreign Intelligence Surveillance Act to enable the FBI and National Security Agency to spy, hopefully with limitations, on private citizens. It increased surveillance of citizens' ordinary business and financial transactions and of private computers and other electronic communication. It expanded the use of warrants and roving wiretaps. It mandated that private companies preserve all electronic records of their customers. It also increased border security, placing travel burdens on American citizens while doing little to stop illegal immigration by land. It monitored ordinary citizens' banking and credit card activity for "terrorist finance." Congressional extensions and various legal maneuvers have kept the main provisions of the law alive ever since.

Then came the Homeland Security Act of 2002, which consolidated various domestic security entities. For decades, congresses and presidents had deliberately dispersed those duties across the government to avoid concentration of power. Now, in the name of fighting terrorism, Bush and Congress merged twenty-two of them into one central concentration of power, emerging in early 2003 as the Department of Homeland Security.[2] Then in 2004 came the third major legislative change, the Intelligence Reform and Terrorism Prevention Act, which created another new government agency, the Office of the Director of National Intelligence (ODNI). ODNI's intended job was to integrate civilian and military intelligence, foreign and internal, to make sure nothing went unshared or slipped between the cracks, in order to keep the American public and U.S. foreign interests safe from terrorist attack.

Those laws and others consolidated a mammoth central apparatus and extraordinary legal authorities for a national security state unprecedented in American history. ODNI mushroomed to a force of two thousand and growing at a brand-new headquarters on the Washington Beltway.[3] The Bush administration sought and received assistance from new tech giants in Silicon Valley and incubated others with grants and contracts arranged on a war footing.

These post-9/11 measures then merged America's intelligence and military machine with progressive San Francisco capital. Few Bush officials or lawmakers truly considered the negative long-term ramifications. In Wild Bill Donovan's spirit, there was no time to waste. Dangerous unintended consequences were baked into the creation, and everyone expected growing pains.

Under Mueller, the FBI created sixty-three new executive positions at headquarters and doubled the size of the bureau. But Mueller also became alarmed at what he saw as illegal surveillance of American citizens in 2004. He handwrote a resignation letter to President Bush, stating his opposition out of principle. Bush had the immediate object of Mueller's complaint corrected, and Mueller stayed on.

By design, the U.S. intelligence community had been decentralized among thirteen autonomous or near-autonomous agencies, civilian and military. Many had no communication with one another, for several none was necessary, and cooperation was limited among those that did. This "stovepiping" meant that intelligence might get to the top of one organization but not be laterally shared with other agencies. That was one of the problems of 9/11. Certain agencies, including the CIA and FBI, had data that, if shared, might have revealed planning of the terrorist attacks. Indeed, through stovepiping—and a large measure of sheer incompetence—the FBI sat on information that probably could have been used to prevent 9/11.

The FBI had maintained its own extra internal checks for more than seventy years, even under Hoover: operational power resided with the director, deputy director, and a small number of assistant directors at the top—as well as about fifty field offices around the country. It was a bottom-up arrangement, as well. The director directed, but the field offices originated the cases and ran them to fruition. Field offices would seek guidance from headquarters as an aid in coordinating with other field offices or agencies as needed, but the cases remained with the originating office, or OO. Especially in the post-Hoover years, that basic practice kept headquarters from running federal investigations from the top. It also limited political abuses from becoming worse.

The bipartisan National Commission on Terrorist Attacks Upon the United States, or 9/11 Commission, and the Commission on Intelligence Capabilities, known as the Robb-Silberman Commission, gave serious consideration to a new domestic intelligence service and dividing the FBI into separate law enforcement and intelligence agencies or even replacing it completely. Laurence Silberman, by then a prominent federal appeals judge, was well aware of the FBI's problems. He had been deputy attorney general in 1975 when President Ford asked him to review the secret archives of the late J. Edgar Hoover and testify about them to Congress.[4] After his commission with Robb submitted its findings, Silberman recommended that the FBI be abolished and its duties scattered elsewhere.

But the FBI defended its turf. With recommendations from the autonomous boards, input and legal authority from Congress, and more, FBI director Mueller and CIA director Tenet altered the functions of their agencies. Their successors, James Comey and ultimately John

Brennan, armed only with presidential executive orders and not laws, set out to politicize them.

Bush 43–era centralization to fight terrorism inadvertently permitted the Obama metamorphosis of the cultures of the FBI, the CIA, and the entire intelligence community under the ODNI oligarchy. Instead of improved performance, this second transformation shocked the system by imposing a governing philosophy of critical theory—a direct descendant of Frankfurt School philosophy—that had nothing to do with enhancing America's intelligence needs. That critical theory would invent a new and permanent terrorist threat which placed half the country under suspicion.

Paradox within the Bureau

In matters of law, evidence is evidence. As a law enforcement agency, the FBI generally dealt truthfully with the public. It had to collect fact-based evidence in a legal fashion that would stand before the scrutiny of a trial, judge, and jury. One is legally innocent until proven guilty.

Intelligence, by contrast, is subject to almost none of those rules. Its facts might not be evidence in a legal or constitutional sense, or, for that matter, for legitimate reasons of national security. Sources might be unreliable. Some of the facts might be intentional distortions or fabrications. Much of the intelligence process and product, by nature, is pure guesswork. Intelligence is not always obtained legally. Even when collected legally, the intelligence might by necessity remain secret—or even be omitted—to protect the sources and the methods of collection. Intelligence conclusions, based on analysis of what is collected, are not always conclusive. Often there are gaps, leaps of logic, caveats, degrees of certainty or uncertainty, and broad conclusions that the community calls "estimates." Even the existence of intelligence is often secret and is sometimes denied. Unless declassified or illegally leaked, intelligence is not subject to independent scrutiny. No right exists to face one's accuser, or even to know that one has been accused at all. Except in rare circumstances, intelligence may not be used as evidence to prosecute an accused citizen.

As a domestic intelligence agency with police powers, the FBI under Mueller in his final years began to look at large elements of the population as potential enemies, as a menace to the government, with intelligence-based evidence that might or might not be true but which could be weaponized against the public based on information that might not stand up in court.

Police might use intelligence as a pretext for probable cause to open a case and collect evidence, or to provide clues about where to look legally, but this thin and blurred constitutional line is perilous to cross. Police use evidence to build cases, to make arrests, and to hand over suspects for prosecution. Secret police use evidence *and* intelligence. This is where the citizen has no recourse to the law. The citizen can be blacklisted without seeing the evidence against him, and even without his knowledge. The post-9/11 FBI can punish its targets through investigative and administrative processes without bothering to prepare cases to put suspects on trial. The process is the punishment.

Chapter 21

"It isn't enough simply to have a conversation with someone. You have to spy on them with an electronic device even if they'd speak to you freely. If you don't do it, you are less likely to advance inside the bureau."

—Former FBI special agent Stephen Friend[1]

Manufacturing Domestic Threats—and the Bounty System

To defend the public against terrorist attack after September 11, 2001, Congress passed draconian new laws that made extraordinary powers legal. Mueller used those laws and policy mandates in ways that turned the bureau into what former FBI special agent Thomas J. Baker called "a threat to democracy."[2] Baker began his career in 1966 under J. Edgar Hoover, retired in 1999, and remained in close professional contact with the bureau as a contractor until 2023. Few living FBI veterans have such breadth of insight.

Mueller crippled the bureau's internal checks by centralizing the director's power. He created two new layers of bureaucracy at headquarters, swelling upper management to more than sixty senior executive service positions, with the highest salaries in the entire federal government.

That top-heavy bureaucracy isolated the entire FBI leadership from the field offices. Mueller cut communication between the director's office and the now fifty-six field offices, forcing special agents in charge to speak to the new high-level bureaucrats instead of to him personally. The open line was gone.

Creation of five dozen new senior positions at the federal government's highest rates of compensation begat aggressive, often hostile competition among the social climbers in the bureau. The careerists now had more ways to grow their power, prestige, and income. They fought for them hard. This had little, if any, positive impact on the bureau's effectiveness, but it did force field agents to work harder.

That's because outside consulting firms convinced Mueller to introduce a bounty system for the upper management to profit personally. The bounty system imposed quotas that forced field agents to check as many boxes as possible as a means of statistically measuring productivity. The criteria were a synthetic construct, invented by green-eyeshade types to assess the quantity of work, not quality, in all the field offices. If every special agent checked as many boxes as possible, the special agent in charge of each field office would be rewarded, as would his supervisor back at headquarters.

Promotions would depend on this system. The FBI top leadership would even collect annual cash bonuses for all the boxes their underlings checked, independent of connection to the ongoing logic of actual investigations.

As the bureau bloated, it became less efficient. The mindless itemized quotas senselessly strained the system. "When we're out doing an investigation we can simply call somebody up and arrange a meeting, and we usually get the basic answers that we want," said Steve Friend, a former special agent in Florida. "But if it's the end of the quarter and we still hadn't run a wiretap on anybody because we didn't need to, our supervisor would pressure us to go to court to ask a judge to issue a warrant to give us legal authority to run electronic surveillance on the person who would have freely talked to us if we had simply asked him. All that waste, all that unnecessary intrusion on a citizen, just to check the box. Just so the top management can get bonuses."[3]

Bounties for You, and You, and You!

The FBI bounty system simultaneously works to gold-plate personnel records and maneuver Congress into appropriating more money. The attempt to quantify FBI personnel performance is built into a strict, cyclical process called Integrated Program Management, or IPM. IPM was developed by a Harvard Business School–educated bureau executive.

From the top levels at the J. Edgar Hoover Building, senior bureau officials develop what they call a TRP, or Threat Review and Prioritization. The TRP establishes the threats and how each FBI field office should prioritize them for action. The field offices then devise a strategic plan. The perceived threats in each field office area of responsibility are displayed on a multicolor field office Threat Issue Matrix, with five levels of urgency. Level I is the highest and Level V the lowest.

"There is a seemingly endless stream of meetings, phone calls, and emails involving supervising agents, intelligence staff, program coordinators, and mission support analysts. The final product is a convoluted matrix marrying the FBI's national, local, and standing threat priorities with mitigation criteria," explained special agent Steve Friend, who was suspended because he objected to being part of a SWAT team to raid homes of people accused of First Amendment misdemeanors.[4] (Friend did not vote for Trump in the 2020 election.)

"It's a pseudo-religion with these people," added a supervisory special agent in the northern field office.[5]

Interviews with more than a dozen current and recently former special agents from field offices across the country confirm that the nature of the IPM process induces FBI personnel to check boxes—fulfill standardized requirements often unnecessary in investigations but quite necessary for the built-in quota system—in order to advance professionally. They have to do what each checked box requires if they wish to get ahead.

"This is a tool that executives use to advance themselves, as well. If they get all their subordinates to do whatever the items next to each box require, they get everyone to do busywork and waste a lot of their time on unnecessary tasks and even techniques," said Friend. "For example, using an electronic device to monitor somebody's conversation" is on the IPM box-checking list. "It isn't enough simply to have a conversation with someone. You have to spy on them with an electronic device even if they'd speak to you freely. If you don't do it, you are less likely to advance inside the bureau."

"The FBI's IPM process applies the principles of *Minority Report* to predict investigative and intelligence-gathering activities in the coming fiscal year. It combines these prophecies with analytics more appropriate for *Moneyball* to measure performance based on how many metrics are achieved," said Friend. "The problem is that, unlike the movies, we do not have the ability to accurately prognosticate criminal activity. Moreover, achieving predetermined benchmarks is tied to FBI executives' compensation. Consequently, the FBI's corrupted incentive structure favors case quantity over quality and encourages employees to deploy their creative faculties to game the system for artificial statistical accomplishments instead of focusing on true casework."[6]

The bounty system also works insidiously with new directives on countering "domestic extremism."

"There are TRP performance metrics for every field office that start at headquarters. At the field office, you have to focus your resources on them," Friend continued. "Counterterrorism is a big one. Busting DVEs [domestic violent extremists] is basically pushed on the field offices from headquarters. The FBI has created the DVE problem by defining ordinary social or political conflicts as violent extremism, which boosts up the numbers of field offices handling violent extremism or terrorist cases."

"The reality is that 90-plus percent of these so-called DVE cases are EDPs," or emotionally disturbed persons. "Ninety percent or more. By tallying everything this way, the field offices report back to headquarters what headquarters want to hear—that domestic violent extremism is on the upswing in the United States and that the FBI is breaking it up," said Friend.

"Each field office sends its IPM statistics to headquarters, which then tabulates them all and sends out a news release or tells Congress how much domestic violent extremism there is out there. Everybody knows the rules with TRP performance. If you want to advance in the FBI, you know what to do," Friend explained.

"Then the director or one of his executives goes before Congress and testifies about the rise in domestic violent extremism, creating headlines about how dangerous the country has become. The phoniness of TRP pushes numbers for the sake of pushing numbers," said Friend. "Congress falls for it every time."

Militarized Agents of Change

The FBI under Bush, Cheney, and Mueller not only centralized but militarized. It introduced the heavy use of tactical paramilitary units, tactical weapons, and military gear in the name of public safety and counterterrorism. As Hoover had been vilified for doing, the FBI ratcheted up intelligence collection against citizens not even suspected of a crime.

That shift changed the FBI's ethos, especially among younger agents who, in their mid- to late twenties, had an idealistic motive to defend the nation against terrorists, often with a postmodern worldview that would motivate them as (illegal) agents of social change and social justice. FBI went out of its way to recruit new people with the agent-of-change mission. It watered down its training and relaxed professional standards. "They won't even do counterintelligence in the academy," said former special agent Stephen Friend. "They had a cross-deputized FBI-CIA guy [teaching]. The only thing they said about Hanssen is that he's incarcerated at the end of an L-shaped corridor. Then they had us watch the movie *Breach*."[7]

The bureau's management tolerated politicization of the workplace. These changes demoralized FBI professionals, young and older, who wanted to bust criminals and foreign spies and fight real terrorism.

Former special agent Baker watched it all play out over three generations. "Americans have lost faith in the Federal Bureau of Investigation, an institution they once regarded as the world's greatest law enforcement agency," he said.[8] He followed the entire careers of younger FBI agents as they rose up through headquarters to executive positions. "I am deeply troubled by this loss of faith," he told a congressional panel in 2023. "Personally it breaks my heart."[9]

Over the past ten years or more, this author has found Baker's concern was not uncommon among active FBI agents, especially younger ones who remained idealistic. Elders from the old school, committed to the FBI as an institution and a brand, shared those worries at the end of their careers or after official retirement. These agents had worked in field offices and other sites across the United States and around the world, and especially in Washington, D.C. Several had been stationed at headquarters. Few of them knew each other at the time. Many of their critiques of the FBI were similar and systematically devastating. Together they formed a distinct pattern.

Most felt they had nowhere to turn to within the bureau with their constructive complaints and concerns.

Senior FBI veterans began punching out before they hit their age limits, taking high-paying and less stressful jobs in the private sector or as contractors, or leaving the field altogether. The author interviewed many for this book but most requested anonymity, citing the bureau's ability to retaliate through administrative means and other abusive options.

This anxiety was not misplaced. A few had become whistleblowers. Those whistleblowers would pay a price.

Failure on Every Front

Even with its expanded powers, Mueller's FBI was unable to find a single al Qaeda member in five years. So it reverted to Hoover's proven efforts against CPUSA and KKK, but without the strategic results: Sting operations. Setups. Entrapment. Quick busts for public accolades. Lots of publicity.

At least the older sting operations worked, up to a point. To Hoover's credit, the FBI deeply penetrated both the party and the KKK, stunting the Communists and crushing the Klan.

But more than half of the known FBI cases from 2007 to 2009 against domestic Islamic terrorists were sting operations that prevented no attacks at all. The FBI generally ferreted out idiots and lowlifes, nobody serious. Albanian losers, video braggarts, a cab driver. The FBI breathlessly portrayed them as real threats from real Islamic extremists. Bureau agents even supplied some of these extremist wannabes with weapons.

During this time, the FBI developed a list of 700,000,000 terrorism-related records with 1.1 million names. The bureau was almost as backward technologically as it had been when its accounting software designer Robert Hanssen was arrested in 2001. As Weiner recounts, only a third of FBI agents and analysts had online access by 2008.[10]

The team of President Obama and Attorney General Eric Holder liked Mueller's work so much that when his congressionally mandated ten-year term ended in 2011, the president asked Congress to allow him to stay on for another two years. By now the Department of Justice was not looking for jihadists—the word was practically forbidden now, for fear of offending the jihadists—and long ago had abandoned concerns about people like, say, Weather Underground veterans and Cuban assets who continued to train new radicals.

By this time, American citizens had become accustomed to warrantless surveillance, militarized police in towns across the country seemingly outfitted for the occupation of Baghdad, electronic strip searches at airports, and Big Data mining all their private information and secretly sharing it with the intelligence community.

"Many willingly surrendered liberties for security," Baker lamented. "They may not have loved big brother, but he was family now."[11]

PART V

Obama's Great Cultural Revolution

"We cannot continue to rely on our military in order to achieve the national security objectives that we've set. We've got to have a civilian national security force that's just as powerful, just as strong, just as well-funded."

—Barack Obama, departure from prepared remarks, 2008 campaign speech[1]

"We are five days away from fundamentally transforming the United States of America."

—Barack Obama, October 30, 2008[2]

Chapter 22

Marching through Institutions

Violent seizure of revolutionary power in a democracy alive with trusted institutions and traditions could never succeed. The built-in defense mechanisms of society's valued foundations would smash such disruption. In the industrialized democracies, successful revolution would have to proceed, for the most part, within the law. Success is all about patience, persistence, and process. Success, in the case of fringe groups taking over institutions, requires a manufacturing of public consent.

For followers of Gramsci and the Frankfurt School, it's also about gradualism, about infiltration, about stretching public opinion and interpretations of law to make incremental gains. It means credentialing extremists in mainstream institutions, and from there cultivating and sustaining new radicals to penetrate and infiltrate and occupy more institutions.

It means electing people to public office, locally and at state or regional levels first, then to national institutions, to change the laws in legislatures and reinterpret them in courts. It means educating and mobilizing young lawyers to become prosecutors, criminal defense attorneys, litigators, prosecutors, and judges. This kind of slow-motion revolution is a difficult, costly, multigeneration trek that others called, with a hat-tip to Chairman Mao, the "long march through the institutions."

With Hoover at the helm, the FBI watched as movement leaders made common cause with Fidel Castro in Cuba, Ho Chi Minh in North Vietnam, Mao Tse-tung in China, and Third World terrorists from Che Guevara to Yasser Arafat. Their older supporters in New York's wealthy progressive society, and stalwarts like Gus Hall and the numerically small but still organizationally important Communist Party, maintained old operational ties with the Soviet KGB. And they cultivated future replacements.

The Soviets and East Germans hardly inspired the New Left. They were gray, bureaucratic, stodgy, old, uncool, and sexually uptight. But they funded and inspired the worldwide liberation movements against the dying postwar West European empires. They opposed American "imperialism," whatever that was, especially the military and CIA that repressed those struggling for Third World "liberation." And the Soviet bloc supported elements of the Black Power and New Left movements fighting the enemy at home. So as far as the New Left was concerned, the Soviets remained allies but were viewed like an embarrassing old dad.

Decades and generations of organization and indoctrination would have to wait for the right national leadership to emerge. That leadership would empower the common-minded radicals planted and cultivated in the established institutions. Its election would mark the tipping point that Marcuse had awaited. Those few elected by the majority would use that margin, however slim, as a mandate for radical change. To Marcuse and his followers, tyranny of the majority would now be morally justified.

Minority rights no longer needed protection from radical transformation. "For Marcuse, it's the majority's duty to shut the minority up if the latter calls for tolerance of views opposed to change," noted Ken Jensen, a critical historian of Marxism-Leninism.[1]

Marcuse himself had marched through those institutions. He began at Germany's prestigious universities, not very radical at first. Then came his uncloseted radical years at the Frankfurt School where he fused Marx and Freud, socialism and psychoanalysis and psychosexuality. After the United States provided refuge and he infiltrated the OSS, Marcuse taught at Harvard, Yale, and Columbia before settling, in the New Left years, at the University of California at San Diego. Since the 1950s he had refined his Marx-Freud fusion.

Human liberation, Marcuse posited in keeping with the Frankfurt School of thought, had little or nothing to do with Marx's 1848 economic dialectics of the *Communist Manifesto* and its exploited working class. A less famous Marx had been a greater prophet earlier, in 1843, when he called for the "ruthless criticism" of everything on earth.

Western culture, the laws and values and traditions of Western civilization, and through them the American founding—those were the real enemies. They inherently repressed everyone and the sexual impulse. The road to human liberation, Marcuse argued, was the orgasmic "libidinal rationality" that would break free of all social, religious, and traditional mores.[2]

In his powerful 1964 work *One-Dimensional Man*, Marcuse released his most politically transformational ideation. American and Western capitalism, he argued, made people "sublimated slaves" of capitalism or free enterprise. In his view, people became modern slaves by desiring nice cars, homes, televisions, and other comforts. Modern capitalist society, he wrote, was repressive, with traditions and laws repressing human sexuality.[3]

There would be no proletariat of the toiling masses enslaved in the smithies of capitalism, as Marx and his early subscribers had envisioned. By the late 1950s and early 1960s, the left's failure to interest the labor movement to serve as a proletariat vanguard "made the New Left turn to Herbert Marcuse," Lawrence Lader wrote in his sympathetic landmark history of American radical movements since 1946. "In his disillusion with the working class as a revolutionary force, Marcuse had built his philosophy around marginal groups. Society could only be shaken, he believed, by the outcasts and outsiders, rebellious students, outraged poor, alienated hippies, oppressed blacks, the unemployed and unemployable."[4]

Black Power, Lader noted, had little to do with the Rev. Martin Luther King's civil rights movement for equal rights in a character-based American society. It was, instead, a prison break from the "surplus repression" of capitalist American society, a raising of "nationalist consciousness—a vision beyond civil rights that stirred blacks to seek economic, political, and social power greater than the gradualism offered by the corporate state."[5]

Its purpose was to put in place a slow-motion Marxist coup to overthrow the American system.

Prepped for Power

The Obama administration took office in 2009 with a carefully conceived plan based on rigorous critical theory and anti-imperialism, designed by brilliant political strategists and ready for implementation by a well-chosen and generally loyal team.

Until that point, Barack Obama had been only a junior United States senator with no legislative accomplishments. Before running for office, he quit work in finance to become a community organizer. He served an undistinguished stint in the Illinois state senate for three terms from 1997 to 2004, handpicked for the seat by the retiring incumbent and her local political machine. Elected to the nation's highest deliberative body in 2004, he held the seat for just over four months before assembling what would become his 2008 presidential campaign.

Obama won the national election with 52.9 percent of the popular vote—a comfortable but not overwhelming majority, and certainly not a mandate. His landslide came thanks to the peculiar calculus of the Electoral College, where he trounced opponent John McCain by better than 2–1. The 365–173 electoral vote victory screamed hope and change.

Obama's candidacy was unique. With no executive experience, he was America's first fully trained, prepackaged political product for the presidency. He was the first president with near-zero education in the American founding. His early childhood education in Indonesia provided him with no study of patriotism and American history that elementary students back home were still receiving, shallow as some of it might have been. His only meaningful feature by then was the promise of being the nation's first African American president.

Dreams from My Father, and from Frank and the Frankfurt School

Obama owed his formation to the many dedicated ideologues who shaped his worldview throughout his life. The future president developed a sound ideological basis for accepting comfort in the critical and cultural theories of the Frankfurt School.

He wrote in one of his autobiographies, *Dreams from My Father*, of a father figure named Frank who mentored him from boyhood on everyday matters of life and introduced him to theories about social and racial justice. Frank was a friend of Stanley Dunham, a white man whose daughter had a son with a man from Kenya. Dunham ultimately introduced Frank to his nine-year-old grandson, Barry, in 1970. He thought that young Barry Obama, raised at that time by neither parent, could relate to a black man like Frank who was married to a white wife. Frank took the bright and articulate boy under his wing. Over the next decade he would introduce young Obama to racial identity politics and the world of critical race theory.[6]

The last time they saw each other was in 1979, when an eighteen-year-old Barry left Hawaii for college. Frank parted with the admonition for Barry to devote his life to always keeping his racial identity first and to go forth as an agent of change. He admonished the hopeful young man to be careful of the American establishment, warning, "They'll train you so good, you'll start believing what they tell you about equal opportunity and the American way and all that shit." As a United States senator, Obama recalled the moment fondly.[7]

In addition to being Barack Obama's beloved mentor, Frank Marshall Davis was a prominent figure in cultural Marxism and critical theory, and he had a very public history. He had fallen afoul of the FBI. And for good reason.

The Davis Coup

Obama had deleted Davis's surname from his memoir *Dreams of My Father.* Only later, after journalist Cliff Kincaid received the FBI file and publicized the connection, did Obama acknowledge Frank's identity as Frank Marshall Davis. We have already briefly met Davis as an underground Comintern man, a sworn servant of Stalin in the battlespace of American culture. Davis was a journalist and poet who made his living writing extremist poetry for a taxpayer-funded salary through a New Deal writers' program.

Davis had been a veteran Communist Party propagandist and community organizer in Chicago from the 1930s to late 1940s, when he moved to Hawaii under the inspiration of fellow party member Paul Robeson. He continued his pro-Stalin writings and activism until the CIA exposed Khrushchev's Secret Speech in 1956, but he remained a party loyalist with or without the card, his writings and arguments putting a party spin on race and racial tension. A poet and sometime musician, Davis made good company with a wide circle of friends. He remained a father figure for Barry Obama.[8] And he never recanted.

Barry to Barack

Davis prepared Obama well. In college, Obama embraced his African patrimony, stopped calling himself Barry, and went by his African given name, Barack, which had been the name of his father. He confirmed in a post-presidential memoir that at Occidental College he studied Marx and other Communist writers, including, he said, Herbert Marcuse. He downplayed it all, saying in *A Promised Land* that he read Marxist works as a way of picking up girls.[9]

In *Dreams from My Father*, Obama wrote that his college circle of friends was "the more politically active black students. The foreign students. The Chicanos. The Marxist professors and structural feminists. . . . At night, in the dorms, we discussed neocolonialism, Frantz Fanon, Eurocentrism, and patriarchy."[10] In other words, Obama spent his college not just reading about Marx but hanging out with Communist faculty and passing evenings with friends discussing and embracing the fundamental elements of critical race theory. It wasn't about picking up girls. It defined his intellectual life, such that it was.

Frantz Fanon was an Afro-French radical from Martinique who based his anti-imperialist views on his childhood and experience in the Free French forces in the Caribbean and Algeria during World War II.

He popularized the Soviet-backed Algerian fight against France and became a prominent Marxist and exponent of critical race theory.[11] He was a strong philosophical influence on the domestic guerrilla warfare strategy of the 1960s Black Panthers under Bobby Seale, Eldridge Cleaver, and Stokely Carmichael.

In that sense Obama found Fanon as an intellectual extension of his father figure in Hawaii. Fanon and Davis both viewed their respective countries, and Western culture at large, as irredeemably racist. Davis, as young Obama's "surrogate father," equated imperialism not with history or ideology or economics but with white supremacy.[12]

By the end of college, Obama had steeped himself in Frankfurt School philosophy. Obama claimed that theologian Reinhold Niebuhr was "my favorite philosopher."[13]

Niebuhr was a fellow traveler of the relocated Frankfurt School in New York, but not a Communist. The Fellowship of Socialist Christians, which he helped found, claimed Christianity and capitalism were incompatible.

After college Obama dabbled in the financial industry, then ditched it to train as a community organizer. He moved to Chicago to seek his political fortune. He got engaged to Michelle Robinson, who worked as an aide to Valerie Bowman Jarrett, deputy chief of staff to the powerful Mayor Richard Daley. The Obamas and Jarrett would remain a close trio of friends.

Obama's favorite philosopher enchanted another future American leader a few years younger. As president, Obama would choose that Niebuhr-infused individual to run the FBI.[14]

His name was James Comey.

CHAPTER 23

The Chicago Marxist Way

Hoover's agents had been in Chicago to infiltrate the founding of Communist Party USA in 1919. Three-quarters of a century later, during the Obamas' time in city politics, the party maintained a presence and power far out of proportion to its withered numerical size. The way to win elections was not to run on the CPUSA ticket, but to infiltrate the one major political party that would welcome well-organized radicals. A radical state senator, Alice Palmer, part of that greater network,[1] had gotten to know Obama and saw he had a future, calling him one of her "Black House babies."[2] She anointed Obama in 1995 to run as her successor so she could run for Congress. In grooming Obama, that senator introduced him to a University of Illinois at Chicago professor of education named Bill Ayers.[3] Ayers and Valerie Jarrett were already good friends. Ayers too saw Obama's limitless potential. He, along with his wife, Bernardine Dohrn, patiently mentored Obama in their living room.

Obama began his political career in the nest of extremist superstars incubated by Marcuse, the old party, and the New Left. Ayers and Dohrn had been 1960s radicals, first as leaders of the Students for a Democratic Society (SDS). Then they lived a clandestine existence as domestic violent extremists in an SDS spinoff, the Weathermen. They created collectives that they called "red armies" to fight "guerrilla war" in more than a dozen American cities, including Chicago, Detroit, New York, and Seattle. Their network was responsible for bombings and shootings and murders across the United States.[4] They organized violence at public schools. Ayers and Dohrn allied with cop-killers, mass shooters and other violent extremists, armored truck robbers, and foreign agents.[5]

"Glorifying violence, cutting themselves off from the campus base, they were substituting themselves—in effect, a personal psychodrama—for a mass movement," sympathetic historian Lawrence Lader recounts. "There were also elements of arrogance, guilt, and the 'spoiled brat' syndrome." Ayers's well-off father ran the Commonwealth Edison Company,[6] the electric utility monopoly in the state. The Weathermen set up armed militias, converged on Chicago in a "Days of Rage" orgy of violence, dynamited a police statue, and attacked the residence of a judge hearing a trial of rioters from the year before. They held a "war council" and then went clandestine. The Weathermen became the Weather Underground.[7]

"SDS failed to learn from the Old Left that any socialist movement must be part of a continuing historical process. This did not necessarily mean the development of a political party. But it did mean a structure and a stable leadership constantly replenished," said Lader. "The Old Left offered noteworthy precedents that SDS ignored—the building of radical cells in every local CIO affiliated union, the development of a block-by-block structure. . . . The Panthers, too, eventually came to the same conclusion, finding community organizing a more productive path to socialism than guerrilla confrontation."[8]

The Vivid Red Thread Binds Fundamental Transformation

And the smarter and more patient elements of the movement went legal. Some organized largely peaceful, semi-violent protests to force universities to hire their radical allies as professors. Ayers and others got university faculty positions on their own long march through the institutions to indoctrinate the next generation of educators and to instruct future trainers. So did Angela Davis, a Black Power militant who bought the murder weapon used to kill a California state judge.[9] She had been one of Marcuse's most promising students.[10] Davis studied under Marcuse before she moved to Communist East Germany to receive a Ph.D. and later, in Moscow, to receive the Lenin Peace Prize from Leonid Brezhnev. The Soviets portrayed Davis as an international heroine for racial justice.[11]

Other Marcuse alumni took a local path. Marcuse had been Bill Ayers's professor and adviser. Here the red thread becomes most vivid. The ideological chain of custody forged at the 1922 meeting of Dzerzhinsky, Lukács, and Münzenberg was passed to Comintern man Marcuse and the others at the Frankfurt School who refined it and brought it to America, then passed directly from Marcuse to Ayers and Dohrn and others of the Black Power/New Left generation, and finally to Valerie Jarrett and onward to Michelle and Barack Obama.

Countless chains of intellectual custody were spun and woven from that Marx-Engels Institute meeting of 1922 to the present. None would ever compare in importance.

Well before the Obamas, Jarrett and Ayers had had a long relationship of trust. FBI documents released under a Freedom of Information

The Radical Coup That Swept Up the FBI

Valerie Jarrett: The Transformer

From her command center in the White House, Valerie Jarrett pushed a transformational workforce agenda throughout the federal government. I believe the old FBI would likely have flagged her for her family's Communist Party connections and her own closeness to domestic violent extremists, even if she was suspected of no crime. (Even if the bureau had flagged Jarrett, Obama as president could overrule any objection. Any president can also designate a security clearance to any person he chooses, regardless of what a background investigation might find.)

Jarrett and the Obamas were so tight that some on Capitol Hill called Jarrett "the Obamas' Harry Hopkins." While President Obama was pleased to have Jarrett at the center of the national leadership's most sensitive discussions, Defense Secretary Robert Gates did have the sense to object to her involvement—and the involvement of Obama's domestic policy team overall—in what he called "micromanagement" of national security. But he did not object personally to the president. Gates acknowledged in his memoir, "I never confronted Obama directly over what I (as well as Clinton, Panetta, and others) saw as the president's determination that the White House tightly control every aspect of national security policy and even operations. His White House was by far the most centralized and controlling in national security of any I had seen since Richard Nixon and Henry Kissinger ruled the roost."[12]

Eric Holder: The Sleeper

The transformation of national security would begin in the Department of Justice. Attorney General Eric Holder had started with a comparatively middle-of-the-road reputation in the nation's capital. He was a liberal Democrat but a comparatively evenhanded professional who prosecuted corrupt members of Congress from his own party. President Reagan appointed him as a District of Columbia superior court associate judge. President Clinton made him U.S. attorney for the District of Columbia, and then tapped him as deputy attorney general under Janet

Reno. Holder, now part of the uniparty Washington establishment, met Obama in 2004, and the two clicked.

Born in 1951, ten years before Obama, Holder came of age at the peak of the New Left. He entered Columbia University in 1969, a year after the famous antiwar riots, and became a student radical. That year, "Columbia SDS had organized on every floor of every dormitory, with movies and meetings twice a week," Lader chronicled.[13] Holder joined the Student Afro-American Society, a militant group tied to the SDS, and became a fanatical devotee of the Black Power cause in general and the Black Panther violent extremists specifically.[14] The Black Panthers embraced Marxism-Leninism and openly called for Maoist-style guerrilla warfare inside the United States.[15] Eric Holder supported those who advocated or committed acts that, as attorney general, he would later redefine as domestic violent extremism.

Holder apparently hewed to Columbia SDS militant Mark Rudd's "action faction," which sought to use "the base" (Arabic translation: al qaeda) as a "vanguard" of attack. He became part of what was described as an "armed" mob that took over a vacant Naval ROTC office for a five-day occupation. He and the mob demanded that the military office be converted to a segregated space for black students and renamed in honor of slain Muslim Black Power leader Malcolm X. They said they needed the space because of "the general racist nature of American society" and because Columbia University, too, was racist.[16]

The Student Afro-American Society, while Holder was a member, supported twenty-one Black Panther members facing felony counts of conspiracy to commit terrorist bombings of department stores, railroad tracks, a police station, and the New York Botanical Gardens.[17]

Holder graduated from law school and landed a job in Washington with the Department of Justice in the Public Integrity Section. By all accounts he was a solid professional working against corrupt politicians, which is how he gained the attention of the Reagan administration.

Yet he remained true to his college-era Black Power recruitment and never publicly renounced his extremist views and associations or exposed the networks. As attorney general of the United States under Obama, Holder recalled those years in speeches.[18]

Holder saw equality of opportunity and equality under the law as insufficient. The real fight was permanent conflict on behalf of an entitled, protected class based on people's immutable traits, such as race.[19] This was, of course, the Frankfurt School and Marcusian notion of critical theory, pioneered at the time in the legal profession as critical legal theory, to manipulate the American legal system for outcomes-based, not evidence-based, solutions in jurisprudence.[20] That didn't stop Holder from wearing expensive suits and working at a white-shoe law firm.[21]

In the Obama cabinet, Holder stood out by returning to his formative roots and radicalizing the civil service employees at the already very liberal Department of Justice.[22] Federal Election Commission statistics show that DOJ was one of the most heavily politicized departments of the United States government. Among Justice employees who made political donations in the 2016 campaign cycle, 91.6 percent gave to Democrats. Homeland Security employees came in at 75 percent Democrat.[23] The Department of Education was as high as 96 percent Democrat.[24]

The tipping point in American history had already occurred when the Justice Department went from very liberal to radical, powered by senior White House and Justice officials as the latest custodians of the red thread chain. It would have a tremendous spillover effect into the FBI.

The FBI Crumbles

Ordinarily the FBI would have presented a hard target. The bureau's power had been largely dispersed among its fifty-six field offices across the country. Mueller's centralization, which added two new layers of bureaucracy at the J. Edgar Hoover headquarters building, eased the fundamental transformations for Obama and Holder. Top-heavy with more than sixty billets of largely useless upper management, the new bureaucracy severed the special agents in charge of the field offices from their traditional direct contact with the director. For any future leaders seeking to abuse their authority and weaponize the FBI for political purposes, Mueller's conversion of the bureau back to a Hoover-like domestic intelligence agency with police powers was a plus.

The Obama administration liked Mueller so much that when the FBI director's legally limited ten-year term approached expiration in 2011, the White House asked Congress to pass a law allowing Mueller to stay on an extra two years.

Act request show that Jarrett's father, maternal grandfather, and father-in-law had been subjects of FBI interest for decades due to their membership in Communist Party–affiliated organizations.[25] Her father, James Bowman, and her maternal grandfather both had a relationship with Soviet spy Alfred Stern, who fled to Czechoslovakia, then under Soviet control. Her father-in-law, Vernon Jarrett, had a relationship with Chicago Communist Party figures going back to the 1940s, including Frank Marshall Davis, who would move to Hawaii and, decades later, mentor the young Barack Obama.[26]

Valerie Jarrett continued down her parents' ideological path. She was well dug in to their old Chicago Communist Party network of activists and organizers. They joined in solidarity with other radicals to turn out votes for chosen Illinois candidates for office, including her old boss, Mayor Harold Washington, and Senator Carol Moseley Braun.[27] Ayers continued with Obama through his three campaigns and terms in the Illinois state senate and then his United States Senate campaign in 2004, and at least through his historic 2008 presidential campaign. Presidential candidate Obama knew Ayers's background well. And he was fine with it.

Obama entered the presidency with the worldview, training, organization, and talent networks in place to fundamentally transform America. He began with a well-defined domestic and social agenda as his staff began that transformation.

Two years into his presidency, Obama would commence the conversion of the CIA, FBI, and the rest of the intelligence community into instruments of this agenda.

Chapter 24

"Vocabulary was so constructed as to give exact and often very subtle expression to every meaning that a Party member could properly wish to express, while excluding all other meanings and also the possibility of arriving at them by indirect methods."

—George Orwell, *1984*

Target: Office of the Director of National Intelligence

Obama began his first term with a bipartisan and apparently balanced national security team, keeping President George W. Bush's Republican defense secretary, Robert Gates, and naming retired general Jim Jones, the former Marine Corps commandant, as his national security adviser. He selected retired admiral Dennis Blair, an uncontroversial and nonpartisan professional, as director of national intelligence. The Senate endorsed Obama's confirmable appointees by the broadest of margins. Some thought Obama was not as radical on national security as they had feared. During a long post-inaugural political honeymoon, Obama aimed his first strike at the top of the centralized seventeen-agency intelligence community. In May 2010, he sacked Admiral Blair.

Now came the revolution. As Mueller had centralized the FBI, the new director of national intelligence post would centralize authority over all American intelligence agencies. Obama replaced Blair with one of the most radical, flawed intelligence figures since the Comintern infiltration of the OSS.

James Clapper had an impressive professional pedigree on paper. He had served in the military, with combat and intelligence duties in Vietnam, and, as a general officer, was chief of Air Force intelligence during the Gulf War of 1991. But being a modern general, in the end, is more of a pay grade than a measure of accomplishment.

Intelligence Gets the Clapper

Insiders hated Clapper. He shut down an Air Force intelligence threat assessment program because he disliked the intelligence that concluded that the Soviet Union still presented a nuclear weapons threat to the United States.[1]

Even so, President George H. W. Bush promoted Clapper to head the Defense Intelligence Agency (DIA) that same year of the Gulf War. The DIA directorship is a uniformed military three-star intelligence post, not a political one. Clapper broke precedent and politicized his position. Several members of the DIA staff and congressional oversight committees at the time told the author that Clapper appeared paranoid, obsessed with enforcing political correctness, and that he often attempted to control intelligence professionals' expressions of beliefs with pressure tactics that they felt unprofessional or unwarranted. Over more than two decades, multiple sources with firsthand knowledge told the author of Clapper video-recording meetings and putting employees through what they sarcastically called Maoist "struggle sessions." No public sources support these accounts, but the author, who has known and trusted his sources for years, is confident of their accuracy.[2]

President Bill Clinton kept Clapper in place until 1995. Then Clapper went into private business, where he cashed in on his insider status as an intelligence contractor.[3] President George W. Bush brought him back into government in 2001 to run the National Geospatial-Intelligence Agency, which controls America's spy satellites. The appointment anguished and angered many Bush political appointees in the Pentagon, but the president's second defense secretary, Robert Gates, got along well with him. In time, Gates would recommend Clapper to Obama.

Clapper was known at the time as a counterintelligence weakling. He wasn't quiet about his leftist, soft-on-Russia views. When he led the DIA, agency officials told the author at the time that Clapper showed preference for a group of female analysts on the Western Hemisphere desk. One of these analysts had grown up with a poster of Communist guerrilla Che Guevara in her bedroom as an icon of devotion.[4] Clapper developed special relations with this group, protected them from criticism, and seemed to ignore counterintelligence concerns, according to my sources.

One of Clapper's favorites in this group, DIA officers told the author, had been in charge of analysis for Nicaragua and El Salvador during the Reagan administration's Communist rollback campaign in Central America. (The author was sensitive to this because those two countries had been in his area of operation at that time.)

The name of the Clapper favorite was Ana Belén Montes.

According to these reports, Clapper protected Montes from critics inside DIA. Apparently on Clapper's recommendation, CIA director George Tenet recognized Montes as an exemplary intelligence professional and posed for her with a ceremonial photograph before the flags of the Army and Marines, the two holding a citation honoring her work.[5] Ultimately, after years of damage, Montes was arrested and convicted as a spy for Fidel Castro in Cuba.[6] She had kept Havana informed of everything U.S. military intelligence knew about the area and passed on information that directly led to the targeted death of at least one American soldier, and likely many more.[7]

Other Communist spies overtly benefited from Clapper's leadership. Former DIA and Pentagon officials told me that Clapper drew vocal resistance when he overstepped his authority to obtain Department of Defense passes for the Russian GRU military intelligence *rezident* and his deputy officers so they could roam the Pentagon freely and unescorted.[8]

Clapper circled time and again through the revolving door from senior official to private government contractor, back to senior official, and private contractor again. He even served two years as head of the Security Affairs Support Association, a pressure group for private intelligence contractors.[9]

Appointments and promotions from both Bush presidents insulated Clapper from criticisms of hyperpoliticization and abuse of position. He made an ideal pick for President Obama in 2010 because he looked like a Republican but acted like a Marxist. Unanimously confirmed in the Senate as director of national intelligence, Clapper would remain in charge of the entire American intelligence community for the rest of the Obama presidency.

As DNI, Clapper found a devoted White House partner in John O. Brennan, the former CIA chief of staff and President Obama's special assistant for homeland security. Brennan called Clapper "my foxhole buddy and good friend."[10] Before long, Obama would name Brennan CIA director.

Clapper provided the sheltering roof, what Russians would call the *krysha*, for the critical theorists in and around the administration to get to work. Almost a year after his appointment as DNI, Clapper quietly sponsored the intelligence community's first annual "Pride Summit." On a rotating basis and out of public view, a different agency would host the summit each year.[11] Clapper's cultural revolution of intelligence would be incremental, done small and quietly at first and escalating gradually, until finally becoming a fait accompli that all must accept if they wanted to continue to serve and keep their jobs.

The Intelligence Cultural Revolution

The great cultural revolution in the intelligence community, as with much of the rest of the government bureaucracy, began on August 18, 2011. On that day Obama issued Executive Order 13583. The title said it all: "Establishing a Coordinated Government-Wide Initiative to Promote Diversity and Inclusion in the Federal Workforce."[12] The executive order was a keystone of the Obama agenda and, consistent with all of his major executive orders, was prepared under the watchful eye of the extraordinarily powerful presidential confidant-without-portfolio Valerie Jarrett. "Obama has said he consults Jarrett on every major decision," the *New Republic* reported in a profile called "The Obama Whisperer," citing corroboration from current and former aides.[13] Jarrett, the identity political strategist, was known to be "the last person the president and/or first lady talk to."[14]

Diversity order 13583 was a social revolutionary *ukase*. It made no reference to enhancing intelligence collection, analysis, operations, or capabilities. It gave no explanation as to how such a diverse force might strengthen the intelligence community with language skills, or knowledge of domestic or foreign cultures, or the benefits of varied personal perspectives, experiences, and backgrounds.

On its face, 13583 looked like a virtue-signaling sop to the various identity groups that funded or mobilized voters for Obama's presidency. But there was nothing superficial about it. It was an ideological palace coup. The executive order was a majoritarian decree to transform the culture of the entire federal bureaucracy through implementation of critical theory. Once the bureaucratic culture changed—as Gramsci and

Marcuse had taught—the proper opinions and policies would follow. Obama knew that personnel is policy.

The Obama White House barely pretended to draw a correlation between increased diversity in the intelligence community and the upgrading of American intelligence capabilities. It issued no guidance on the actual skill sets that a more diverse workforce would require. The criteria kept shifting. First it was diversity and inclusion; later "equity" would be inserted between the two. Persons with disabilities, known as PWDs, became "persons with targeted disabilities," or PWTDs, "targeted" meaning more severe—to include advancement for people with psychological disorders and mental illness.

Agency meetings advertised as inviting open exchanges of ideas fizzled into presentations that mandated policies and stifled discussion and constructive feedback. All personnel were invited to voice concerns, but it was clear that any intelligence professional who did so risked paying a price. One might mark oneself for professional oblivion by dissenting at all.

Chapter 25

Target: Critical Race Theory at CIA

Obama's surprising pick of Leon Panetta brought a serious, capable leader to the CIA. For years Panetta had been a prominent and powerful member of Congress. He served as White House chief of staff under the very challenging Bill Clinton. Yet now, at Langley, Panetta appeared not to comprehend the gravity of what he was being told to do. The CIA's top operational mission under Panetta was to track and help the military kill Osama bin Laden. At the same time, Panetta carried out White House orders to begin an ethnic diversification of the agency, consistent with his own beliefs and Obama's stated policies, ostensibly to make the CIA look more like a cross section of America.[1]

In its 2009 report on intelligence reform, released under Panetta's name, the CIA made no mention of diversity, equity, inclusion, gender, sex, LGBT, or anything similar.[2] That would change. The very liberal CIA director seemed powerless to moderate the radicalism of what would follow.

Panetta wrote in his memoir that the Obama White House staff displayed what he diplomatically called a "penchant for control" over the CIA and the intelligence community at large. He named no names.[3] The White House seemed more obsessed with taking over the levers of power through its cultural Marxist revolution than it did with terminating bin Laden.

Georgetown University professor John Gentry, a former CIA analyst, penned several studies in a professional journal about the forces Obama was unleashing. Panetta, he recounted, "wrote later that Obama's White House staff tightly controlled the policies and activities of agency heads, including himself as DCIA [Director of the Central Intelligence Agency], making it clear that Obama was behind the IC's diversity initiatives. By the end of the Obama administration, such efforts had appreciably altered the demography of the IC."[4]

The intelligence community and military's extraordinary work in destroying al Qaeda and killing bin Laden in May 2011 called for a victory lap and changed everyone's focus. The next month, with his mission complete, Defense Secretary Gates returned to private life. Panetta left the CIA to replace Gates at the Pentagon. Obama named former Army general David Petraeus as the next CIA director. Petraeus lasted only fourteen months and resigned in a scandal late in 2012.[5] Obama waited until his second term, in March 2013, to appoint his aide John O. Brennan, Clapper's man, as CIA director.

The team was being pieced into place to execute fundamental transformation.

Brennan may have been a career CIA man with the nonpartisan credentials of having served at the top of the CIA under presidents

Clinton and Bush 43, but he had a radical past. He shared Obama's views that the administration should transform the country through incrementalism. He also had a political background not unlike that of Holder and especially Jarrett. When Brennan first applied to the CIA during the Carter administration, the CIA somehow cleared him despite his recent vote for a controlled Soviet asset, Communist Party chief Gus Hall, as president of the United States. In his memoir, Brennan drew no lessons from the experience, dismissing it as "a lark."[6]

After a shipboard United States Navy Islamic ceremony carefully prepared and prayed over bin Laden's body before setting it into the Indian Ocean, Director Brennan executed Obama diversity order 13583 with gusto. He mandated diversity offices be set up within CIA components. He increased hiring and promotions consistent with Obama's critical theory criteria. And he instituted explicit preferential promotion by sex (not gender, which would come later) in response to a study on the status of women at the CIA, regardless of the best qualified for a particular job.

Managers on the CIA Directorate of Support punished their subordinates who failed to comply with the new politicized atmosphere. Even female employees felt threatened.[7] Retired CIA analyst Nicholas Dujmovic said that some in the analysis directorate called Brennan's politicization "soft totalitarianism."[8]

Nowhere in his four-hundred-page memoir did Brennan ever claim that the goal was to make intelligence more efficient or its deliverables more productive.[9] According to Gentry, excellence was never the plan. "Brennan did not argue that Obama wanted to improve the performance of government in general, let alone the IC," Gentry wrote.[10] Yet Brennan began a constant refrain that the cultural revolution in the CIA would make America's intelligence machinery stronger. He just never explained how.

Target: Transforming the FBI

Once Robert Mueller served out the additional two years beyond his legal ten-year term as bureau director, Obama picked a lifelong Republican to replace the FBI's fidelity, bravery, and integrity with diversity, equity, and inclusion. Plus, his pick would be a Niebuhr acolyte like himself.

Early in his second term, Obama reached out to James Comey, a federal prosecutor who had served just over a year as Bush 43's deputy attorney general, to run the FBI. Obama's 2013 pick of Comey had the appearance of keeping a level, nonpartisan approach to running the FBI domestic-intelligence-with-police-powers apparat. Comey had investigated the Clintons' Whitewater scandal and now, heading the bureau, would lead the probe of Secretary of State Hillary Clinton's illegal use of a private email server while conducting State Department business.

Rise of the Niebuhr-lectuals

The Obama team screened its appointees with a microscope. Some in the administration would have learned of Comey's intellectual journey to show that this Republican lawyer was predisposed to what Obama wanted the FBI to become. Comey's worldview borrowed openly from Reinhold Niebuhr, the influential and widely respected Christian theologian who had imported the Frankfurt School's Paul Tillich to New York. Niebuhr was the thought leader whom Obama had called "my favorite philosopher."

Niebuhr was never a Communist but had been a fellow traveler. He came around later in life to support Truman's containment policy against Stalin. He always clung to socialism. He became an intellectual powerhouse at the State Department, especially with the milquetoast Secretary of State Dean Acheson and his policy-planning staff formerly headed by Alger Hiss.

But Niebuhr's move from 1930s pro-Communism stopped short of full opposition. In 1962, he joined the National Committee to Abolish the House Un-American Activities Committee, a Communist Party front devoted to shutting down the congressional panel that had plagued the party and its allies since before World War II.[11]

Niebuhr died in 1971, obscured by the rise of the New Left, but his ideas continued to influence the next generation. Hillary Clinton admired him, as did Republican senator John McCain. Though he'd been deceased for nearly forty years, the Obama administration cast Niebuhr as "the philosopher of the post-9/11 era."[12]

A year older than Obama, Comey had discovered Niebuhr in the early 1980s. He studied the philosopher while at the College of William & Mary. By chance he took a religion course with Professor James C. Livingston, who had studied under Niebuhr at the Union Theological Seminary thirty years before.

Journalist Diana West traces the intellectual chain of custody. It went from the Frankfurt School's Paul Tillich and the American importers, like Niebuhr, of critical Marxist scholars from Germany who were comfortable in, and never resolutely opposed to, NKVD circles on both sides of the Atlantic. They passed it on to the likes of Livingston, who relayed it to the future director of the FBI. A similar custody chain exists with Hillary Clinton, Obama's secretary of state whose journey from her original Goldwater conservatism owed much to Tillich and Niebuhr before she progressed to Saul Alinsky and Marcuse.[13]

Comey remained a Niebuhr devotee through his entire government career. "Comey's honors thesis, then, becomes a case study in the dissemination of these ideas over a couple of academic generations," wrote West, who read the former FBI director's ninety-five-page thesis multiple times. Comey's political views shifted back and forth, with no real roots. "In college, I was left of center," he told *New York* magazine.

Comey voted for Jimmy Carter in 1980. But by 1984, he said, "I voted for Reagan—I'd moved from Communist to whatever I am now. I'm not even sure how to characterize myself politically. Maybe at some point, I'll have to figure it out."[14]

But Niebuhr's code of justice remained solid, fundamental to Comey's lifelong legal worldview. In Comey's words, "Niebuhr's notion of justice is valid for all nations and time." Comey stayed true to his honors thesis: "Justice is distributive, says Niebuhr, and must be accomplished through power, with one eye on the standard of love and the other on the regulative principle of equality. He clearly believes the duty to establish this justice to lie with the government."[15]

Comey's formative Niebuhrian approach is more consistent with Old World monarchy and modern dictatorship than American founding principles. But it remained consistent through Comey's social justice warrior life that peaked during his time as Obama's FBI director.

In Comey's view, Christians must leave their moral beliefs at the door, not out of some postmodern American secularism but because "it is the duty of a Christian in politics to have no specific 'Christian politics,'" in other words, no moral guideposts at all. "By this Niebuhr does not mean a Christian viewpoint is irrelevant but that a set of Christian political decisions is impossible given the evil present in such decisions."[16]

Post-Ethical Ethics

Comey found a moral obligation to dispense with ethics. He saw that doing the unethical was ethical in the name of some higher human but not divine power. In Comey's words, "The Christian in politics must be willing to transgress any purely Christian ethic. He must be willing to sin in the name of justice."[17] This was progressive Christian-lite J. Edgar Hooverism.

Views can and do evolve after college, but Comey nursed an unusual personal devotion to Niebuhr. In 2009, in his late forties, Comey anonymized his Instagram and Twitter accounts as @ReinholdNiebuhr. The profile picture featured the real Niebuhr over the weird biographic summary, "I'm the dude, disguised as a dude, playing another dude," a line spoken by Robert Downey Jr. in Ben Stiller's *Tropic Thunder.* A journalist discovered the account in early 2017, while Comey was FBI director.[18] Comey later confirmed that the Twitter account was his.[19]

In his 2018 memoir, Comey began with a Niebuhr quote at the top of page one.[20] He recalled how the chance college course had transformed his life, shifting his future to law. "I took the course, and everything changed," he wrote. "The religion department introduced me to the philosopher and theologian Reinhold Niebuhr, whose work resonated with me deeply. Niebuhr saw the evil in the world, understood that human limitations make it impossible for any of us to really love another as ourselves, but still painted a compelling picture of our obligation to try to seek justice in a flawed world," Comey recalled.

Justice would not come from converting men's hearts and consciences through evidence, faith, and reason. For Comey it would be social justice, coming through the coercive hands of an administrative state: "And justice, Niebuhr believed, could be best sought through the instruments of government power."[21]

Chapter 26

Whole-of-Government Cultural Shift

As Obama's Jarrett-led team envisioned in the diversity-mandating Executive Order 13583, this would be a whole-of-government transformation. The transformation, cloaked in the Aesopian language that Hoover had warned about, was preceded through a cultural whole-of-society transformation led by mega-donors and think tanks, news and entertainment industries, universities, Big Data, and woke capital.

Leaks, Freedom of Information Act requests, and official disclosures would trickle out over time. A decade would pass before the scope was understood. The *Wall Street Journal* sifted through hundreds of pages of federal government diversity and inclusion manuals obtained under the Freedom of Information Act. It summed up its findings in a late December 2022 editorial: "The Department of Veterans Affairs has a gender gingerbread person. NASA says beware of micro-inequities.

And if U.S. Army servicewomen express 'discomfort showering with a female who has male genitalia,' what's the brass's reply? Talk to your commanding officer, but toughen up."[1]

Comey and Wray Push Critical Theory on Entire FBI

Back at the FBI, Director Comey made A. Tonya Odom effectively the bureau's diversity commissar after Odom pushed him to create a top diversity management position.[2] "As the chief diversity officer, she was responsible for developing and executing diversity and inclusion strategies to improve workplace inclusion and increase workforce diversity across the FBI," the bureau would later say in a fawning press release.[3]

Odom's titles were section chief in the Office of Diversity and Inclusion and the FBI's chief diversity officer. "One of the first things I did was to lobby to have diversity as a core value," Odom later said, hitting the points from the Clapper diversity initiative. "Existing core values included respect, integrity, fairness, and compassion, among others. Initially, there was a little pushback, because some people thought diversity was encompassed in all the other values. Making diversity a core value elevated the office and made it relevant. Before, diversity was not thought of as mission-critical or really helping us do better as an organization."[4]

After President Donald Trump fired Comey in 2017, new director Christopher Wray not only allowed Odom to continue her work, but promoted her to assistant director shortly before the November 2020 election.[5] She left the Office of Diversity and Inclusion in 2021 and was replaced by Scott McMillion, with the FBI marking the occasion in a published interview.

That year, the FBI acknowledged that the workforce had become even whiter than it had been in 2016—83.4 percent.[6] "It is frustrating," Odom said, reflecting on her diversity work. "Our workforce is not that diverse." The diversity recruits didn't make the cut at Quantico. "Our recruitment of women and minorities special agents has gone up significantly, but they don't all show up at new agent training. We've got to look at where we're losing people and then see what we can do to improve that process."[7]

The Odom-McMillion transition under Wray marked the start of an aggressive, extreme, psychologically manipulative diversity program that the FBI waged against personnel. Former FBI special agent Steve Friend, suspended indefinitely without pay for being a whistleblower, commented, "FBI requires two separate diversity trainings per year. No instruction on due process or cruel and unusual punishment rights."[8]

DEI Decoded

Three scholars who dissented from critical race theory mandates published a "Cheat Sheet for Policymakers" to help people understand DEI in brief.

Diversity in DEI doctrine, according to the scholars, is an "identity-based approach to society; includes only those who agree with Social Justice, which is a violation of individual identity; enforced intellectual conformity; political quotas; an attack on merit and a form of soft bigotry."

Equity, under DEI, is a manufactured inequality, or "equality of outcomes plus reparations, which is a violation of equality before the law, a dismantling of the foundations of a free society, [and] state management of society by redistributing resources, opportunity, and access."

Inclusion in DEI-speak is "restricted speech and justification for purges" of those deemed guilty of improper thinking, "an attack on freedoms of association and speech, [and] an enforced separation of people by race ('neo-segregation')."[9]

Marcusian Five-Year Plan

By Obama's second term, about half of the agencies of the intelligence community housed their own standing offices for diversity. That achievement enabled Director of National Intelligence Clapper to impose a political commissariat on the entire IC by creating an Intelligence Community Equal Employment Opportunity and Diversity Council. The ODNI Diversity Council would sign off on the work of others to create a five-year plan called the *IC Equal Employment Opportunity and Diversity Enterprise Strategy*, unveiled in 2015.[10]

It was the dawn of the new cultural Marxist commissariat that would come to be known as DEI.

All Diversity Council members ensured execution of Clapper's *Enterprise Strategy*. The obsessive bureaucratese of the DEI commissars followed: members included the ODNI's Chief of IC Equal Employment Opportunity and Diversity, the Director of the Center of Mission Diversity & Inclusion (CMDI) of the CIA, the Chief of the Equal Opportunity and Diversity Office of the Defense Intelligence Agency, the Director of the Office of Diversity Management and EEO at the National Geospatial-Intelligence Agency, the Chief of Diversity and Inclusion Section of the Human Resources Division of an unnamed agency (a check would reveal it to be the FBI), the Director of EEO and Diversity at the National Security Agency, the Director of EEO & Diversity Management at the National Reconnaissance Office, and the Chief Diversity Officer of the Department of State.

The ODNI Diversity Council included the respective officials at agencies and services that hadn't yet gotten with the program to insert the magic word in their titles: the intelligence and counterintelligence unit of the Department of Energy (responsible for nuclear weapons), the Drug Enforcement Administration, the Department of the Treasury, the Department of Homeland Security, the Department of Defense, and the Army, Navy, Air Force, Marines, and Coast Guard.

Sign On—or Else

Everyone was to be a co-conspirator. DNI Clapper required the handwritten signatures of designated officials at every intelligence agency to appear in the document.[11] The official, authorized record would show that the strategy was not a party line from a Chicago red diaper baby at the White House, but the entire intelligence community's own carefully considered consensus strategy.

Marcuse's repressive tolerance now ruled. There must be no dissent.

A very few intelligence officers did dissent—but they promptly had to leave government service. One was CIA operations officer Scott Uehlinger, who resigned and went public in 2017. "The twin serpents of politicization and political correctness—a Soviet term, by the way—walk hand in hand throughout the intelligence community," he said, "as well as every other government agency."[12]

Like others, Uehlinger saw many new CIA recruits as carriers of the politically correct plague from university to agency. "The PC mindset that now dominates every college campus is also positioned firmly throughout our government—particularly within the intelligence community, which saw its greatest personnel influx ever in the post-9/11 environment," Uehlinger said. "Today's intelligence community, the average age of which I would estimate at 32, was raised under the beleaguered Bush administration and reached professional maturity under the Obama administration, immersed in a PC environment."

Demoralized professionals saw a bleak future. "The U.S. intelligence community is in the midst of a severe crisis," Uehlinger said. "It has been used, or perhaps allowed itself to be used, as a tool of political destruction, against some of the same U.S. citizens it was created to protect."

As the Obama-era political abuses began to surface, Uehlinger said, "We are seeing the widespread abuse of intelligence by an incumbent administration to target political opposition. Long a technique in the developing world—a tactic I often witnessed as a CIA station chief working abroad—the Third World has come to roost in the United States."

Palace Coup: How to Hijack an Intelligence Community

The Jarrett-Clapper *Enterprise Strategy* listed three goals, with objectives under each. Every definition of the word "stultifying" applies to the numbing, nagging mantra of required Newspeak and behavior to implement the current truth. What follows is tedious but necessary to understanding the fanaticism of intelligence transformation.

Goal 1 placed the intelligence community leadership on notice and held agency chiefs personally accountable for making diversity and inclusion front and center, with metrics to prove results. Within that goal, Objective 1.1 was to "implement efforts to hold all IC leaders accountable for advancing EEO, diversity, and inclusion and for achieving measureable [*sic*] results." Objective 1.2 was to "create opportunities for the exchange of ideas and solutions to challenges among IC EEO and Diversity professionals." Objective 1.3 showed how the ODNI instructed the IC leadership to empower the preexisting, horizontally integrated identity networks established throughout the intelligence community years before.[13]

This was literally a twenty-first-century version of intra-bureaucratic, Frankfurt-School-in-action critical theory within the intelligence community. The operational nodes in the horizontal networks, identity cells called employee resource groups or ERGs in most agencies, but Agency Resource Groups or ARGs in the CIA, were already a done deal. These pre-existing cell groups housed the similarly organized and indoctrinated cadre for each intelligence service leader to tap per the ODNI's instruction. One CIA ARG is the Agency Network of Gay, Lesbian, Bisexual, and Transgender Officers (ANGLE), which pushed trans ideology on other employees with exhibits like "'HEART: Sharing Our LGBT Families with Our Agency Family' to showcase officers' reflections on family, diversity and inclusion."[14]

ERGs were not new. Though different ideologically, in organization and function they were similar to the Old Left's building of party cells in unions and government offices. The identity cells had proliferated in the private sector a decade before penetrating the intelligence community and most of the rest of government. They extended from within agencies and crossed to other agencies. Then they spread to ERGs that sprang up among government contractors. Normal security compartmentation was scrapped to accommodate the class-privileged ERG identitarians.

The ODNI *Enterprise Strategy* specifically instructed: "Collaborate with seniors [that is, agency chiefs] to leverage their positions of leadership and visibility in support of employee resource groups and diversity programs, as a means to identify and seek resolution to diversity, inclusion, and EEO issues in the workforce." Diversity and inclusion in, equal opportunity on the way out.[15]

Goal 2 would push diversity first to be accepted and internalized in the intelligence workforce. Enforcement of that voluntary acceptance would come from the top. The injection point was the Grade Scale 13–15 section of higher midlevel management or their equivalents, plus those in "senior positions" and "core occupations" to "ensure that diversity is a critical consideration in succession planning and other human capital initiatives."[16] Again, equal opportunity and professional excellence would be shunted as of secondary concern.

Succession planning is a business management term for the preparation and elevation of new cadres to replace those who would be promoted up or attrited out. DEI would ensure the selection and pre-positioning of favored classes of people for rapid promotion once more senior positions opened. This built-in favoritism would ensure a faster takeover of the levers of control, a palace coup within the intelligence bureaucracies.

Goal 2 mandated that IC chiefs "integrate diversity, inclusion and EEO into broader workforce planning processes." Objective 2.1 shoved equal opportunity out the back of the bus by not mentioning it at all: "Ensure that IC Element workforce shaping activities include diversity and inclusion—in its broadest context—as a mission critical imperative."[17]

That language made clear that the United States intelligence community would have no greater priority than DEI.

Goal 3 concerned recruitment, hiring, and retention of the intelligence community's workforce. Once again, equal employment opportunity was out. Skill and expertise didn't make the cut. Fixation on diversity "at all levels within the IC" was in.[18] Objective 3.2 mandated that the entire IC "partner with diverse external organizations and academic institutions to gain greater access to diverse candidates," an apparent reference to NGOs, pressure groups, and university diversity committees as recruitment grounds or feeders for desired recruits into the intelligence community.

Mandated Struggle Sessions

Goal 4 ostensibly mandated career development and advancement for "all IC employees." Objective 4.3 gave away the real agenda, which was to "partner with internal and external stakeholders" to plan and execute psychological conditioning of all IC personnel, "including training in diversity and inclusion." DEI training became mandatory for intelligence career advancement and thus a professional instrument for behavior modification and the purging or self-purging of the noncompliant.[19]

This smacked of the alleged Maoist-style "struggle sessions" my sources tell me Clapper had run when he was DIA director years earlier.

Goal 5, to maintain equal employment opportunity for all, seemed more status quo, with little for anyone to disagree about. The goal appears to be nothing more than a blandly worded means to equip the intelligence community to handle the mass of confusion and complaints expected with the planned imposition of DEI.

Not even the successive plans to break up the inter-bureaucratic stovepipes that had crippled intelligence would work anywhere nearly as quickly or efficiently as the Jarrett-Clapper *Enterprise Strategy.* ODNI had yet to show significant progress in leveraging data, metrics, studies, research, and technology to inform the president and his decision-makers with first-class intelligence. Instead of fixing those huge problems, Clapper made it a priority to force DEI, now as a mission-critical imperative, to ditch equal opportunity and impose critical race theory.

All the intelligence chiefs, and the department, agency, and service chiefs among them, went along without complaint, either to Congress or to the public. None resigned in protest. None even spoke out.

Systemic Revolution

Clapper's *Enterprise Strategy* was just the intelligence community portion of Obama's carefully planned White House initiative to inject critical race theory into the entire federal workforce, and to use that workforce as an engine of societal change.

This federal workforce shift would be a crucial engine for Obama's vision of fundamental transformation. It fulfilled the government-as-vanguard model of the Frankfurt School, Gramsci, and Niebuhr. "You can say General Donovan was a trailblazer for promoting diversity, equity, and inclusion within the IC," the agency implausibly claimed in a 2021 social media post.[20]

With a few exceptions, everything continued apace through the end of Obama's second term, remained practically undisturbed by Trump, and emerged re-energized on the first day of the Biden administration.

Chapter 27

"Culture is the unwritten rules. So by definition, you can't train your way to a change in culture. . . . We have an opportunity to shape our culture."

—James Comey, FBI director, 2016[1]

Pride before the Fall

For five years, starting in 2011, the Obama administration's Office of the Director of National Intelligence held Pride Summits in the closet. It was as if they were secret operations. During those closeted times, the Marcusian diversity initiatives charged ahead. The FBI established its Office of Diversity and Inclusion.[2] It issued an internal use–only Diversity and Inclusion Program Policy Directive in 2014. Director Comey added diversity as a "core value" of the FBI in 2015.

Then, in 2016, with the summits embedded and celebrated throughout the intelligence community, Clapper's office issued a public statement about what it considered an extraordinary historic event:

> Director of National Intelligence James Clapper, FBI Director James Comey and DIA Director Vincent Stewart will address the Fifth Annual Intelligence Community Pride Summit,

> entitled "Count on Your Community." The trio—who rarely together address one assembly outside the houses of Congress—will applaud LGBTA—A is for Allies—officers for sharing their authentic selves at work each day, empowering the mission of each one of the 17 elements of the Intelligence Community.[3]

The "A is for Allies" had nothing to do with the Five Eyes or NATO, or allies against jihadists or Putin or Communist China (although the start of the summit in 2011 coincided with a public rainbow offensive across the Atlantic at Britain's MI6). "A is for Allies" had nothing to do with ethnicity, linguistic skills, cultural background, professional expertise, technological prowess, or other attributes befitting a strong intelligence community. It was Marcusian social revolution. Clapper had piloted it all along in near secrecy. With a reference to the spy services leading American public opinion on a divisive political and cultural issue, he told the 2016 summiteers:

> When I spoke at this summit two years ago, I mentioned that I was serving in the Air Force when [President Bill Clinton's] "Don't Ask, Don't Tell" was enacted. . . . I am thankful that—as a nation—we have put that policy behind us. . . . I won't dwell on the issue of Transgender rights. . . . I know our nation is currently engaged in a complex conversation . . . with strong feelings on both sides. But here in the IC, we have the chance to lead by example. . . . So I'll say without equivocation . . . in IC facilities . . . you can use whatever restroom you feel comfortable and safe in.[4]

The head of the entire intelligence community of the United States of America had spoken. The spooks would lead national social change by example. ODNI's press release even bore its own hashtags: #LGBTSPIES and #2016ICPRIDE.

The only senior participant not quoted as pushing a revolutionary line was Marine Corps Lt. Gen. Vincent Stewart, at the time DIA director. Because the annual ODNI pride events rotated from agency to agency, Stewart hosted the Pride Summit. Stewart said, "This summit isn't about a complicated, abstract idea. It's about treating others as we would like to be treated: with dignity, respect and kindness."[5]

Stewart seemed out of the loop. That wasn't the theme at all. Then FBI director James Comey spoke. He certainly understood what Stewart did not. Comey took a swipe at "socially confused, awkward white people."[6] Inappropriately for a sitting FBI chief, he made an indirect reference to Hillary Clinton, then a presidential candidate. And then he turned to tragedy: "We actually face a crisis in the FBI," he said solemnly. "Eighty-three percent of our special agents are white."[7]

The bureau chief committed himself to transforming the FBI's internal culture. "Culture is the way things are really done no matter what they tell you in training. Culture is the unwritten rules. So by definition, you can't train your way to a change in culture."[8]

Recalling his diversity initiative in his memoir, Comey spouted the same programmed, trendy banalities. "Diversifying the Bureau was the key to our sustained effectiveness," he wrote. He then commented on the "high-potential black and Latino men and women" who "thought of the FBI as 'The Man.'"[9]

Global Spy Pride

ODNI said that about one thousand intelligence personnel participated, "in-person and via video teleconference from posts around the world," in the Pride Summit breakout sessions. This means that CIA stations and other intelligence outposts worldwide were simultaneously open, or had staff on duty, in most of the world's thirty-eight time zones to participate in the Pride Summit.

Five breakout sessions provided focus. The first described the revolutionary pull from above: "Seniors Helping Drive Change." In this case, ODNI said, "seniors" meant not the elderly but senior military and civilian officers. The second involved the training of the united front cadres, the allies: "LGBT Ally Training." The third went over the practicalities of implementation, "Extended Enterprise Management: Getting Inclusive." The fourth concerned coming out: "Boots to Rainbow Suits: Successfully Transitioning from Military to Civilian Life." The fifth breakout session, and most controversial even among lesbian, gay, and bisexual intelligence personnel, was about the "T+" part of the ever-changing alphabetical soup: "Building Trans Inclusivity."[10]

Now fully mobilized to progress ahead, the ODNI came out to the world. An officially approved, ODNI-run Tumblr account featured a defaced black-and-white Old Glory with stars in rainbow colors. ODNI artists blacked out the bottom half of the flag to feature the official ODNI logo and the slogan, "AMERICA'S LGBT SPIES / Secret Agents . . . of Change."[11]

It was the unveiling of an unimaginable achievement that would have awed cultural gradualist Gramsci, culture warrior Lukács, front-*gruppenführer* Münzenberg, Cheka commissar Dzerzhinsky, and the whole of their critical theory spawn at the Frankfurt School. After years of work, the horizontally networked identity groups had not only burrowed into the heart of the American intelligence community; they had fused with its vertical bureaucratic command structure to mobilize as secret agents of change across Uncle Sam's intelligence and counterintelligence defenses. They had received official sanction from the top to change the culture of American society.

"This Whole Woke Thing Is Just Vile"

The 2016 summit marked a sea change. The CIA had lost its more objective basis for recruitment. It actively sought out emotionally damaged and fragile personnel who immediately became a drag on the professionals.

"Their judgment has become subjective," said a recently retired intelligence veteran of thirty-five years. "We see this throughout the community: 'I was injured by your factual statement.' 'My feelings were hurt.' 'I didn't feel safe.'"

The veteran asked for anonymity because he makes his living as a contractor, but he still has a sense of mission. He spoke in early 2023 with the bitter language of a real professional at the end of his rope: "Can you imagine an intelligence officer, in some of the most secure compounds on earth, complaining that he or she doesn't 'feel safe'? What a bunch of fucking horse shit. This whole woke thing is just vile. It's an excuse to get your way, to demonize other people, to purge."[12]

Obama's COINTELPRO

In eight years, the Obama administration built upon the centralized levers of control that the George W. Bush administration had redesigned and Congress enacted into law, and primed the intelligence community for weaponization against the public. The 2016 election, with Hillary Clinton as Obama's hoped-for successor, would involve the FBI and other elements of the intelligence community in a political dirty-tricks campaign of a scope never before seen in American politics.

The dirty-tricks campaign was code-named Crossfire Hurricane. It was run not as a criminal investigation but, as if cribbing from Hoover's COINTELPRO, as a counterintelligence program. It was run by senior FBI counterintelligence officers. But COINTELPRO, despite some benighted excesses, had been narrowly focused. COINTELPRO was not a descendant of the Comintern's program of stealth Marxism. COINTELPRO had targeted Kremlin agents and those who collaborated with them; foreign-backed, racial-identity violent extremists; foreign-backed elements of the New Left; supporters of military enemies like the North Vietnamese regime and its Vietcong proxies; and the Ku Klux Klan.

The Obama-Comey 2016 variant targeted the front-runner and nominee of the Republican Party in order to elect Democrat nominee Hillary Clinton. Crossfire Hurricane undoubtedly was an operation directed against a broad swath of the American people. Once the undesired candidate Donald Trump became president, the FBI continued Crossfire Hurricane to cripple his administration.

Suspicions and piecemeal evidence were there all along to show that the "Russia collusion narrative" against Trump was a lie, but Trump's lack of a coherent national security team and his own defensive behavior didn't help his case. For four years, the narrative that Trump and those around him ran America as Russian traitors was pounded into the political psyche. This received widespread credibility because of the leaks spewing from the FBI and other "intelligence sources," later with the personal imprints of former top Obama intelligence officials like James Clapper and John Brennan.

Former FBI director Robert Mueller, as special prosecutor, led an investigation that found in 2019 that the Steele dossier that fueled Crossfire Hurricane was a complete fabrication.[13] By then, the Mueller fans who had once appreciated his inadvertent teeing up of the FBI for Obama had discarded him as no longer useful. Almost no senior former intelligence official who had promoted the Steele dossier falsehoods made a public retraction or apology. Now it was time to find the wrongdoers. The following year, John H. Durham was appointed special counsel to "investigate whether any federal official, employee, or any other person or entity violated the law in connection with the intelligence, counter-intelligence, or law-enforcement activities directed at the 2016 presidential campaigns."[14]

Durham issued his report in 2023. He and his team conducted more than 480 interviews, issued 190 grand jury subpoenas, and collected 6 million pages of documents. Some key individuals, Durham reported, "had important and relevant information about the topics under investigation" but "refused to be interviewed" or cooperate.[15]

Durham's findings were unequivocal. They showed that the entire FBI had become rotten to the core. The crimes and abuses were not confined to a few senior bureau leaders who had been fired. Certain counterintelligence officers' refusal to cooperate with Durham's probe, and FBI director Christopher Wray's pointed failure to order their full cooperation, indicated as much.

The main drivers of Crossfire Hurricane, according to Durham, were FBI deputy director Andrew McCabe and Deputy Assistant Director for Counterintelligence Peter Strzok. There were others. Both McCabe and especially Strzok were openly hostile in a partisan manner that broke all FBI rules of professionalism. Strzok had manipulated counterintelligence for partisan political purposes under McCabe, also a counterintelligence man.

The FBI opened Crossfire Hurricane without following the most basic rule, which was to interview the accusers and evaluate whether their information merited investigation. Durham found that the bureau started the operation without "any significant review of its own intelligence databases," with no "collection and examination of any relevant intelligence from other U.S. intelligence entities," without bothering with "interviews of witnesses essential to understand the raw information it had received," and neglecting to use "any of the standard analytical tools typically employed by the FBI in evaluating raw intelligence."[16]

This was systematic neglect, not a failure of imagination.

Had it done those basic things, Durham concluded,

> the FBI would have learned that their own experienced Russia analysts had no information about Trump being involved with Russian leadership officials, nor were others in sensitive positions at the CIA, the NSA, and the Department of State aware of such evidence concerning the subject. In addition, FBI records prepared by Strzok in February and March 2017 show that at the time of the opening of Crossfire Hurricane, the FBI had no information in its holdings indicating that at any time during the campaign anyone in the Trump campaign had been in contact with any Russian intelligence officials.[17]

There never was a case on which to base the operation.

Durham documented a total breakdown in FBI investigative and counterintelligence procedures and practices, from top to bottom. For reasons Durham explained but that an average citizen would not understand, FBI director James Comey got away unscathed. Even so, Durham observed that something institutionally was terribly wrong: "The speed and manner in which the FBI opened and investigated Crossfire Hurricane during the presidential election season based on raw, unanalyzed, and uncorroborated intelligence also reflected a noticeable departure from how it approached prior matters involving possible attempted foreign election interference plans aimed at the Clinton campaign."[18]

That speed stood in marked contrast to FBI investigations of Clinton, in which Durham said the "FBI moved with considerable caution."[19] The investigations of Clinton, Durham said, "are also markedly different from the FBI's actions with respect to other highly significant intelligence it received from a trusted foreign source pointing to a

Clinton campaign plan to vilify Trump by tying him to Vladimir Putin so as to divert attention from her own concerns relating to her use of a private email server"[20] while she was secretary of state.

Crossfire Hurricane polluted the entire intelligence community and chain of command. Durham continued:

> Unlike the FBI's opening of a full investigation of unknown members of the Trump campaign based on raw, uncorroborated information, in this separate matter involving a purported Clinton campaign plan, the FBI never opened any type of inquiry, issued any taskings, employed any analytical personnel, or produced any analytical products in connection with the information.[21]

When the FBI learns that foreign intelligence services have targeted senior officials or other public figures, it offers them what is called a defensive briefing. A defensive briefing alerts them that they have been targeted and provides advice about what they can do to defend themselves and their teams and help foil the attempts. Durham found that the FBI provided defensive briefings to Clinton and her team but not to Trump and his team. "Instead, the FBI began working on requests for the use of FISA authorities" against two Trump campaign people, one allegedly overheard by an Australian official in a bar, to obtain secret Foreign Intelligence Surveillance court orders to allow the FBI to use foreign spy information against them.[22]

Durham found a partisan motive for this discrepancy. Among the documentation, he published excerpts of texts between Strzok and his lover, FBI lawyer Lisa Page. Strzok: "We'll stop it," it being Trump becoming president.[23] Said Durham, "Indeed, the day before the Australian information was received at FBI Headquarters, Page sent a message to Strzok stating, 'Have we opened on him yet? [angry-faced emoji]' and referenced an article titled *Trump & Putin. Yes, It's Really a Thing.*"[24]

Even though Comey, McCabe, and Strzok had been fired by the time Durham began his investigation, *senior counterintelligence officials still refused to cooperate with the probe.* This suggests that the FBI spy-catchers, years after the fact, remained part of an old-boy (and old-girl) network with Strzok and perhaps others, or had become a politicized cell diverted from the counterintelligence mission. Or something worse.

Critics note that the Durham team failed to ask or seek answers to certain key questions, failed to compel certain figures to cooperate, and declined to file criminal charges against many who could still be charged. Still, Durham's findings were damning:

> The government possessed no verified intelligence reflecting that Trump or the Trump campaign was involved in a conspiracy or collaborative relationship with officials of the Russian government. . . . [Furthermore,] neither U.S. law enforcement nor the Intelligence Community appears to have possessed any actual evidence of collusion in their holdings at the commencement of the Crossfire Hurricane investigation.[25]

Chapter 28

Main Sources of the Allegations: Foreign Spies

But there was more. The Clinton campaign relied on foreign sources as the pretext to trigger and leak news of Crossfire Hurricane. The first was Christopher Steele himself, formerly of the British MI6 foreign intelligence service. Michael Sussman, Clinton campaign general counsel at the Perkins Coie law firm, hired the opposition research company Fusion GPS,[1] which paid Steele to come up with material to discredit Trump.

Steele wasn't just a former British intelligence officer. In the 1980s, before joining MI6, he had been an activist in the Campaign for Nuclear Disarmament (CND). CND was a British anti-nuclear movement loosely affiliated with a Soviet-backed active measures operation to defeat Prime Minister Margaret Thatcher's and President Ronald Reagan's strategic nuclear modernization against the USSR, and to freeze in Moscow's then-qualitative and quantitative nuclear weapons superiority. CND was not under Soviet control, but it was under Kremlin influence. A declassified CIA report from the early 1980s on Soviet disarmament active measures said, in cautious language, that the CND amplified Kremlin propaganda against the United States: "The largest and most influential peace groups—such as . . . the Campaign for Nuclear Disarmament (CND) in the UK—are not dominated by Communists or by those explicitly sympathetic to Soviet objectives per se, and on occasion are influenced by pro-Soviet activists only to amplify their denunciations of NATO and US motives."[2] A CIA diagram of international "peace" movements controlled or influenced by Soviet active measures against the United States includes the CND.[3]

A Russian national named Igor Danchenko was Steele's sub-source. The Durham investigation found that Danchenko had been the target of an FBI national security investigation from 2009 to 2011 for allegedly trying to recruit Brookings Institution staff to spy for the Russian government once they entered the Obama administration.[4]

The FBI ran Steele as a confidential human source, or CHS, as soon as Crossfire Hurricane began, if not earlier. Steele provided the first of his reports "to his FBI handler" on July 5, 2016, according to the Durham report.[5]

The FBI also ran Danchenko as a paid CHS for Crossfire Hurricane. Durham found that the FBI had known since 2009 that Danchenko was in contact with Russian intelligence officers and seeking to recruit Americans to spy for the Putin regime. The FBI identified Danchenko as Steele's "primary sub-source" in 2016. Under questioning, "Danchenko was unable to provide any corroborating evidence to support the Steele allegations," and even admitted that his own sub-source conversations were only "rumor and speculation," according to Durham. Even so, the FBI in 2017 "engaged Danchenko as a CHS and began making regular financial payments to him for information—none of which corroborated Steele's reporting."[6] The FBI either allowed itself to be hoodwinked or knowingly enriched someone it had long suspected to be a Russian spy.

The false allegations tore the country apart for the entire four years of the Trump administration. A similar operation took place during the next election cycle, in 2020. By this time, some of the biggest names in the American intelligence community had convinced themselves and half the country, with no corroborating evidence, that Trump was a Putin tool. A derangement syndrome had swept some of the most respected, or at least prestigious, names in U.S. intelligence.

In October 2020, senior intelligence community figures manufactured a fake story to generate a false headline that news of the Hunter Biden laptop was another Russian disinformation operation to keep former vice president Joe Biden from winning the presidency. More than fifty former national security and intelligence officials, including five former CIA directors, signed the misleading document, with nine signatories hiding behind anonymity.[7] The false letter came out just days before Biden's debate with Trump, allowing Biden to use it as a prop to show that the protectors of American national security were on his side and that the Putin regime wanted Trump to win. We will look at that letter in a separate chapter.

Before the *New York Post* broke the laptop story, the FBI warned Facebook, Twitter, and social media companies to beware of an upcoming Russian disinformation story intended to manipulate the election. But that would not be learned until congressional hearings almost three years later. One of the top Twitter officials liaising with the FBI and recommending which accounts should be censored or suspended was a new legal executive, former FBI general counsel Jim Baker.

Durham Exposes the FBI's Own Rap Sheet

Durham concluded in the summary of his massive report on government wrongdoing in pushing the false Trump collusion narrative, "Based on the review of Crossfire Hurricane and related intelligence activities, we conclude that the Department [of Justice] and the FBI failed to uphold their important mission of strict fidelity to the law in connection with certain events described in this report."[8]

The independent counsel continued to rattle off a chain of FBI abuses, unprofessionalism, negligence, and crime: "a criminal offense by fabricating language in an email" to deceive a judge and get a surveillance order; "at best, a cavalier attitude towards accuracy and completeness"; "FBI personnel . . . repeatedly disregarded important requirements when . . . they did not genuinely believe there was probable cause"; "certain personnel disregarded significant exculpatory information that should have prompted investigative restraint and re-examination."[9]

The decay spread across the bureau, at all levels, all the way to the top, Durham reported: "Senior FBI personnel displayed a serious lack of analytical rigor towards the information that they received, especially information received from politically affiliated persons and entities," which "in part triggered and sustained Crossfire Hurricane and contributed to the subsequent need for Special Counsel Mueller's investigation," which found that the allegations were false. "In particular, there was significant reliance on investigative leads provided or funded (directly or indirectly) by Trump's political opponents. The [Justice] Department did not adequately examine or question these materials and the motivations of those providing them, even when at about the same time the Director of the FBI and others learned of significant and potentially contrary intelligence."[10]

Durham found intellectual rot, bias, politicization, groupthink, and sheer recklessness throughout the bureau:

> In light of the foregoing, there is a continuing need for the FBI and the Department to recognize that lack of analytical rigor, apparent confirmation bias, and an over-willingness to rely on information from individuals connected to political opponents caused investigators to fail to adequately consider alternative hypotheses and to act without appropriate objectivity or restraint in pursuing allegations of collusion or conspiracy between a U.S. political campaign and a foreign power. Although recognizing that in hindsight much is clearer, much of this also seems to have been clear at the time.[11]

The Real Goal Was Subversion of the Institutions

Any intelligence service's basic psychological profile of the candidates would have revealed what buttons to push and when. "Trump has reacted to the Steele report exactly as the Russians wanted him to—by denouncing the intelligence community that leaked it and saying that their actions were like 'something out of Nazi Germany,'" journalist David Satter, a former Moscow correspondent for the *Financial Times*, noted as the scandal unfolded.[12] "The same pattern of Russian interference was evident in the release by WikiLeaks of the e-mails from the Democratic National Committee and the personal account of Hillary Clinton's campaign manager, Joe Podesta," Satter said. "Had the e-mails been published as the result of investigative reporting, they would have been a major contribution to our knowledge of the candidates. In this case, however, the 'investigative reporters' were the agents of a foreign intelligence service."[13] The same was true of the Steele dossier.

It was a byzantine operation of multiple deflections to polarize Americans further. The dossier seemed to be, as Satter put it, "primarily an attempt to destroy the Clinton candidacy," when in fact it was "an effort to discredit the American system as a whole." It was, he said, "a carefully constructed attempt to disrupt American political life for years to come."[14]

Americans ordinarily would expect their sprawling intelligence community, led by the CIA and FBI, to detect, neutralize, and expose such destructive foreign active measures—especially the FBI, whose Counterintelligence Division is tasked precisely for this job. Under the disturbed and bitter Peter Strzok, certain of his underlings, that division was compromised. Under the direction of Strzok's superior, FBI deputy director Andrew McCabe, the entire bureau was compromised. All was done with the full protection of FBI director James Comey, and in collusion with figures at the CIA, both active and retired, including Director John Brennan and with the enthusiastic backing of the director of national intelligence, James Clapper.

It was a triumvirate of direct descendants of the Frankfurt School.

With angry glee, leading figures in the intelligence establishment claimed inside information that it was all true. Biden's future national security advisor Jake Sullivan pushed the false story.[15] So did former CIA Moscow station chief John Sipher, a Biden campaign surrogate who self-identified in a *Washington Post* column as an expert on disinformation. In time for the 2020 campaign, Sipher joined the advisory board of the Lincoln Project, a group cofounded by a registered agent of the Russian government.[16] Like Brennan, Sipher would sign the infamous letter from fifty-one former intelligence officials claiming that the Hunter Biden laptop story was Russian disinformation, a letter that Biden would go on to use as a prop in his debate with Trump.[17] They seemed to speak in the name of the entire intelligence community.

They were all completely wrong.

The intelligence establishment's unified line was that if you didn't go along with the Steele disinformation, you were a conspiracy theorist, perhaps even a traitor. The truth mattered not. Before Durham completed his findings, Senators Chuck Grassley and Ron Johnson found out that the FBI knew all along about Russian disinformation in the Steele dossier. The mainstream press and many of their Senate colleagues keelhauled Grassley and Johnson for it.[18] The Durham investigation proved them completely right, but it didn't matter.

The 2020 presidential campaign would see a repeat performance from that same intelligence establishment. Trump's decapitation of the FBI over the Steele dossier had no effect on improving professionalism and reducing politicization. Under Trump's appointee, Christopher Wray, it was the FBI itself, not the political campaign of Trump's rival, that spread the falsehoods in 2020. Building on the continued widespread public belief in the Russian collusion narrative, the FBI warned social media companies of an impending Kremlin disinformation campaign to discredit Hunter Biden. The FBI prompted Facebook, Twitter, and others to censor the *New York Post* reporting on the laptop.[19] In 2023, whistleblowers gave sworn testimony before Congress to reveal that the FBI knew all along that the laptop story was true.[20]

Wray had quickly proved Comey's equal and more when it came to information operations run out of FBI headquarters. He built on Comey's foundation to turn the bureau into a weapon of cultural revolution.

Chapter 29

"We don't really think of threats in terms of left, right, at the FBI. We're focused on the violence, not the ideology."

—FBI director Christopher Wray, 2020[1]

Antifa Is Just an Idea

By now, a shameless, willful blindness had embedded itself in the top levels of the FBI, CIA, and other elements of the United States intelligence community. Given the policies, it would be fair for one to suspect that it wasn't blindness at all, but deception to conceal an agenda, an agenda that was being implemented by underlings in the name of job security and professional advancement. In key areas, leaders of the intelligence community denied the nature of certain threats and sometimes even downplayed or denied their existence.

In early 2011, while the Obama administration was backing a Muslim Brotherhood color revolution to overthrow the pro-American government of Egypt,[2] Director of National Intelligence James Clapper told the House Intelligence Committee that the Egyptian Muslim Brotherhood was nothing to worry about. It was a harmless organization, "largely secular," and it had "pursued social ends, a betterment of the political order in Egypt, et cetera," he testified, "not necessarily with a view to promoting violence or overthrow of the state."[3]

In fact, the Muslim Brotherhood is an Islamic extremist organization that was banned in Egypt and in the process of overthrowing the Egyptian government. It shares the same end goal as al Qaeda—that is, to impose an extreme Islamic caliphate on the entire world. A backlash forced Clapper's office to issue a clarification.

While the hyper-violent Antifa network raged across the United States in 2020, some top politicians denied the violence even existed. Confronted with questions about Antifa violence in Oregon and elsewhere, House Judiciary Committee chairman Jerrold Nadler, the New York Democrat who ran oversight of the FBI, dismissed the issue entirely. "That's a myth that's being spread only in Washington, D.C.," Nadler said.[4] Nadler is a former member of Democratic Socialists of America (DSA).[5] DSA says it seeks to "build broader united fronts" against what it broadly deems "outright fascist elements." It has an Antifascist Working Group to help the loose Antifa and related networks become better organized, and to "work in coalition with others in creating mass mobilizations."[6] Presidential candidate Joe Biden brushed off Antifa as "an idea, not an organization. Not a militia, that's what his [Trump's] FBI director said." Biden said that white supremacists present a far greater threat.[7]

Testifying before a House Homeland Security Committee hearing on terrorism shortly before the presidential debate, FBI director Chris Wray claimed that Antifa was not an "organization" but an "ideology." Antifa is a "real thing," Wray said, adding that the FBI had launched "any number of properly predicated investigations into what we would describe as violent anarchist extremists." However, he went on to claim, "It's not a group or an organization. It's a movement or an ideology." He did not describe it as a network. He made no attempt to define or explain that ideology or its foreign origins and continued transnational connections.[8]

That represented a fundamental flaw in FBI intelligence collection and analysis. Antifa is, in fact, a horizontally integrated transnational network of networks. The present network is a revival, in deliberate spirit if not in fact, of the Comintern's Anti-Fascist Action in Weimar Germany. It has the same short name and the exact same logo.

"As a subversive and violent extremist international movement committed to anarcho-communist ideologies, Antifa is fundamentally committed to the abolition of the U.S. government and the violent overthrow of the United States Constitution," Kyle Shideler, a specialist on ideological extremism, testified to the Senate Judiciary Committee one month before Wray's Senate appearance. "It is committed to the use of both subversion and violent extremism to enforce its political views by terrorizing American citizens. Antifa's activities clearly meet the definition of an organized criminal conspiracy and terrorism established by federal law," he said.[9]

Shideler provided Congress what the FBI could not before or since: a description of Antifa's networked grouping and organization. "American law enforcement and domestic intelligence have largely failed to understand the nature of the movement," he said.[10]

> Seeking a rigidly hierarchical organization, such as historically found in transnational criminal organizations such as the American Mafia or the Soviet-controlled Communist Party USA, some analysts have concluded, against all evidence, that Antifa does not exist in any meaningful sense. This obsolete form of intelligence analysis of seeking out vertically integrated command-and-control is precisely what handicapped the U.S. from understanding horizontally

> organized or even un-structured networks like al Qaeda nearly two decades ago.[11]

"Neither the FBI nor the Department of Homeland Security have given any indication that they have prioritized intelligence collection and analysis of this growing domestic threat," Kyle said at the end of his testimony. "It is clear that the threat has been underestimated and swept under the rug for too long."[12]

The FBI presented Congress with no significant descriptions of Antifa and certain other left-wing domestic violent extremist groups, preferring to focus on a political narrative of right-wing and white supremacist violent extremism.

The Germans Get Antifa Right

Wray did not tell Congress that Germany, a key American ally that works closely with the FBI on counterterrorism, had prepared a report several months earlier on Antifa. Since the Allied occupation after World War II, the Federal Republic of Germany has been mindful of any white supremacist, fascist, or neo-Nazi activity, though it has been spotty at best on anarchist and Communist subversion. Germany's Office for the Protection of the Constitution, the BfV internal security service, has infiltrated, disrupted, and shut down extreme right-wing illegal networks. Its annual report, the *Verfassungsschutzbericht*, in recent years has shown a fairly consistent, evenhanded approach against all extremists that threaten the German constitution from left and right.

Antifa, according to the BfV, is an organized "left-wing violent extremist" network with ideological goals "to eliminate the existing state and social order and thus the free democratic basic order."[13] No public FBI statement had ever been so clear.

The German Dissection of Antifa

"The 'Anti-Fascist Action' ('Antifa' for short) is not a clearly defined single organization or structurally consolidated group," *V2019* said of today's German network. The long and short names were identical to the original Comintern network of nearly ninety years before.

"The term 'Antifa' is currently coined by 'autonomous anti-fascism,' which acts on a case-by-case or campaign-oriented basis. Under the motto 'Antifa means attack,' left-wing extremists regularly call for 'counter-actions' as part of the 'Antifascism' action field, to the disadvantage of 'fascist' people, groups or institutions, in their opinion. Ultimately, this means the commission of criminal offenses such as property damage, arson or, in some cases, serious bodily harm, in some cases at least including the death of people is accepted," according to *V2019*.

Symbols matter, which is why Antifa destroys those it doesn't like, including statues, and makes careful use of its own iconography, a practice that dates to the Comintern. Antifa's symbolism in Germany remains as it was under Stalin's sponsorship and is identical to that in the United States today: a red banner and parallel black banner superimposed over a white field and within a broad black circle. This symbol has special meaning, according to the *V2019* report.

The black flag element pertains to the "autonomous zones" such as those in Seattle, Portland, and elsewhere. The red stands for building socialism and Communism.

The Antifa symbol "is widely used, particularly in violent left-wing extremism. The symbol of 'Antifa' therefore does not only stand for a confrontation with right-wing extremism, but also for the demarcation of 'bourgeois' or 'state-conforming' struggle against right-wing extremism with the rule of law," *V2019* said.

"For example, the black flag, which is used next to the red one in the 'Antifa' symbol, stands for autonomous anarchism. Autonomous zones are primarily formed in large and/or university cities. The respective zone usually has a central point of contact around which a network of small groups, individuals, and local branches of national or nationwide organizations and structures is formed," according to *V2019*.

In Germany, the biggest zones were in Berlin, Hamburg, and Leipzig. "Not only do they have an above-average level of action and mobilization potential, they also commit a large number of criminal and violent acts. In addition there is a wide, sympathetic and occasionally mobilizable zone environment," *V2019* continued.[14]

The German report, part of an annual extremism summary nearly four hundred pages long, provides a good basic, unclassified overview as seen by a Western professional security and counterintelligence service. Titled *Verfassungsschutzbericht 2019* but shortened here as *V2019*, the report gives substantial attention to Antifa within Germany. It is a useful guide to understanding the networks in the United States.

Antifa's Ideology: Progressing toward the Total Destruction of Free Society

Germany has more experience than almost any other country in dealing with extremist intellectualism and politics, having been the incubator of much of it since the 1800s, and *V2019* drew distinctions that few American security and counterintelligence professionals are trained to address still.

"The foundation of this ideological worldview is the 'historical materialism' propagated by Marx as a scientific fact," the report said.

Anarchists versus Constitutional Republican Democracy

The other dimension of Antifa—the anarchist element—is different in its approach to overthrow constitutional society. *V2019* explains: "Anarchists set themselves the goal of abolishing all forms of human rule over other people, unlike Communists who make absolute the value of socio-economic equality. Anarchists reject socialism just as much as 'historical materialism.' They are consistently hostile to the state and want to replace the parliamentary democracy directly with a 'grassroots democratic' organized society."[15]

It seems that the anarchists and Communists would hate one another. But they didn't during other stages in history, such as in 1928 with the Comintern extremism policy to tear Germany apart, or the Spanish Civil War of the 1930s. And they don't today.

The Communists and anarchists of Antifa agree: the Constitution must be overthrown by violence. This is the motivation that the FBI refuses to acknowledge.

Overthrowing a Constitution Takes Time

Shortly before FBI director Wray's Homeland Security Committee testimony in the fall of 2020, German domestic intelligence issued another, more urgent warning: Antifa and its allies were going to get more destructive and more violent.

"There is a change in the forms of action from mass militancy to clandestine small group actions," the updated report said.[16]

"The target selection of left-wing extremist attacks is shifting more and more often from an institutional level to a personal level. *Serious physical injuries to the victims up to possible death are accepted with approval,*" the report said. German analysts said that "*the formation of terrorist structures in left-wing extremism appears possible under these conditions.*"

The official report pertained to the Antifa networks and other violent extremist groups in Germany. American experts like Shideler noted that Antifa tactics in the United States lagged behind those in Europe, making the German reports useful predictors of what American authorities could expect.

Terrorist Danger

Director Wray's failures to understand Antifa's horizontal network-of-networks structure, its ideology, and its strategic end goals undermined the Trump Justice Department's efforts to stop the violence. That internal FBI ideological bias stems from poor hiring, poor training, and poor management that built an unprofessional intelligence analytical workforce, and from the cultural Marxism that prejudices objective intelligence analysis. The FBI management under Comey and Wray has damaged American domestic counterterrorism efforts, resulting in billions of dollars[17] in vandalism[18] and sabotage,[19] and the violent deaths of innocent citizens, including police officers.[20]

The FBI analytical failure undermined then attorney general William Barr's proposals to dismantle Antifa networks using legal tools such as material support for terrorism, the Racketeer Influenced and Corrupt Organizations (RICO) Act, and seditious conspiracy. The failure also damaged state and local law enforcement by denying them the strategic understanding of Antifa and its associated networks and movements in other states and internationally. One must presume that the CIA does not collect on Antifa as an organized network of networks outside U.S. borders, or, less likely, that if it does it does not share this intelligence with the FBI.

The bureau broke from its tendency to assume leadership of combating crime at the state and local levels to produce a "domestic terrorism" "primer" which noted that, in the case of extreme leftists, "much of the criminal activities of anarchist extremists fall under local jurisdiction, so they're investigated by local police."[21] If that were true, it would be helpful to strengthen state and local police.

As Shideler put it, "This inaccurate, uninformed view appears to have been institutionalized within the FBI. It does not seem to address—and indeed avoids—the Bureau's legal responsibility to investigate interstate subversive threats to the Constitution and to enforce the internal security provisions of U.S. federal law, which are directly applicable to Antifa. This myopic, artificial view has allowed Antifa violence to run rampant in cities and states where local and state political conditions have discouraged the enforcement of the state law against Antifa offenders."[22]

The FBI generally palmed off Antifa's interstate organized violence as a problem for local authorities. Conversely, by the time the Biden administration took office in 2021, the FBI had centralized control to focus on a nation allegedly full of right-wing, white-supremacist nationalists. The bureau was now in full thrall of the Frankfurt School's critical theory.

See No Evil

The Office of the Director of National Intelligence identified "domestic violent extremists" in its annual worldwide threat assessment for the first time when Biden became president in 2021. ODNI placed them under the heading of "global terrorism." It made no mention of Antifa specifically or anarchists or Marxists in general.[23] The old Obama team was back, and it had an agenda.

By late 2023, the FBI website contained only two documents that even mentioned Antifa. One was a general statement from the director, who denounced "anarchists like Antifa" with "violent, extremist agendas" who exploit social unrest and harm innocent citizens, including law enforcement officers.

The second document was a strategic threat assessment of terrorism for 2022. It mentioned Antifa twice in its forty-five pages, the first time in passing as a lone-wolf matter, and the second as a phantom of right-wingers' imaginations.[24]

In a sub-report, the FBI fired a bullet into the head of any idea that Antifa or anarchists form a network of networks: "We assess AVEs are not organized at the countrywide level."[25]

Yet the ability of anarchist extremists to move personnel around the country was fully demonstrated in the 2020 riots, or uprising, as anarchist participants often called it. Private researchers, and one state investigative service, have assessed what the FBI could not. "By their nature, anarchist extremists organize on the basis of local cells, termed affinity groups," said Kyle Shideler.

Formal or semi-formal bodies exist to help forge anarchist networks at the national level. "They include the Indigenous Anarchist Federation, the Anarchist Black Cross Federation, which is an American branch of the international Anarchist Black Cross, and the Black Rose/Rosa Negra Anarchist Federation," Shideler said. "Claims by federal law enforcement that anarchist extremists are not organized at the national level are clear evidence of never having done even a modicum of due diligence on anarchist violent extremism."[26]

Chapter 30

"Let me tell you: You take on the intelligence community—they have six ways from Sunday at getting back at you."

—Senate majority leader Chuck Schumer, January 3, 2017[1]

Trump and the Apparat

Whatever can be said about President Donald Trump, he never sought to politicize or weaponize the FBI or CIA.

He also did nothing serious to undo the Obama administration's top-down damage. Unlike his predecessor and successor, Trump assumed the presidency with no intelligence reform agenda, no strategy, no unified transition team or even personnel. He had no plan of any kind to combat the critical theory and exorcise the wokeness of cultural Marxism from the system, nothing to reverse the overall politicization of the FBI and CIA led by his chief false accusers of Russia collusion, Clapper and Brennan.

Trump knew that the intelligence community needed drastic executive oversight and reforms. His administration raised high expectations of reviving "a potentially powerful board capable of intimately reviewing intelligence agency conduct on his direct orders."[2] That was the President's Intelligence Advisory Board, generally an honorary body with few resources and no authority. Long known as the President's Foreign Intelligence Advisory Board—the "foreign" deleted after 9/11 to include domestic spying—the group traced its roots back to the Eisenhower administration and could act legally under the president's direct orders. Trump did not deploy it to stop the stormtroopers of wokeness within the intelligence community, even when sages like Angelo Codevilla urged him on and volunteered to join.

Snowflake Spies

The annual intelligence community rainbow summits continued seamlessly. Demonization and purging surfaced at FBI headquarters during the June 2017 event. The summit had yet another new name, "LGBTA Summit." The ODNI celebrated, "LGBTA—A for Allies."[3] As before, not allies of the United States, but allies of the horizontally-networked identity cell groups, the ARGs and ERGs. Summit host Andrew McCabe, then FBI acting director after James Comey's firing, explained that the summit's purpose was "amplifying" voices.

McCabe never defined the mission as anything but pushing cultural and social change. But he did recite the obligatory slogan: Diversity is strength.

"The bedrock of the Intelligence Community is our credibility," McCabe said. "To maintain that credibility, we must understand and reflect the people we protect, across the full spectrum of diversity that is the strength of our country."[4]

And then the mandatory solidarity: "We all need to be allies, to walk in each other's shoes, to try to understand what it's like, for example, to be gay, a person of color, or transgender or all of these at the same time."[5]

Back in the ODNI and CIA, senior personnel went along unquestioningly with the entire agenda, obligingly adopting and repeating the Big Sibling slogans: "Diversity is strength," "Diversity is our greatest strength."

But others quit in droves, citing a toxic, unprofessional atmosphere. "Lots of us are punching out once we put in our thirty years," a former CIA station chief in a vital Arab country told the author as he packed up his Washington-area house, never to return. Some didn't even wait that long. "Many are quitting at age fifty," before the minimum retirement age of fifty-five, sacrificing much of the pensions they had earned.

Lost Opportunity

Trump nibbled on the edges, having fired FBI director James Comey and soon forcing out some underlings like McCabe and counterintelligence chief Strzok in response to the bureau's Russia collusion falsehoods, but that's generally where it ended. The Trump team seemed not to understand the critical theory agenda behind many of the Obama administration's executive orders. The president could have modified or repealed them in a short executive order of his own. With both houses of Congress in friendly hands during the first half of his term, he could have freed completely the intelligence community, even the entire government, of the Obama executive orders under force of law and defunded the woke critical theory agenda.

Trump did not seek a political loyalist FBI director who would settle personal scores for him. He uncharacteristically wanted an FBI director that his most extreme political enemies agreed on, not somebody who would shake up the bureau's inefficiencies and politicization. Former New Jersey governor Chris Christie recommended millionaire lawyer Christopher Wray. Unlike most Trump appointees, Wray's nomination received almost-unanimous confirmation from the Senate. Only one Republican senator, Rand Paul of Kentucky, voted against Wray.

Trump's FBI director had no effect on returning things to normal. Whether by design or by passively letting militant underlings run him as their top cover agent of change, Wray accelerated internal politicization and swung the bureau into a Hoover-meets-Marcuse political enforcement machine. Meanwhile the country plunged into anarchist and critical race violence from coast to coast.

In response to political pressure, Director Wray announced the FBI would stop using the term "black identity extremism" to categorize black identity extremist groups whose members murdered law enforcement officers.[6] The Black Lives Matter and Antifa rioting and murder sprees cost billions of dollars in property damage and innocent lives. For a long time, the FBI leadership balked at calling it domestic violent extremism. It refrained when the organized violence became such a threat that it forced the first two floors of businesses and government buildings in the center of the nation's capital to be boarded up, and when mobs converged on Lafayette Square to storm the White House, with the unprecedented effect of forcing the president to retreat to the nuclear bunker.

Wray shepherded the full politicization of the FBI along the entire cultural Marxist spectrum of the time, expanding it as that agenda progressed. The bureau joined or endorsed public "LGBT" events nationwide in 2018 "to celebrate #PrideMonth."[7] Internally, FBI Pride Month 2018 art featured a mocking image of Lady Justice, who brandished a sword in her right hand with the scales of justice in her left, her wild hair in pale blue-and-pink transgender colors and her gown like a billowing rainbow flag. Then came the slogans, all in capital letters: "BUREAU EQUALITY" and "LESBIAN, GAY, BISEXUAL & TRANSGENDER PRIDE MONTH."[8]

Wray's graphics team redesigned the official artwork for Pride Month 2019 with a succession of rainbow flags.[9] FBI Pride Month 2020 revived 2018 queer Lady Justice, but never called her "lady."[10] One FBI tweet took a united-front approach, bestowing Lady Justice, in caps, with the slogan "THE POWER OF ALLIES."[11]

Take the Knee—or Else

During a June 2020 Black Lives Matter march in the nation's capital, members of the FBI's Washington Field Office stood on the sidewalk on Pennsylvania Avenue near the Justice Department. Unlike police, the FBI has no escalation-of-force protocol, and is trained to use deadly force after issuing only a verbal warning.[12] The lead special agent on the scene was morbidly obese.

Despite the loud BLM mob in the avenue, there was no visible threat to either the National Archives, a stone-clad building closed by huge bronze doors, or FBI headquarters, the brutalist concrete fortress a block away. The FBI personnel appeared calm and relaxed. None looked on edge or even on alert. Some were obviously out of shape. An obese agent in a Covid mask appeared physically incapable of firing a weapon from a prone position. Some stood or knelt alone. Others sat by a flower bed or lounged against a wall. Several could be seen smiling and clapping in support of the BLM marchers. One agent just shook his head.[13]

Wearing external body armor emblazoned with "FBI" in large yellow letters, some with their FBI badges on their belts and several with visible sidearms, the FBI personnel drew the attention of demonstrators, who told them to kneel. Incredibly, several FBI agents and staff did so.

Photos of the genuflecting FBI employees appeared in BLM-fueled Russian propaganda against the United States, with the Kremlin's RT outlet running a story on the day of the protest.[14]

Instead of being disciplined for taking political positions while on duty, the opposite happened. One agent present, Kyle Seraphin, said that the Washington Field Office special agent in charge for counterterrorism praised those who took the knee, calling them "heroes" and claiming that the show of solidarity "de-escalated" a potentially violent situation. She gave them each a hug.

By contrast, the FBI punished agents who, as private citizens on their own time, joined hundreds of thousands of their countrymen protesting in Washington on January 6, 2021, even though none had committed a crime or gone near the Capitol building. A former FBI employee said that the bureau rescinded their security clearances, meaning that the agents could no longer work. The Capitol Police severely disciplined a heroic officer, Lt. Tarik Johnson, who answered an emergency call to rescue sixteen fellow police who the dispatcher said were trapped in the portico of the Rotunda during the riots. Against what he feared were thousands of hostile protesters, Johnson cleared a path by borrowing a protester's MAGA hat as a virtual "helmet" to ease the crowd so he could evacuate his colleagues who, a police alert said, had been in danger. The Capitol Police demoted the twenty-three-year veteran to private and destroyed his career. Johnson successfully fought for reinstatement and retired from the force.[15] An officer who shot and killed a protester got promoted to captain.[16]

FBI director Wray promoted one of the bureau's BLM march kneelers to assistant special agent in charge of the Washington Field Office.[17]

"During my 25-year career, I was privileged and honored to work alongside FBI agents who killed or captured Top Ten fugitives and violent, dangerous, murderous felons," said former FBI supervisory special agent James A. Gagliano. None to his knowledge received a token of appreciation. "I have come to grips with the fact that my beloved FBI has been irreparably broken by woke activists serving amongst its senior ranks."[18]

Special Agent Seraphin, who was present with the Washington Field Office staff at the BLM march but did not kneel, blew the whistle on that and other FBI wrongdoing. In 2022 the FBI permanently suspended him without pay. He started a social media movement, The Suspendables, to join forces with other whistleblowers. The Biden Justice Department then found ways to accuse him of crimes, including felonies, the process being the punishment. In a March 31, 2013, letter, the FBI told Seraphin that a bureau administrative inquiry alleged that he had committed a range of abuses and offenses, including "disparaging remarks about the FBI." The letter, from headquarters, was unsigned.[19]

Grenell Shows Grit

Director of National Intelligence Dan Coats could have put a stop to this early on, but he didn't stick around. In his absence, the CIA celebrated Pride Month 2019 by posting an image of headquarters bathed in rainbow colors on Twitter.[20]

Where Coats had passively stayed away, his interim successor, Ambassador Ric Grenell, leaned into it. Trump's appointment of Grenell marked the first openly gay intelligence chief and cabinet-rank official in American history, but this won Trump no points from the rainbow flaggers. It did, though, provide a powerful and creative opportunity to crush critical theory and cultural Marxism across the intelligence community. Acting DNI Grenell gave an official interview for the 2020 ODNI Pride Summit, which had renamed itself once more, this time as Inside Out.

In a single sentence, Grenell stomped on everything that ODNI had been working on for a decade. "I've made it clear that I am not asking for special treatment or special rights," he said, "just equal access and consideration."[21]

"It's important to me that I not be defined by my sexual orientation—I want to be defined by my experience and skills. It undercuts all that I want to do in my career when I'm narrowly defined as a gay ambassador," Grenell heretically asserted.[22]

Grenell placed professional accomplishments first. No entitled victimhood in him. Critical theory was off his agenda. To the horror of many in his audience, Grenell said kind words about "the Bible and modern Christianity."[23] He spoke of family. No salutes to the horizontally networked ARG and ERG cell groups. No odes to diversity. Equality, not equity. And not a peep about inclusion.

He didn't trash the United States and its history, or twist the intelligence mission with the latest progression of cultural Marxism. To the contrary. Reflecting on his international travel, Grenell said, "The United States is the best country in the world for gays and lesbians, and there are still many people from around the world—including the LGBTQ+ community—who are desperate to come to America."[24]

Grenell's interim tenure was short. His successor, an upright former congressman named John Ratcliffe, faced an onslaught of DEI agendas but prioritized them far below other intelligence matters.

There would be no CIA course correction from its critical theory route. Trump's CIA director, Mike Pompeo, did nothing effective to brake the wokeness seething through the agency. Named secretary of state after a year, Pompeo ensured the Obama-Jarret-Clapper-Brennan team's entrenchment when he enthusiastically recommended Gina Haspel as his replacement. Trump agreed to this "historic" first of a female CIA director, letting the agency run itself as a sovereign state-within-a-state for the rest of his term while he flailed against the "Deep State."

Haspel—DEI First, Last, and Always

Inside the CIA, Gina Haspel made little of her status as the first female CIA director, but focused as hard on promoting diversity and inclusion as Pompeo, now secretary of state, did fighting Chinese subversion. It was a different world. Haspel launched a "Diversity in Leadership Study" for "increasing equity" to advance personnel, based on favored racial, ethnic, and self-identification silos, to senior leadership positions and to develop "a diverse pool of future leaders" under the *2020–2023 CIA Diversity and Inclusion Strategy*.[25]

Haspel built the strategy on a human resources bureaucracy that was 80 percent female—typical of human resources but quite the opposite of what the policies were allegedly supposed to avoid.[26] The strategy mobilized CIA Directorate Diversity and Inclusion Program Managers (DDPMs), the ubiquitous Agency Resource Group (ARG) critical theory cells, and an Executive Diversity and Inclusion Council (EDIC) which, the strategy said, "acts on behalf of all the workforce and senior leadership across all Directorates and Mission Centers to enhance workforce diversity and promote inclusion of all employees."[27]

The new cultural competence was all about intelligence workers' mastery and acceptance of the CIA's own "Cultural Norms Framework" of critical race theory.

The Newspeak Manual

According to the *CIA Diversity and Inclusion Glossary*—yes, there is such a thing—"Cultural Competence is the ability to understand, appreciate, and interact with persons from cultures and/or belief systems other than one's own and apply insights learned for better outcomes." For normal people it may seem a decent basic definition.

Among practitioners of Aesopian doubletalk, however, it means a form of Gramscian consciousness-changing and critical theory behavior modification. The agency says as much by calling its Cultural Norms Framework "a tool that helps decision makers identify and promote patterns of behavior" within the bureaucracy itself.[28]

The *CIA Diversity and Inclusion Strategy* lays out an internal psychological conditioning campaign against intelligence community professionals. It is diversity for diversity's sake: subjective, always changing, never compromising, and never-ending. It is not for mission success. "Weaving diversity and inclusion principles and practices throughout the talent cycle—performance management, talent development, and learning—allows employees and managers to fully benefit from a diverse and inclusive workplace and is a hallmark of this strategy," the document says.[29]

Haspel laid out the strategy for an agency-wide cultural revolution, alienating personnel from merit and commitment to defense of American founding principles, psychologically conditioning intelligence personnel, reinforcing behavior modification, and bestowing preferential mobility along Marcusian logic. As was happening simultaneously among her old London liaison colleagues at MI6, the CIA director was imposing cultural Marxism on the agency. Enforcement was implied, with details to follow.

Finally, in September 2020, Trump issued Executive Order 13950 on Combating Race and Sex Stereotyping. That order banned diversity training across the federal government and in companies that contracted with the government.[30]

It was too late. It had no force of law. In the chaos of the election and transfer of political power, everything fell apart. On President Joe Biden's first day in office, as an indication of their critical theory agenda, his handlers' well-prepared and unified team repealed Trump's belated executive order.

Miss Intersectionality

Days before Biden took office, the agency launched a "Humans of the CIA" video campaign. Director Haspel had developed the recruitment redesign during the Trump administration. The first in the 2021 series, titled "Michael: Serving with Pride," gave away the unsurprising real agenda. Michael isn't just a CIA librarian who happens to be gay. He is part of a cell. "Michael is an active member of ANGLE, our ARG for LGBTQ officers. He also takes part in LGBTQ outreach with our recruiters," the CIA recruitment device said. A sidebar followed about how more trans and queer ideology in the workplace would help the CIA make the world a better place: "I want other members of the LGBTQ community to know that the Agency offers a supportive environment for them to really make a difference in the world."[31]

The most widely publicized video featured a Latina CIA employee talking about herself in a two-and-a-half-minute monologue. The mid-level intelligence careerist describes herself as an intersectional cisgender millennial of color who suffers from mental disorders. She wears a black pantsuit. Her black jersey forms the backdrop for a large pink fist stylized within an ancient Egyptian hieroglyphic ankh symbol appropriated to represent militant feminism. Her real name is not given. She refers to herself only as "Mija," a Spanish contraction of "My Daughter."

The full text of the Mija monologue, with the author's observations in brackets, shows a self-absorbed, emotionally disturbed, ideologically supercharged individual:

> When I was seventeen, I quoted Zora Neale Hurston's "How It Feels to Be Colored Me" in my college application essay. The line that spoke to me stated simply, "I am not tragically colored. There is no sorrow dammed up in my soul nor lurking behind my eyes. I do not mind at all." [At 0:23, the camera pans her from toes to head, focusing on the pink fist.]

> At seventeen, I had no idea what life would bring, but Zora's sentiment articulated so beautifully how I felt as a daughter of immigrants then and now. Nothing about me was or is tragic. I am perfectly made. I can wax eloquent on complex legal issues in English while also belting "Guayaquil de Mis Amores" in Spanish. I can change a diaper with one hand and console a crying toddler with the other. I am a woman of color. I am a mom. I am a cisgender millennial who has been diagnosed with generalized anxiety disorder. [At 0:56, the camera again focuses on the militant fist.]
>
> I am intersectional. But my existence is not a box-checking exercise. I am a walking declaration. . . . [At 1:02, the camera follows her walking slowly down a corridor, her back to the audience, past dignified oil portraits of all the previous CIA directors.]
>
> Sometimes I struggle. I struggle feeling like I could do more, be more to my two sons. And I struggle leaving the office when I feel there's so much more to do. . . . [The video shows her walking down a corridor alongside a CIA billboard with an exhortation to "Celebrate the Spirit of Inclusion."]
>
> But at thirty-six, I refuse to internalize misguided patriarchal ideas of what a woman can or should be. I am tired of feeling like I'm supposed to apologize for the space I occupy, rather than intoxicate people with my effort, my brilliance. I am proud of me, full stop. [Video shows her smiling broadly and laughing.][32]

Not a single word about public service. Nothing about defending the country. Not a hint of a sense of mission. It's all me, me, me—pure vanity and hubris—plus her ethnicity, color, gender identification, and mental disorder. This individual sounds empty, angry, selfish, resentful, devoid of meaning. Almost everything she says in the monologue is about herself.

Chapter 31

"The FBI's strength is in its diversity."

—FBI, official statement while the bureau was 84 percent white and 98.5 percent straight, 2017[1]

"Our Workforce: The FBI Family . . . 1.6 % LGBT+"

—*FBI Diversity Report*, 2023[2]

Team Biden

During the 2020 presidential campaign, Joe Biden railed against Russian or any foreign interference in the election. A Biden administration would "treat foreign interference in our election as an adversarial act that significantly affects the relationship between the United States and the interfering nation's government," said Biden.[3]

It was a good, solid statement. But there was a catch: Just days before, a top veteran Communist Party USA figure, a slavish servant of Moscow for nearly a half-century, got on Kremlin television to throw her support behind Biden. Angela Davis, who had been Herbert Marcuse's most promising student and twice a running mate of Gus Hall, went on Vladimir Putin's RT channel to tell her supporters that now was the time.[4]

The Biden team entered the White House in 2021 with a carefully formulated, strategic plan. Much of the team had worked together

Angela Davis Uses Putin's Outlet to Tell Supporters to Back Biden

The correlation of forces in American politics reached a point in mid-2020 when old Soviet- and Chinese-backed political fringe parties threw their considerable activist support behind a mainstream candidate and backed Joe Biden for president.

Former Black Liberation extremist and Communist Party standard-bearer Angela Davis took to Moscow's RT channel to announce that her cadres were backing the former vice president.

She appeared on RT's *Going Underground* program. Davis had no love for Biden, but the election was going to be close, and the growing mob movement had to tip the scales. She had spent most of her adult life advocating for domestic violent extremism and for abolishing prisons, defunding the police, and overthrowing the United States government. She saw Biden as a Trojan horse who could bring radicals into his administration and would go along with much of what BLM/Antifa wants.

The Soviet-trained militant made three main points:

Biden can be pressured to bend to BLM/Antifa's will: "It will be about choosing a candidate who can be most effectively pressured" to bow to the BLM/Antifa movement.[5]

Biden is receptive, weak, and malleable: "Biden is far more likely to take mass demands seriously."[6]

A vote for Biden is a vote for BLM/Antifa: "To vote for ourselves . . . means that we will have to campaign for a vote for Biden."[7]

In full context, Davis told RT:

> I don't see this election as being about choosing a candidate who will be able to lead us in the right direction. It will be about choosing a candidate who can be most effectively pressured into allowing more space for the evolving anti-racist [BLM/Antifa] movement.
>
> Biden is very problematic in many ways. He is, not only in terms of his past and the role that he played in pushing toward

> mass incarceration, but he's indicated that he's opposed to disbanding the police, and this is definitely what we need, we need to reconceptualize the very notion of public safety.
>
> But—I say but—Biden is far more likely to take mass demands seriously. Far more likely than the current occupant of the White House. So that this coming November the election will ask us not so much to vote for the best candidate, but to vote for or against ourselves, and to vote for ourselves, I think, means that we will have to campaign for a vote for Biden.[8]

in the Obama administration. They had lifelong friends and allies in the senior levels of all the bureaucracies. They took office with all the needed strategic vision and the pre-formulation of what to do to get there.

Executive orders are presidential diktats, allowed by the Constitution and the law, that require substantial research, internal discussion, interagency review, and other vetting. They are literally presidential commands to the executive branch. A well-prepared incoming administration will take office with pre-written executive orders. The Trump administration had failed to do that. The Biden team arrived at the White House with extended magazines of transformational executive orders. So began implementation of the DEI doctrine across the government, including the intelligence community.

On his first day as president in 2021, Joe Biden repealed Trump's executive order against diversity training and issued a far more comprehensive one of his own. He restored the Obama diversity training commissariat and expanded it under Executive Order 13985.[9] On his sixth day, he issued an executive order allowing transgender people to serve in the U.S. military.[10]

Two weeks before Biden was inaugurated, his team received a colossal windfall that turbocharged the most extreme elements of his agenda. It was the January 6 violence at the United States Capitol and it took place literally on, around, under, and behind the temporary plywood-and-scaffolding inaugural platform where Biden would be sworn in. A more perfect setting could not have been planned.

The vandalism, assaults, mayhem, and violence at the Capitol, aided by professional agitators channeling destruction with a few Confederate battle flags strategically placed high and up-front to drive a narrative, gave Team Biden a visible and believable pretext for a massive national crackdown against domestic violent extremists, insurrectionists, terrorists, white supremacists, and anybody else who could be lumped in with them.

Confusion, panic, and opportunism gave the new Biden team and its politicized supporters in the Department of Justice and elsewhere all the latitude they needed. Trump, the immediate overcharged narrative went, had personally incited the spontaneous insurrection. That was false. Seasoned observers, including the author, witnessed signs that the violence was professionally coordinated and planned in advance.[11] Trump supported the insurrectionism, the reasoning went. Half the country had voted for Trump. That half of the country was extremist, wanted to overthrow Congress, and harbored countless domestic terrorists. No good crisis should go to waste.

Strategic Offensive

Biden picked William Burns as his CIA director. Burns expanded DEI to diversity, equity, inclusion, and accessibility (DEIA). DEIA, the CIA's latest diversity communiqué said, is centered "on the concept of belonging" to ensure that CIA personnel "have the psychological safety" to "bring their best selves to work."[12]

Burns was a well-known figure in the Washington foreign policy establishment who worked with both parties. Before taking his new post in Langley, he had served as head of the prestigious Carnegie Endowment for International Peace, which still had on its wall a photo of its former leader, Alger Hiss.[13]

Over the spring of 2021, Team Biden put together a *National Strategy for Countering Domestic Terrorism*. The document drew directly from critical race theory by presuming that the dominant domestic terror threat came from white people. The document appeared five months after the Capitol riot, which the administration and its allies continued to insist was an insurrectionist act of white supremacism.

According to the strategy, the undesirable extremists' "insistence on violence can, at times, be explicit. It also can, at times, be less explicit, lurking in ideologies rooted in a perception of the superiority of the white race that call for violence in furtherance of perverse and abhorrent notions of 'racial purity' or 'cleansing.'"[14]

As terrible as chauvinism and racism are, they pose no existential threat to the nation as the strategy claimed. But they do comport with critical race theory's insatiable need to find white devils to justify the next level of permanent discrimination, as cultural Marxism calls for. As the Obama-appointed chairman of the Joint Chiefs of Staff had done under Trump, the Biden administration promoted a leading and extreme critical race theorist, Ibram X. Kendi, as mandatory reading[15] for much of the defense and intelligence communities as a justification for the diversity, equity, and inclusion triad.

The strategy establishes that the clear and present danger is both white supremacism and citizens suspicious of the central administrative state. It proceeds with the assumption that critical race theory is the solution. It never says "critical race theory" or "cultural Marxism," and it does make passing reference to leftist extremism, but even that is lost in the strategy's constant railing against the real devil.

The strategy describes that devil in some detail: "Self-proclaimed 'militias' and militia violent extremists who take steps to violently resist government authority or facilitate the overthrow of the US Government based on perceived overreach; anarchists or violent extremists, who violently oppose all forms of capitalism, corporate globalization, and governing institutions, which they perceive as harmful to society; sovereign citizen violent extremists, who believe they are immune from government authority and laws; or any other individual or group who engages in violence—or incites imminent violence—in opposition to legislative, regulatory, or other actions taken by the government."[16]

In practice, taken to the extreme that the White House intended, such "terrorism" and "violence" doesn't really include the anarchists and Communists burning up the country. But it does include parents who, during the Covid lockdown, discovered the anti-American and pornographic material that public schools were feeding their children and took their complaints with righteous anger to local school boards. The FBI got involved in these local issues because of these potentially violent extremist moms and dads.[17] Ditto for a completely peaceful pro-life activist, who had his house stormed by an FBI SWAT team and was arrested under the same violent extremist rubric. A jury later acquitted the man on all counts in a slashing rebuke to the FBI's abuse.[18] And then, through a whistleblower network, emerged an FBI memo about traditional Catholics being an extremist threat, with language on infiltrating churches.[19] The FBI's war on American citizens resisting cultural Marxism had begun.

The strategy made passing reference to "other domestic terrorists" who "may be motivated to violence by single-issue ideologies related to abortion-, animal rights-, environmental-, or involuntary celibate-violent extremism, as well as other grievances, or a combination of ideological influences," in groups or as loners.[20]

Those lone terrorists can "connect and intersect with conspiracy theories and other forms of disinformation and misinformation," the strategy said.[21] That comment sheds light on the administration's fatally

The Dog Ate My Homework

After more than a year and a half of COVID-19 pandemic agony, the entire foreign spy machinery of the United States issued its long-awaited assessment of the origins of the virus said to have killed millions.

It was a conclusion of America's seventeen main foreign intelligence services, the best known of which is the CIA, all coordinated by a gigantic central apparat called the Office of the Director of National Intelligence, or ODNI.

The assessment concluded nothing.

ODNI waffled. The unclassified October 2021 document effectively said that the intelligence community's immense force of human talent and technology could make no real assessment of the COVID-19 pandemic's origins because the Communist Chinese made it hard to collect information.

Four of the seventeen intelligence services, which ODNI did not name, asserted with "low confidence" that the SARS-CoV-2 virus broke out naturally. A fifth expressed "moderate confidence" that the virus was "the result of a laboratory-associated incident, probably involving experimentation, animal handling, or sampling by the Wuhan Institute of Virology."[22] Analysts at three other services couldn't agree at all. According to the summary, not one element of the U.S. intelligence community expressed "high confidence" of anything about the pandemic's origins.

It was a dog-ate-my-homework moment for spies.

The non-assessment about the pandemic's origins let the Chinese Communist Party off the hook. To ODNI, it wasn't the fault of the world's most powerful spy services for failing to find the origin of the virus with the slightest degree of confidence.

The reason why the CIA and others couldn't do their job was because the Chinese Communists weren't being team players.

"China's cooperation most likely would be needed to reach a conclusive assessment of the origins of COVID-19," the intelligence community summary said. "Beijing, however, continues to hinder the global investigation, resist sharing information and blame other countries, including the United States."[23]

Which is the reason, of course, that countries have foreign intelligence services: to find out what other governments don't want known.

As if that weak non-assessment weren't enough, the spooks gave Xi Jinping a pass. Beijing's hindrances, lack of cooperation, and disinformation—the assessment didn't use the latter word, but we all know it was a factor—"reflect, in part, China's government's own uncertainty about where an investigation could lead as well as its frustration the international community is using the issue to exert political pressure on China."[24]

Thus the American intelligence product meant to pinpoint the source of the destruction and grief that the Chinese regime wreaked on practically every single person on earth concluded by excusing China in advance and chiding the rest of the free world.

The CIA had effectively died of COVID.

flawed disinformation office at the Department of Homeland Security and FBI and its meddling in social media companies to get them to shut down or censor unapproved facts and ideas. "Internet-based communications platforms such as social media, file-upload sites, and end-to-end encrypted platforms," the strategy said, "can combine and amplify threats to public safety"[25] and, implicitly, must be constantly monitored and censored by federal government agents and contractors.

The strategy then reproduced an intelligence community assessment of the "Domestic Violent Extremism Threat," or DVE threat.

"Enduring DVE motivations pertaining to biases against minority populations and perceived government overreach will almost certainly continue to drive DVE radicalization and mobilization to violence," the intelligence assessment claimed. "Newer sociopolitical developments—such as narratives of fraud in the recent general election, the emboldening impact of the violent breach of the U.S. Capitol, conditions related to the COVID-19 pandemic, and conspiracy theories promoting violence—will almost certainly spur some DVEs to try to engage in violence this year."[26]

Others have recounted the facts in investigative articles and congressional investigations, and more will piece the facts together in future books, but the puzzle here is that, by all appearances, the intelligence community failed to provide the Capitol Police information necessary to prepare against organized violence in early 2021. It completely failed to warn Congress in advance even though it had assets among the organizers.[27] And it refused to provide Congress with any further information, in open testimony or in written responses to lawmakers' letters, after the fact.

The intelligence assessment in the strategy said that several factors could worsen the domestic violent extremism problem in the future, including "growing perceptions of government overreach related to legal or policy changes and disruptions." The intelligence community added one more problem to be dealt with among the citizens: "access to firearms."[28]

Since it viewed the American public at large as the problem, the Biden administration proposed a comprehensive solution. "We will forge a government-wide effort," the strategy said, promising that "particular investigatory and prosecutorial decisions are for law enforcement alone, unaffected by and insulated from any political influence or bias."[29]

The strategy reads like an implementation plan for Obama's cryptic, unscripted comment in 2008 about building a massive domestic security apparat: "We cannot continue to rely on our military in order to achieve the national security objectives that we've set. We've got to have *a civilian national security force* that's just as powerful, just as strong, *just as well-funded*" [emphasis added].[30]

What was needed, the strategy says, was "a new systematic approach" for using non-governmental sources of "specialized areas and types of analysis, including ways in which gender-motivated violence can have implications for domestic terrorist threats."[31]

The prescription includes online censorship, programs against "disinformation and misinformation online for domestic audiences," and gun control—the type of central government overreach that causes citizens to wish to resist and, by the strategy's logic, potentially become DVEs. "The Department of State and United States Agency for International Development are doing similar work globally."[32]

The strategy recognizes that the central government isn't always best placed to take the initiative, which is why it calls to "equip" people and governments at the local levels to prevent terrorist violence.[33]

Biden's strategy envisions resources for citizens to inform on one another. Funds for this purpose are to be channeled through the Departments of Justice, Health and Human Services, Education, and Homeland Security, with all the necessary data on "an easily accessible and navigable one-stop website."[34]

Domestic spying is normalized beyond the abuses of the PATRIOT Act to make the federal authorities enforcers of pre-crime: "Beyond particular intelligence, investigatory, and prosecutorial work, Federal law enforcement serves as a critical resource for countering domestic terrorism nationwide." More money for the FBI, more money and training for federal prosecutors to "match the heightened priority already being assigned by the Department [of Justice] to domestic terrorism investigations and prosecutions."[35]

Under the strategy, the central state security apparat would grow and grow: "The Department of Justice will strengthen and expand the use of the Domestic Terrorism Executive Committee to ensure nationwide interagency collaboration on countering domestic terrorism and ensure that Anti-Terrorism Advisory Councils across the country focus on the elevated domestic terrorism threat, ensuring that every U.S. Attorney's Office has the expertise, training, and guidance needed to identify and address domestic terrorism to the fullest extent of the law." More cash would go into state, local, tribal, and territorial law enforcement,[36] with snarls of strings attached, adding to the central government's ability to exercise control over local authorities through the ability to hand out technology, equipment, and cash.

The next step of the strategy is a political purge of career government employees. The document doesn't say "purge" but uses words like "screening and vetting" and "additional scrutiny."[37] Of course, screening, vetting, and scrutiny are already done in spades through the onerous security clearance and disclosure processes. More civil rights and civil liberties talk, and then the real point: "individual known or suspected terrorists" might somehow manage to sneak through the full-field background investigations and polygraphs. The implication is obvious, as defense secretary Lloyd Austin said when purging the uniformed military of wrong-thinkers. The intent of the strategy is a political purge of the federal government's civil service, diplomatic service, intelligence services, and law enforcement services.

The strategy presumes that the federal workforce is swarming with prospective terrorists and real terrorists who have managed to escape detection.

This might explain the merciless rigidity of purging federal employees, including in the military and FBI, who opted out of taking the COVID vaccines or who refused to order their subordinates to submit. Certainly the professionals on the receiving end consider themselves politically purged.

"I objected on religious grounds, which I'm entitled to do," said former FBI special agent Kyle Seraphin, "but they wanted me out because I'm a conservative Catholic who saw through the politicization of the bureau. They didn't even consider my objection. They just emailed me an unsigned form letter."[38]

The purge swept through the military. The hundreds of highly trained officers and personnel who refused either resigned or were discharged from the service.[39]

Those who resisted the COVID mandates tended to be observant Christians and politically conservative. During a door-to-door vaccine tour with Washington, D.C., mayor Muriel Bowser, then director of the National Institute of Allergy and Infectious Diseases Anthony Fauci said to Bowser about those not complying with the mandates, "They're Republicans. They don't like to be told what to do. And we gotta break that, you know, unpack that."[40]

Toward the end of the strategy, the critical race theory and gun control agendas reemerge openly. To fight domestic terrorism over the long haul, the strategy says, "means tackling racism in America."[41]

The 2021 DVE strategy is, in the end, all based on a critical theory worldview to destroy through relentless criticism and Marcusian forms of tolerance. "Although the U.S. Government must do everything it can to address enduring challenges like racism and bigotry in America, the Federal Government alone cannot simply 'solve' these challenges quickly or on its own."[42]

This is pure critical race theory when one understands the Aesopian language of cultural Marxism. "This approach must apply to our efforts to counter domestic terrorism by addressing underlying racism and bigotry." Like all things Marxist, that would necessitate political commissars high and low across the apparat. "That imperative includes ensuring that domestic terrorism threats are properly identified and categorized as such and addressed accordingly."[43]

With the radicals in control of the levers of power, the strategy requires the public to trust Big Brother. It lists what it called a "broader priority: enhancing faith in government and addressing the extreme polarization, fueled by a crisis of disinformation and misinformation often channeled through social media platforms, which can tear

Americans apart and lead some to violence. . . . We will work toward finding ways to counter the influence and impact of dangerous conspiracy theories that can provide a gateway to terrorist violence."[44]

CHAPTER 32

"The American people need to be assured that never again will an agency of the government be permitted to conduct a secret war against those citizens it considers threats to the established order."

—bipartisan Senate report, 1976[1]

Five Former CIA Directors Run Their Own Election Op—with CIA Help

After the Steele dossier and Crossfire Hurricane in 2016, some sort of spook-driven reprise was all but expected for the 2020 presidential election.

Months after former FBI director Robert Mueller issued his 2019 special counsel report to conclude that the Steele dossier contents were falsified, the FBI planted disinformation with social media corporate leaders to allege that upcoming news about a Hunter Biden laptop was Russian disinformation.[2] After the *New York Post* broke the story on October 14, 2020, sixty former intelligence and national security professionals, nine of whom hid behind anonymity, made unsubstantiated allegations in a public letter that news of the laptop showed all the hallmarks of Russian disinformation.

The laptop case showed just how politicized and sloppy much of the U.S. intelligence community had become, and that the FBI, long after the removal of Comey, McCabe, and Strzok, continued to deceive the public to try to influence a presidential election.

During his final debate with President Donald Trump in the 2020 campaign, Biden repeatedly called the story about his son's laptop and email contents "Russian disinformation."

"There are fifty former national intelligence folks who said that what he's accusing me of is a Russian plant," Biden said during the October 22 debate.[3]

That wasn't true.

Biden was referring to a statement that was written, signed, leaked, and published three days earlier in *Politico*, just in time for Biden to raise it during the debate.[4] The headline read, "Hunter Biden Story Is Russian Disinfo, Dozens of Former Intel Officials Say."[5]

The document was not an honest intelligence assessment. It was fed, like an op, through a dishonest journalist at a political media outlet to disinform the American public, for the purpose of confusing the electorate to influence a domestic political outcome.

More properly, it wasn't "like an op." It was an op. Not against foreign adversaries, but against the American public. Former acting CIA director Mike Morell told a congressional committee three years later that he personally orchestrated the activity at the request of Anthony Blinken, then the Biden campaigner slated to become secretary of state.[6]

The op used the truth to convey distortions or falsehoods as fact. Thought-leader Jeff Giesea gave this type of op, and its product, a name: establishment disinformation.[7] Former public figures create establishment disinformation when they write or sign falsehoods, distortions, and misinformation to be circulated in the press, with their names and impressive former titles attached, to mislead the public for a political or policy purpose. More clever ones use truths to convey a lie. The public, not having access to the real facts, pays attention to the prestige, not the substance.

In this case, the stunt employed the credentials of sixty former intelligence, security, and defense professionals and officials, nine of whom hid behind anonymity, to plant an engineered news story with a phony headline. It was as if many were unaware of what they were signing. At the top of the list: former director of national intelligence James Clapper, former CIA and National Security Agency director Michael V. Hayden, former CIA directors Leon Panetta and John Brennan, and former acting CIA directors John McLaughlin and Michael Morell.

The signers personified the heart of the American intelligence community establishment, many of them being careerists with distinguished records. They included former chairmen of the National Intelligence Council, one of whom had literally written the textbooks on intelligence; senior leaders in intelligence analysis and research across various agencies; former top Pentagon intelligence and Defense Intelligence Agency officials; seasoned top CIA analytical and operations leaders, including those who ran intelligence analysis for the entire agency plus a former Moscow station chief; a former head of the National Counterterrorism Center; several former CIA chiefs of staff; a former director of the White House Situation Room; former agency general counsels and inspectors general; and more. They were Democrats and Republicans. They made a powerful, overwhelming, believable lineup.

One can only presume that most signers simply agreed to let their names and titles be used after getting a request presumably from former CIA acting director Morell, without asking or being told why. One of Brennan's former aides allegedly fed the misleading story to *Politico*.[8] Some of the same intelligence people who spread the Steele dossier disinformation were at it again.

The thrust of the statement claimed to debunk the October 14, 2020, *New York Post* revelation about Hunter Biden's incriminating laptop and emails, and an apparent scheme to sell his father's influence in exchange for dubious business deals with Russian, Ukrainian, and Communist Chinese entities.[9] The core concern: the revelation "has all the classic earmarks of a Russian information operation."

Responsible intelligence analysts indeed should have thought that. And they would have investigated. But they would not have gone public with mere "classic earmarks." (Disclosure—this author played a role in the release of the Hunter Biden laptop story. In the weeks before the contents went public, the author screened many of the emails to evaluate them for release. His first concern was that the material could be Russian or Chinese disinformation, but on learning the provenance of the laptop and its chain of custody, and on studying his portion of the contents, he assessed that the material was genuine.)

Contrary to the fake *Politico* headline or what Biden would say, the former intelligence officials admitted in the statement that they had no proof of anything—including Russian disinformation.

The statement neglected to mention that many of the signatories, including Clapper and Brennan, were campaigning for Biden, and that signee John Sipher was on the advisory board of a pro-Biden group called the Lincoln Project, whose cofounder was a registered agent of the Russian government.[10] It failed to mention that, like the Steele dossier, the disinformation was commissioned by a presidential campaign.

Suspicions are fine. They prompt alertness and lead to the search for truth. The signers acknowledged that they had no facts at all—only vague guesses in an extremely polarized political environment a few days before a presidential debate.

"If we are right, this is Russia trying to influence how Americans vote in this election, and we believe strongly that Americans need to be aware of this," they wrote.[11]

But as far as the laptop was concerned, they were all completely wrong.

Evidence or none, they claimed to presume that the whole thing was a Putin operation, or in their term, a "laptop op."[12] Here lies the establishment disinformation. It was a disposable distortion, a timely prop, useful only for a few crucial days through the presidential debate, after which questions about its veracity would not matter.

This was intelligence synthesis of the worst possible kind. Lots of normal investigative journalism and political activism, to say nothing of politicians' campaigns, could be "consistent with Russian objectives," depending on how people choose to interpret them. Yet very few are indeed Russian operations. The intelligence analysis and conclusions from some of the top brand names in the United States intelligence community were unprofessional and reckless.

If the signers had held out for the possibility that in addition to Trump, the Russians might have targeted Joe Biden with *kompromat* through corrupt foreign influence deals by way of his son with the missing laptop, and that perhaps voters ought to be aware of such possibilities when casting their ballots, one could take seriously their stated concern about Russian interference in American politics.

But not a single one of them did. Instead, all attacked the very idea.

Here is what they said, one year after Special Prosecutor Mueller determined that the Steele dossier was a hoax: "For the Russians at this point . . . there is incentive for Moscow to pull out the stops to do anything possible to help Trump win and/or to weaken Biden should he win. A 'laptop op' fits the bill, as the publication of the emails are clearly designed to discredit Biden."[13]

Intelligence professionals, even retired ones, are held to a much higher standard than politicians. They have the prestige of their previous positions and professions, paid for at taxpayer expense. Many, if not most, still hold clearances. Senior officials continue to call on them. Government agencies continue to contract their services. Senior former officials are the unofficial public face of the American intelligence community.

The statement said that a Ukrainian figure whom the United States had identified as a Russian agent had passed Hunter Biden–related materials to Giuliani. It did not allege that the agent had given Giuliani the computer drive or its contents. They leapt to the conclusion that because the individual was (indeed) a Russian agent and was trying to influence Giuliani to help Trump win the election, then everything that the highly controversial Giuliani did was a Russian setup.

This was a monstrously irresponsible leap of logic. Serious former prosecutors and aggressive lawyers like Giuliani—to say nothing of journalists and intelligence officers working in the gray zone—routinely associate with such figures as part of their jobs. Associating with sleaze is what people in their professions are supposed to do. It's what they do with those associations that matters, and the sixty signers simply jumped to politicized conclusions.

Dishonest Intelligence Assessment

All sixty affixed their signatures, with nine names hidden from the public, to a presumption that Giuliani was a knowing Russian asset. They based their "view" on a single report in the *Washington Post*. The *Post* said that the White House had been provided intelligence that the Russians had targeted Giuliani in an influence operation. Obviously a targeted person, especially a national figure and presidential counsel like Giuliani, who had held a security clearance, would—or should—have been alerted, under normal circumstances, that he had been targeted. The FBI calls this routine warning a "defensive briefing." One would anticipate that the forewarned Giuliani was immunized against any Russian op.

But all sixty signers apparently presumed that Giuliani was a traitor—a willful conspirator with a known Russian agent to spread Putin regime disinformation. That presumption was an irresponsible intelligence assessment. It was a political trash job. It was disinformation from a Washington establishment network that sought a political outcome.

The signers made inexcusable errors for intelligence professionals. They got the sources wrong. They falsely single-sourced all the Hunter Biden–related emails to Giuliani. In fact, much of the material originated and emerged from a source apart from the presidential lawyer: former Biden business associate Bevan Cooney, who provided full access to his Gmail account to investigative journalists Peter Schweizer and Matthew Tyrmand, a fact that was public at the time. This author had worked with both Schweizer and Tyrmand to analyze a portion of the Hunter Biden documents before they went public. Those analyses survived all scrutiny. There was a third independent primary source of emails, texts, and other inside information in the form of ex–Biden business colleague Tony Bobulinski, who was providing a separate flow of data but whose involvement might not have been known publicly at the time. Hunter Biden's lawyer later admitted that the contents were real.

Those who exposed the laptop data as genuine were triple-sourced, and all had possession of primary-source documentation.

All the Signers Admitted That They Really Didn't Know the Facts

Then, after having used the reports as blocks on which to build their misleading argument, the signers conceded, "We do not know whether these press reports are accurate."

So they admitted that they never even saw the Hunter Biden computer contents in Giuliani's possession or emails that they (wrongly) attributed to him. *They admitted that they didn't examine any of the facts at all.*

This was sloppy, unprofessional work. Yet this is the analytical product of some of the most senior and widely respected leaders in the American intelligence community. What does this say about the community overall?

Even as Private Citizens, Former Top Intelligence Officers Still Reflect the Intelligence Community

For decades, intelligence community members at large considered themselves, even in private life or retirement, as reflective of the integrity of their professional community. That generally remained the tradition until the statement of October 2020.

All the signers publicly stuck to their position for more than two years, though some wavered along the way. Not until the Steele dossier had been publicly discredited and the Hunter Biden laptop contents authenticated did Clapper start to change his tune.

Speaking in the passive voice—a voice that intelligence analysts and lawyers routinely use to hedge in writing or speaking about a conclusion or assessment—Clapper told the *Washington Post* for a "Fact Checker" feature in 2023, "There was a message distortion."[14] Clapper held himself and the others blameless. "All we were doing was raising a yellow flag that this could be Russian disinformation," said the man who imposed cultural Marxism on the entire intelligence community. It was *Politico*'s fault. "Politico deliberately distorted what we said. It was clear in paragraph five," Clapper claimed.[15] Clapper never objected when his objection would have mattered. It took him twenty-seven months to point the finger at the messenger.

Roll Call of Shame

The signers of the "Public Statement on the Hunter Biden Emails" follow, in order of appearance and with descriptions from the original as posted by *Politico*:[16]

Jim Clapper, Former Director of National Intelligence; Former Under Secretary of Defense for Intelligence; Former Director of the National Geospatial Intelligence Agency; and Former Director of the Defense Intelligence Agency;

Mike Hayden, Former Director, Central Intelligence Agency; Former Director, National Security Agency; Former Principal Deputy Director of National Intelligence;

Leon Panetta, Former Director, Central Intelligence Agency; Former Secretary of Defense;

John Brennan, Former Director, Central Intelligence Agency; Former White House Homeland Security and Counterterrorism Advisor; Former Director, Terrorism Threat Integration Center; Former Analyst and Operations Officer, Central Intelligence Agency;

Thomas Finger, Former Deputy Director of National Intelligence for Analysis; Former Assistant Secretary for Intelligence and Research, Department of State; Former Chair, National Intelligence Council;

Rick Ledgett, Former Deputy Director, National Security Agency;

John McLaughlin, Former Acting Director, Central Intelligence Agency; Former Deputy Director, Central Intelligence Agency; Former Director of Analysis, Central Intelligence Agency; Former Director, Slavic and Eurasian Analysis, Central Intelligence Agency;

Michael Morell, Former Acting Director, Central Intelligence Agency; Former Deputy Director, Central Intelligence Agency; Former Director of Analysis, Central Intelligence Agency;

Mike Vickers, Former Under Secretary of Defense for Intelligence; Former Operations Officer, Central Intelligence Agency;

Doug Wise, Former Deputy Director, Defense Intelligence Agency; Former Senior CIA Operations Officer;

Nick Rasmussen, Former Director, National Counterterrorism Center;

Russ Travers, Former Acting Director, National Counterterrorism Center; Former Deputy Director, National Counterterrorism Center; Former Analyst of the Soviet Union and Russia, Defense Intelligence Agency;

Andy Liepman, Former Deputy Director, National Counterterrorism Center; Former Senior Intelligence Officer, Central Intelligence Agency;

John Moseman, Former Chief of Staff, Central Intelligence Agency; Former Director of Congressional Affairs, Central Intelligence Agency; Former Minority Staff Director, Senate Select Committee on Intelligence;

Larry Pfeiffer, Former Chief of Staff, Central Intelligence Agency; Former Director, White House Situation Room;

Jeremy Bash, Former Chief of Staff, Central Intelligence Agency; Former Chief of Staff, Department of Defense; Former Chief Counsel, House Permanent Select Committee on Intelligence;

Rodney Snyder, Former Chief of Staff, Central Intelligence Agency; Former Director of Intelligence Programs, National Security Council; Chief of Station, Central Intelligence Agency;

Glenn Gerstell, Former General Counsel, National Security Agency;

David B. Buckley, Former Inspector General, Central Intelligence Agency; Former Democratic Staff Director, House Permanent Select Committee on Intelligence; Former Counterespionage Case Officer, United States Air Force;

Nada Bakos, Former Analyst and Targeting Officer, Central Intelligence Agency;

Patty Brandmaier, Former Senior Intelligence Officer, Central Intelligence Agency; Former Deputy Associate Director for Military Affairs, Central

Intelligence Agency; Former Deputy Director of Congressional Affairs, Central Intelligence Agency;

James B. Bruce, Former Senior Intelligence Officer, Central Intelligence Agency; Former Senior Intelligence Officer, National Intelligence Council; Considerable work related to Russia;

David Cariens, Former Intelligence Analyst, Central Intelligence Agency; 50+ Years Working in the Intelligence Community;

Janice Cariens, Former Operational Support Officer, Central Intelligence Agency;

Paul Kolbe, Former Senior Operations Officer, Central Intelligence Agency; Former Chief, Central Eurasia Division, Central Intelligence Agency;

Peter Corsell, Former Analyst, Central Intelligence Agency;

Brett Davis, Former Senior Intelligence Officer, Central Intelligence Agency; Former Deputy Director of the Special Activities Center for Expeditionary Operations, CIA;

Roger Zane George, Former National Intelligence Officer;

Steven L. Hall, Former Senior Intelligence Officer, Central Intelligence Agency; Former Chief of Russian Operations, Central Intelligence Agency;

Kent Harrington, Former National Intelligence Officer for East Asia, Central Intelligence Agency; Former Director of Public Affairs, Central Intelligence Agency; Former Chief of Station, Central Intelligence Agency; Former Analyst, Central Intelligence Agency;

Don Hepburn, Former Senior National Security Executive;

Timothy D. Kilbourn, Former Dean, Sherman Kent School of Intelligence Analysis, Central Intelligence Agency; Former PDB [President's Daily Brief] Briefer to President George W. Bush, Central Intelligence Agency;

Ron Marks, Former Officer, Central Intelligence Agency; Twice former staff of the Republican Majority Leader;

Jonna Hiestand Mendez, Technical Operations Officer, Central Intelligence Agency;

Emile Nakhleh, Former Director of the Political Islam Strategic Analysis Program, Central Intelligence Agency; Former Senior Intelligence Analyst, Central Intelligence Agency;

Gerald A. O'Shea, Senior Operations Officer, Central Intelligence Agency; Served four tours as Chief of Station, Central Intelligence Agency;

David Priess, Former Analyst and Manager, Central Intelligence Agency; Former PDB Briefer, Central Intelligence Agency;

Pam Purcilly, Former Deputy Director of Analysis, Central Intelligence Agency; Former Director of the Office of Russian and European Analysis, Central Intelligence Agency; Former PDB Briefer to President George W. Bush, Central Intelligence Agency;

Marc Polymeropoulos, Former Senior Operations Officer, Central Intelligence Agency; Former Acting Chief of Operations for Europe and Eurasia, Central Intelligence Agency;

Chris Savos, Former Senior Intelligence Officer, Central Intelligence Officer;

Nick Shapiro, Former Deputy Chief of Staff and Senior Advisor to the Director, Central Intelligence Agency;

John Sipher, Former Senior Operations Officer, Central Intelligence Agency; Former Deputy Chief of Russian Operations, Central Intelligence Agency [and advisory board member of the Lincoln Project];

Stephen Slick, Former Senior Director for Intelligence Programs, National Security Council; Former Senior Operations Office, Central Intelligence Agency;

Cynthia Strand, Former Deputy Assistant Director for Global Issues, Central Intelligence Agency;

Greg Tarbell, Former Deputy Executive Director, Central Intelligence Agency; Former Analyst of the Soviet Union and Russia, Central Intelligence Agency;

David Terry, Former Chairman of the National Intelligence Collection Board; Former Chief of the PDB, Central Intelligence Agency; Former PDB Briefer to Vice President Dick Cheney, Central Intelligence Agency;

Greg Treverton, Former Chair, National Intelligence Council [and a noted author of some of the most important textbooks on intelligence];

John Tullius, Former Senior Intelligence Officer, Central Intelligence Agency;

David A. Vanell, Former Senior Operations Officer, Central Intelligence Agency;

Winston Wiley, Former Director of Analysis, Central Intelligence Agency; Former Chief, Counterterrorism Center, Central Intelligence Agency;

Kristin Wood, Former Senior Intelligence Officer, Central Intelligence Agency; Former PDB Briefer, Central Intelligence Agency;

"In addition, nine additional former IC officers who cannot be named publicly also support the arguments in this letter," *Politico* added.[17]

Chapter 33

The Incident at the Capitol

For more than two years, senior FBI officials, including Director Chris Wray, refused to answer questions from federal lawmakers about whether or not FBI agents or assets were involved in the planning or execution of criminal acts of violence at the United States Capitol on January 6, 2021.

The congressmen and senators had a right to know, as they sat on the oversight committees that governed the FBI's budget and conduct. The senior FBI officials knew in advance that they would be asked. They were given simple yes-or-no questions, without being asked to reveal classified information.

Instead of putting rumors to rest that the FBI had been involved in instigating or orchestrating the January 6 mob violence, the FBI leadership fueled them. The FBI never offered to testify in executive or closed session to inform oversight committees without jeopardizing sources and methods. It never answered lawmakers' written questions. Its leaders, from Wray down, simply refused to give an answer. A dramatic exchange aired in public a year after the incident, when then executive assistant director Jill Sanborn testified to the Senate Judiciary Committee. The senior FBI official was in a unique position to know the answers. She had previously confirmed to the Senate this author's eyewitness observations that the violence appeared organized in advance. This time, she would neither confirm nor deny a set of yes-or-no questions from Senator Ted Cruz (R-TX):

> **Senator Cruz:** "Did any FBI agents or confidential informants actively participate in the events of January 6, yes or no?"
> **Sanborn:** "Sir, I can't answer that."
> **Cruz:** "Did any FBI agents or confidential informants commit crimes of violence on January 6?"
> **Sanborn:** "I can't answer that, sir."
> **Cruz:** "Did any FBI agents or FBI informants actively encourage and incite crimes of violence on January 6?"
> **Sanborn:** "Sir, I can't answer that."[1]

We do not yet know the truth about FBI involvement in instigating the Capitol violence, but we do know that the FBI had assets—confidential human sources—in the leadership of some of the groups involved.[2] We know that some of the violence was professionally regimented and coordinated, as any trained eye could see at the time, and as was later confirmed in criminal trials and hearings.[3]

It is now agreed that the FBI, as the lead domestic agency against domestic violent extremism, failed to detect the planning and organization of violence in advance of January 6, or, if it did know of it, that the FBI failed to warn the United States Capitol Police.[4] Steven A. Sund, who was Capitol Police chief on that fateful day, testified to Congress that the FBI had provided his force with only the vaguest advance information about radical groups planning to protest at the Capitol, saying that the assessment was that the likelihood of violence was "remote."[5] Sund wrote a book and gave an extensive interview describing how the FBI, Pentagon, and Department of Homeland Security had failed the Capitol Police that day.[6]

The FBI has been unable to explain why a certain identified ringleader of the organized violence first appeared on its "Most Wanted" list and then was mysteriously removed.[7] It never publicly explained why Steven D'Antuono, the special agent in charge of the Detroit Field Office at the time of the planning and execution of the FBI sting operation to organize a fake plot to kidnap or assassinate the governor of Michigan,[8] was suddenly transferred to run the Washington Field Office right before the fateful Capitol violence.[9]

What we can conclude is that the FBI's handling of the "insurrection" recklessly endangered Congress as an institution and the personal safety of individual lawmakers, and developed a storyline to fit a prevailing White House narrative that white supremacists present the single greatest domestic threat to the country.

Internal communications at the FBI Washington Field Office in the weeks after the violence show a dedicated team working overtime to solve crimes committed at the Capitol that day. They did not use politicized words like "insurrection." Those terms would come later.

Chapter 34

"I'm Special Agent Jones, I use he/him pronouns. Thanks for talking to me today! First, what name and pronouns should I use to refer to you?"

—FBI training course for all personnel, 2021[1]

Agents of Change

Apart from hunting down every last protester who was in the Capitol unlawfully parading, sexual orientation and gender identity training arose as FBI director Wray's top 2021 priority. Wray compelled all FBI personnel to take it. General Clapper's lead-by-example mandate from the Obama years had survived Trump and was now soaking into the intelligence community's cellular structure.

As laid out under Clapper's direction a decade earlier, the designers of the FBI training program created a psychological manipulation process to force employees to modify their thought, manipulate their behavior, overcome their moral or ethical qualms, take direct action against their values, and become activist agents of cultural change.

The training was explicitly not developed to assist agents and analysts in understanding people within a cultural demographic as part of street-level law enforcement or criminal and national security investigations or analysis, or in relating to juries. It was pure politicization. The program mapped out an agent-of-change strategy to transform the FBI's entire culture and ethos. The training program is a fifty-six-page document, which is fully detailed here for the first time. Unless otherwise sourced, all quotes are from the document, provided by FBI whistleblower Kyle Seraphin.

"This course is sponsored by the Office of Diversity and Inclusion and was created with assistance from Bureau equality," the presentation began, decorated with a narrow rainbow bar across the top margin.

"Objectives," said the next slide, with the rainbow bar above a photo of a billowing rainbow flag, are to "provide awareness of the LGBT+ community and to promote an inclusive workplace environment." It addressed "terms for sexual orientation and gender identity (SOGI)," "appropriate behaviors for an inclusive work environment," and "how to be an ally for LGBT+ colleagues." Psychological reshaping would program a new behavior, or so Wray's office hoped.

The third slide: "Inclusion is MISSION ESSENTIAL." All capital letters. The blindfolded Lady Justice, brandishing her sword in her left hand and raising the scales of justice in her right—all superimposed over a rainbow flag—illustrated the page. FBI personnel were instructed how to behave in front of "LGBT+ employees." It did not tell "LGBT+ employees" how to behave in front of the 98.4 percent of FBI personnel who are non-"LGBT+" and therefore straight. (By May 2023, the FBI reported that 1.6 percent of its personnel are "LGBT+."[2]) The slide cautioned everyone in the bureau to go along with whatever fads and changes they might encounter, or in the FBI's exact words, "Remember, the LGBT+ community is very diverse and always evolving. This course cannot cover every hypothetical situation. However, it will provide a broad overview of ground rules for engaging each other with respect." Respect was explicitly unilateral.

And so on from page to page, all with the little rainbow line across the top.

Candy Rainbow Betrayal

A segment titled "What is SOGI?" explained all the latest passing sexual and gender identity terms and symbols that every FBI employee needed to know for that 1.6 percent of the force, or more specifically, the militant fraction among that 1.6 percent who required special treatment.

The next segment described the "Plus+" spectrum of "Queer/Intersex/Asexual/Non-binary/And more, including everyone under the transgender umbrella." Some agents suspected "And more" to be code language for what advocates call "minor-attracted persons," but since acts of pedophilia are crimes that the overall LGBT+ community would denounce, those agents suspected that FBI management left it vague for a reason.

And so on and so on, with buttons for all personnel to select to learn more. Again, not to arm agents and analysts with knowledge in their areas of responsibility, but to appease the thinnest sliver of radicals. Then the FBI presented a rainbow-colored pinwheel about "Sexual Orientation and Gender Identity," which one would read from the top in a clockwise direction from Lesbian to Asexual to Gay to Bisexual to Queer to Questioning to Heterosexual. Nothing about "And more." The slide invited FBI agents to learn more by pushing the pinwheel.

A simpler, purple-to-blue-to-green wheel on the next slide taught about cisgender, transgender, and such profound observations as "assigned female at birth, and then gender identity is a woman, is cisgender," while "assigned female at birth, and their gender identity is a man, is transgender" (who did the assigning is not explained), with another invitation to push the virtual wheel.

The FBI pulled agents off investigations to track Chinese spies and bust kiddie porn rings to take this course.[3]

Then came a segment on good transgender manners. "When writing or talking about a transgender person keep in mind that the word 'transgender' describes a person but does not define or name a person. You can say they are [*sic*] a transgender person. However, it is inappropriate to say they are [*sic*] 'transgendered.' Saying that a person is transgendered is like saying they are [*sic*] an object and not a person."

Lesson: "Do not: Call someone 'a transgender'" or "add an unnecessary 'ed' or 's' to transgender." These grammatical rules were mandatory, as was mutilating the English language with plural pronouns to avoid gender confusion sown from insensitive use of the proper (wrong) singular. After that, a handy checklist of dos and don'ts, complete with more invented grammar. A green checkmark indicated that it's OK to say, "They are [*sic*] a transgender person." Just as long as an insensitive FBI employee doesn't add the hurtful "ed" or "s."

Then a five-page quiz, or "Knowledge Check #1," to make sure that FBI workforce grammar is properly butchered.

Guide to Identity Goose-Stepping

After the quiz—we are only a third of the way through the class right now—comes the discussion, "Is Queer a Derogatory Term?" Those who were raised never to hurt homosexual people by calling them queer are now re-educated that it really is OK after all to apply that long-demeaning word to homosexuals and others. Under the proper circumstances. But that, like so much else, the criteria are purely subjective. Keeping flammable words completely out of the workplace is off the table. "Some, within the FBI workforce and LGBT+ community, may find it offensive or a reminder of the pain it infers. It's all about context," the training course said. FBI personnel were advised neither to say queer or avoid saying queer, but to comply passively as indicated in each random situation: "Mirror the language a person uses when referring to themselves [*sic*] and use good judgment!"

Illustrating the slide is a photograph of a small piece of notepaper held between two hands and marked in handwritten, capitalized, underlined letters, "I'm QUEER."

Then there's a segment on "Gender Expression." This is so that everybody understands that "how one outwardly presents their [*sic*] gender, expressed through one's clothing, haircut, behavior, or body characteristics" is "not their [*sic*] gender identity." This is followed by examples of women with a "stereotypically masculine haircut" or men who paint their fingernails. And then a six-page quiz called "Knowledge Check #2."

Next is a section on how to question fellow FBI personnel about the various sexualities and genders that they flaunt in America's premier federal law enforcement and domestic intelligence agency. After all, there are boundaries. "Ask yourself: Is it any of my business?" The training did not address the question of whether said individual flaunted anything. Even so, every FBI employee had to consider, "Would I ask my straight, cisgender coworkers these questions?" (The course did not provide the authorized and politically correct meaning of "cisgender.")

While stressing personnel genitalia, identity, and sexual practices, it is "inappropriate and offensive," FBI employees were told, to refer to things, body parts, and acts that are generally considered very private. The best practice was essentially for the heterosexual 98.4 percent of FBI personnel to comply in silence.

Now, halfway through the course, came the "Respect Toolkit." Respect means calling professional colleagues by their made-up names, not by their real names. Indeed, there is no longer such a thing as a "real name," according to the FBI training course. In the course, personnel are told it is forbidden to ask a colleague "What is your 'real' name?" or

"Are you in the right restroom?" FBI people were no longer allowed to ask if one is "male or female." It was OK for human resources, medical, and legal departments to ask bureau employees for their "legal name" and to ask properly, "How does your name appear on your government ID?"

Erasure of Personal Ethics

"Personal beliefs" is the next section, with a big reminder for heterosexual FBI personnel to "focus on appropriate behavior, not beliefs." To be sure that this order is properly understood, and that no reciprocity to cisgenders will be offered or considered, a photo accompanies the text showing bureau recruiters behind an FBI crest that hangs from a table beneath a rainbow flag.

The thirtieth slide hints more broadly at the truth about an agenda to change the FBI's culture. "SELECT THE CORRECT ANSWER BELOW," says the scenario. "Can transgender people be Special Agents?" is the question. First choice: "Yes, new talent is always welcome to the FBI." Second choice: "No, unfortunately you may not fit into the FBI culture." There is no third choice, let alone a blank area to provide an unapproved answer. The "wrong" answer rules out the possibility that transgender people might have a higher incidence than most of mental and emotional disorders, hormonal imbalances, side effects of mood-altering medications, medical issues manufactured through elective sex-change surgery, and other issues that would preclude a large number of them from being effective special agents carrying firearms in public.

The next scenario covers roommates and religious beliefs, which looks fair enough until the only permitted answer is shown. The scenario is all about counseling an FBI trainee named Jack. Jack is having a difficult time sharing a room with an assigned roommate who is a homosexual. Personnel are not told whether Jack is homosexual or heterosexual. The question is, "If you were Jack's Class Counselor, how would you respond?" Four answers are provided. The first: "I agree, you shouldn't be subjected to living with a gay roommate." The second: "I can't approve a roommate transfer based on your religious beliefs." The third: "You have a point, I wouldn't want to live with him, either." The fourth: "Your religious beliefs exempt you from rooming with someone who is gay."

The answer is that all four answers are wrong. The FBI explains why: "Leave your personal beliefs at home. Personal discomfort, personal beliefs, or lack of understanding is not a justification for discrimination."

"You have completed the scenario," the PowerPoint slide announces in lavender letters.

After a Cloying Section on Pronoun Usage Comes the Kicker: You Are Expected to Squeal

"If you have been discriminated against due to SOGI status"—"discriminated" in the curriculum meaning inadequately pronoun'ed beyond the transgressor's allotted introductory mistakes—one more link is provided for the victimized to inform on their colleagues. If FBI employees witness someone else doing it—or even hear a rumor or other "information" about it—they can snitch to an office via a different link. Privileged status needs an unwritten reminder. On this slide, the inform-against-your-colleagues guidelines are illustrated with a photo of a judge's gavel, a pile of bookmarks, and a rainbow flag.

Now comes the political organization. This is the activist, the mobilization, part. The true "special agents" of the FBI are agents of change. Or what the training curriculum calls #UnexpectedAgents. This is about forcing a cultural change of the FBI itself. It is a neo-Freudian, critical theorist, Marcusian approach to compelling FBI employees to dispense with their personal morals and beliefs. It's about infusing the bureau with critical theorists, cultural Marxists, and other social revolutionaries whose self-identities precede the FBI's real mission.

As Willi Münzenberg, the Comintern, and the Frankfurt School people preached, and as J. Edgar Hoover and all early FBI agents knew, successful infiltration of the few requires a broad front with others. And so Christopher Wray's mandatory FBI course asks the question on slide fifty-two: "What is an Ally?"

Yet another rainbow flag variation, this one a bold, rainbow-striped emblem shaped like the Russian letter "L," is superimposed over a striped background of stark black and white. The interpretation: Allies are good. Non-allies are bad. There are no gray areas.

Then the requisite instructional slogans: "Allies: Are open minded; Are good listeners; Create a safe atmosphere; Accept the identities of others; Do not use slang or derogatory language; Use inclusive language"—this last point linked to a politically sanitized word-term index. "Speak out and defend; Always model good behavior." It reads like the Cheka's old instruction to be nice to people before taking them away to be shot. The FBI LGBT+ "allies" are what were called, in another age and place, the *zampolits*, the political officers assigned to police speech and attitude among military personnel, this time a digital-age rainbow army. The heavy Cyrillic rainbow "L" on the flag, which looks like an inverted "V," could be a stylized "A" for Ally, but the course makes no attempt to explain the symbolism, which always has a meaning behind it.

They Who Must Be Obeyed

By now, the FBI diversity course has established the privileged and protected-class status for the aggressive few. The FBI has dictated its authorized words, its twisting of language to distort grammar and change meaning. It has made clear the expectations of employees' modified behavior—that they will break their values to comply with the new privileged order—plus the enforcement tools of the Word Police and the electronic, anonymous, secret-informant system.

Now that all that has been established comes the fourth scenario. It's a word-and-behavior scenario for the allies, the political commissars, the *zampolits*. Even though the scenario implies there is more than one correct answer among the five offered, the opposite is true. Pushing the ironically named "submit" button brings the next slide, which declares that no matter what answer you picked, you are wrong.

Silence and minding one's own business is toxic workplace hostility. So is good-natured or awkward laughter. The bureau people are cautioned, "Be brave, recognize inappropriate behavior and speak up in a respectful manner. If you say nothing or laugh along, you could be enabling a potentially hostile work environment. All FBI employees should be aware that derogatory and inappropriate language serves no purpose in the workplace and is contrary to our core values."

This, of course, is generally true. But the graphics and images in the course numb the FBI employees with the true demand for total and unquestioning compliance down this one-way street. It was no secret. The FBI publicly announced that the architect of this program, Tanya Odom, had persuaded Wray to make diversity jargon a core value.

The step after being an "Ally" is to go "The Extra Mile." It isn't enough to be privately compliant, an obedient employee loyally doing what xe or zhe is told. Nor is it enough to be a *zampolit* or commissar to toe and enforce the party line. For the good of the order, FBI personnel who disagree must break with their values permanently and completely, not only in the workplace but in public.

The expectation is for all FBI agents to dump their religious or traditional values, or whatever family or personal priorities they might have, and explicitly take to the streets for Pride. A large image on slide fifty-five reinforces the messages in rainbow colors: Well over a dozen FBI agents in the street wearing FBI shorts or FBI shirts and waving rainbow flags. One carries the end of an eight-foot, blue, FBI #UnexpectedAgent rainbow-scales-of-justice banner with "www.fbi-jobs.gov" above the same thin rainbow bar that matches the graphic design of the entire course. The FBI person sports a Rolling Stones logo on her denim shorts, the protruding tongue lapping her crotch.

The text on slide fifty-five is explicit. Director Wray was directing all FBI personnel to "Make your support visible; Continue self-educating; Participate in regional Pride events and support field office LGBT+ events" and "Contact your Diversity and Inclusion Coordinator or Bureau Equality for more information."

The final segment is more of the same numbness-inducing material: a compact list of six sources of approved information, including an appropriate glossary; plus suggestions to find "resources" among local, state, and national activist groups, with half the slide featuring a golden statue of the blindfolded Lady Justice, this time with the sword in her right hand and the scales in her left, mockingly superimposed over yet another rainbow flag.

Anyone who has lived in a totalitarian country recognizes the esoteric communication to obey the order of the banner. It's as though the FBI diversity program was drawn from an enemy template for internal coup d'état. Any decent Sovietologist or survivor of the Chinese Great Cultural Revolution would recognize the pattern. So would any disciple of Gramsci or Marcuse.

Coalition of the Sane Resists

A militant fringe minority organizes within the FBI *apparatchiki*. Officials at the top, either appointed to execute the job or just following orders, empower that militant fringe by imposing an extreme agenda on everyone else. They anticipate resistance along the way, but with enough pressure, the breaking point comes when professionals are forced to junk their moral beliefs and adopt the ever-changing artificial vocabulary and obligatory speech codes. Words change perception, which changes behavior. All employees must conform. They face secret informant and arbitrary enforcement mechanisms of punishment, re-education, and reward. Those devices create narrower thinking, sow mutual distrust, enforce political obedience, and identify or purge the non-compliant.

After being acclimated to conforming and informing, the employees, out of conviction or self-preservation or some false hope that this too shall pass, help the fringe broaden its cadres. The remaining professionals now recruit at the street level to metamorphose the culture of the institution.

That metamorphosis will break and rebuild the institution's ethics, subdue the consciences and behaviors of the now demoralized personnel, diminish operational capabilities, and empower the new cadres. The rainbow ecosystem of life, death, and decay purges or isolates the non-compliant or, better yet, forces them to self-purge.

If the self-purged remain quiet and go along, their compliance reports and pensions and reputations might be safe. If they make an issue of it, even under whistleblower mechanisms established by law, the apparat will attack. Portions of their confidential personnel files will leak to the public. Few of their former colleagues will support them, some will denounce them, and most will stay silent, leaving the incompliant ones' reputations in tatters. The apparat will suspend the unbroken indefinitely without pay, revoke their clearances, illegally leak the contents of their personnel records, and deny their right to work elsewhere because they are merely suspended and not terminated, as happened to former special agents Kyle Seraphin, Stephen Friend, and others. The apparat will

Was J. Edgar Hoover a Rainbow Justice Warrior?

Before continuing, let's address the elephant in the room: the very private life of J. Edgar Hoover.

After his mother passed away, Hoover roomed with his best friend and confidant, Clyde Tolson. Neither man had married, leading to the usual rumors. Critics in Congress and the Roosevelt administration wondered if Hoover was secretly gay. Wild Bill Donovan gleefully raised questions about Hoover's sexuality. Homosexuality was a taboo subject in American society. It could subject people to blackmail and increase the likelihood of security risks. But FDR saw no problem as long as Hoover could run the FBI, and no evidence ever surfaced.

The rumors persisted for decades. In the early 1960s, Attorney General Bobby Kennedy called the FBI chief "J. Edna" behind his back. Once when Tolson was hospitalized, Kennedy joked that Hoover's roommate had undergone a hysterectomy.[4] Kennedy ordered an investigation into Hoover's private life and found nothing more than Hoover being, in the words of critical biographer Beverly Gage, "the restrained, self-disciplined workaholic he had always seemed to be."

In her thorough, heavily documented work, Gage demolished the rumor that Hoover had been a cross-dresser.[5] Pulitzer Prize–winner Tim Weiner, in *Enemies*, his extraordinary critical history of the FBI based entirely on primary sources, determined that rumors of homosexuality were "almost surely false."[6]

Foreign intelligence services excelled at exploiting people's secret personal lives. Hoover watched prominent figures' sex lives, not for prurient reasons as often alleged but because he, like others, believed that, in addition to vulnerability to blackmail by foreign spies, illicit or repressed homosexuals were especially likely to lash out secretly against the society that would never accept them. British and OSS analysts shared that conclusion during World War II.[7] Senior political leaders of both parties tended to agree, and President Eisenhower formally banned the hiring of homosexuals in the federal government.

Hoover did occasionally exploit what he found for political purposes.

The Soviets took note of the Hoover rumors and began an active measures campaign to discredit the FBI director. Former KGB archivist Vasili Mitrokhin smuggled notes to the West describing what the Chekists had planned. "To compromise E. Hoover as a homosexual, letters were sent to the main newspapers on behalf of an anonymous organization," Mitrokhin said. The KGB letters criticized Hoover as a hypocrite, saying he projected himself as "a moralist and a pillar of American society" while he "turned the FBI into a faggots' den."[8] Less serious future biographies and films of Hoover would accept this Soviet disinformation and spread it as fact. Even many FBI agents today believe the stories.

provide prosecutors with the means to press criminal charges against those, like Seraphin, considered whistleblower ringleaders.[9]

And the slogans. Always the slogans. Another march through another institution. This has happened time and again in modern history. And it is happening to the American intelligence community.

Fortunately, all is not lost. Not yet.

The rainbow course didn't go as FBI director Christopher Wray and his diversity commissars had planned. The Gramscian Feds were not astute followers of Gramsci. They pushed too far, too quickly. Wray's course provoked bitter indignation at the bureau's fifty-six field offices and at headquarters. Agents, analysts, lawyers, and other employees refused to comply. Many refused to complete the course. By late 2021, Wray faced what was, for the FBI, an internal rebellion. Without a word, Wray quietly withdrew the course. Then he tried to hide the evidence. The fifty-six-page set of course slides vanished from the FBI servers to erase the embarrassment from the record. Nobody would know.

But good FBI agents save evidence. Some saved the incriminating slides.

Chapter 35

"How many soldiers and Marines, coalition partners, and innocent civilians would be alive today if it wasn't for PC?"

—former U.S. intelligence officer who served in Iraq and Afghanistan

Defending against Communist Chinese Spies Is Racist

Early in 2022, the Biden Justice Department ended the Trump administration's successful interagency counterintelligence program against Communist Chinese agents, arguing that it was racist.[1] The termination came amid a nationwide pressure campaign for the administration to drop the China Initiative, which Attorney General William Barr and Secretary of State Michael Pompeo started in 2018 to combat Beijing's aggressive espionage, much of it run out of American universities.

This was an orchestrated campaign. In a publicized case, 192 Yale professors signed a letter to Attorney General Merrick Garland, complaining about bias against people of generally Asian extraction. In place of the China Initiative, DOJ said it would start a new "Strategy for Countering Nation-State Threats," and counterintelligence work against Communist Chinese agents continued.[2]

The China Initiative had been directed specifically against Chinese Communist Party (CCP) espionage. To pressure the administration, Beijing ran a short and successful active measures operation on American universities. Chinese students loyal to the regime ran nationwide protests against any anti-CCP activity at universities.[3] Chinese Communist Party media ripped the George Washington University as an "asylum for racism" because it allowed a Chinese human rights activist there to display posters protesting Beijing's sponsorship of the 2002 Olympics.[4]

The Beijing-based media worked in tandem, United Front Work–style, with a certain GWU-based Chinese students' association with identical lines of attack. The controversy prompted outrage from George Washington University president Mark Wrighton—not at the persecution of the dissident, but at the dissident's offenses against the CCP.[5] Could it be Wrighton felt protective of his school's substantial income from Communist China and certain CCP-approved joint academic programs? He acted as the CCP censor on the campus next to the White House, sniffing that the dissident art "personally offended" him. He called the poster campaign a "terrible event" and pledged to "determine who is responsible." Then, as a CCP proxy sensor, Wrighton ordered the posters taken down.[6]

GWU is one of the nation's top feeder schools for future CIA and other intelligence professionals, diplomats, Justice Department lawyers, and FBI personnel.

"We are ending the China Initiative," Assistant Attorney General for National Security Matthew Olsen announced. "By grouping cases under the China Initiative rubric, we helped give rise to a harmful perception that the [Justice] Department applies a lower standard to investigate and prosecute criminal conduct related to that country or that we in some way view people with racial, ethnic, or familial ties to China differently." The program, or at least some elements thereof, would continue under a different name, he said.[7]

Olsen added that there was no basis to the misperception that the program was racist. "I have not seen any indication of bias or prejudice in any of the decision making I've seen by the Department of Justice," he said. "Full stop."[8] If there was no basis to the misperception of racism, the Justice Department could have debunked that misperception and attacked what was clearly a CCP disinformation campaign to disrupt American counterintelligence.

PC Costs Lives

Some saw it coming. "We developed very detailed intelligence on what we could call top Islamist clerics and terrorist leaders whose private behavior, if exposed to their peers and subordinates, would have destroyed them," said a former intelligence officer who served in Iraq and Afghanistan who is still in the system as a contractor and requested anonymity.

"It was cocaine use. It was drunkenness, getting it on with boys, having some male Filipino lover boy stashed in one of the Gulf states. All the types of behaviors that their belief system rejected. The kind of information that just would have wrecked the images of these targets and demoralized and divided their loyalists," he said. "We had it all. We even had it on the Gulfies [the sheikhs, emirs, and princes in the Arabian or Persian Gulf] who were funding the terrorism.

"And it was graphic. Really, really gross. But people in the system were, and are, too PC or risk-averse or whatever to suggest weaponizing this intelligence. There's a mirror-imaging in the IC that just because the analysts or supervisors don't think something's bad, they don't see the utility of the intelligence from the enemy's perspective.

And then there's the general risk-averse nature, and the fear of giving offense."[9]

Fear of giving offense, at least, to their peers and to the jihadis.

The former intelligence officer left with a parting question: "How many soldiers and Marines, coalition partners, and innocent civilians would be alive today if it wasn't for PC?"

The FBI's Woke New Headquarters

Woke jargon even peppered the federal government requirements for choosing the site of a new FBI headquarters.

The J. Edgar Hoover FBI Building hulks across Pennsylvania Avenue from the Justice Department. The deteriorating headquarters represents the worst of 1960s paranoid brutalism: a massive concrete bunker elevated on colossal stilts three stories above the sidewalk. Ugly, menacing, fearful, inhuman. Obsolete by any fair standard, headquarters has always been a poorly designed, architecturally unsalvageable waste of open space. Now it's a deteriorated wreck. The perennially dead flowers in heavy concrete planters at the southern entrance show that the FBI has given up trying to make the place look civil. A modern law enforcement and counterintelligence service needs something better.

In 2022, Congress authorized funding to begin construction of a new FBI headquarters in the Maryland or Virginia suburbs. The current Hoover building footprint is under two city blocks. The vision is to build a gargantuan, multibillion-dollar megaplex on land at least twice the size of the Pentagon. Wokeness is baked into the plan.

The General Services Administration, which manages federal property, chose three prospective sites ranging from fifty-eight to eighty acres.[10] The Pentagon, one of the largest office buildings in the world, has a footprint of twenty-nine acres, excluding its courtyard.[11] By comparison, the Kremlin, a walled fortress containing four villages that house presidential offices, residences, the former Supreme Soviet assembly chambers, administrative buildings, security complexes, museums, and several churches, sits on sixty-seven acres.[12] The new FBI headquarters complex could dwarf the Kremlin.

Neither the Justice Department nor the White House, to say nothing of the FBI itself, ever explained to Congress or the public why the bureau needs such a sprawling new complex. The bureau doesn't plan to consolidate other facilities in the Washington area. Regardless of the new headquarters, the FBI plans to keep its large Washington Field Office and build a new, unspecified downtown office complex to liaise with the Justice Department and other government agencies. The FBI just dictated the supersized site without rationale.

A Biden executive order framed critical race theory as one of the five main criteria for selecting a new FBI megaplex. "This criterion considers the likelihood that selecting the site will advance the policies and goals contained in Executive Orders 13985 and 14057 to: Advance racial equity and support for underserved communities through the Federal Government; and Promote sustainable locations for Federal facilities and strengthen the vitality and livability of the communities in which Federal facilities are located," according to the General Services Administration.[13]

The policy would turn the new FBI headquarters into a petri dish of the latest progressive fads, from person-made climate change to race and gender. It would require "sustainable land use that promotes conservation of natural resources, reduced GHG [greenhouse gas] emissions, and increased resilience to the impacts of climate change," according to GSA, along with "equitable development that promotes environmental justice."[14]

The federal government weighted this criterion as 50 percent more important than the actual cost of buying and developing the land.[15]

Though almost everyone agreed the FBI needed to move out of its obsolete and decaying space, Congress never debated why such a gigantic complex was needed. Not one single lawmaker questioned it on the record as they approved the omnibus spending bill in 2022 with Biden's diversity diktat, authorized one of the three sites, and appropriated $375 million to get it started.[16]

Nobody in Congress even asked if the nation might be best served by a reconfiguration of law enforcement that might efficiently reduce the duties and size of the FBI, or remove the extensive duplication between the FBI and other agencies. No lawmaker raised the bipartisan recommendations that came up after 9/11 to dismember the FBI and parcel out its functions to other agencies or create something new.

Instead, Congress voted unquestioningly to appropriate and authorize the money, following politically trendy and woke themes that have nothing to do with the FBI's mission.

The mood changed as Congress switched hands in 2023 and lawmakers sought action against FBI biases, abuses, and the imperious attitude that the bureau leadership took toward the few lawmakers who did demand answers to unapproved questions. House appropriators made significant cuts to the FBI budget and zeroed out funding for the new headquarters, with some suggesting the leadership of the bureau should be moved to the new $2.5 billion FBI facility in Huntsville, Alabama.[17]

Part VI

Rebuilding American Intelligence

Chapter 36

It's Been Done Before

The American national security community saw its last fundamental redesign in the late 1940s. It is based on the National Security Act of 1947 and related laws of the early Cold War. That was after the United States first became a superpower, with Nazism and fascism crushed, and Stalin's Communists challenging all of America's national interests. The world—and American national interests—have changed radically since then, as has the bipartisan consensus that designed the system that served the nation well over the years.

Failure to adapt facilitated the rise of Vladimir Putin, Islamic jihadism, the Chinese Communist Party, and the psychological and philosophical threats—foreign and domestic—of critical theory and cultural Marxism. Nobody in the bipartisan consensus that built the post–World War II national security community would have foreseen, let alone accepted, the infiltration of the Comintern's ideological subversion into the FBI, CIA, and the rest of the intelligence community. Not even Lukács, Münzenberg, and Dzerzhinsky could have foreseen what they unleashed, let alone the West's absorption of their Frankfurt School line of attack.

One of the greatest of the great American intelligence leaders, Wild Bill Donovan, never saw it coming, even right under his nose. J. Edgar Hoover saw it happening from the very start and warned against it for a half-century, but almost always under his personal and the FBI's institutional brands. One wonders how much better off the country would have been had Hoover shared his knowledge of the Venona decrypts with President Truman as the National Security Act of 1947 was being conceived, or with Allen Dulles and his inner circle of great men as they built the CIA to fight Communism. Certainly the solid early leaders in the CIA would have been more mindful to weed out and ban the Frankfurt School's missionaries from the intelligence profession.

The CIA and FBI—or at least their essential functions—are far from lost. But as those mid-level careerists, to whom mandatory DEI is normal if not essential, advance up the professional ladders, they recruit new people, often without regard to knowledge, talent, and aptitude, into the latest generation of careerists. At the current rate, they will take total and permanent bureaucratic control. This is normal for any self-perpetuating and politicized civil service or its equivalent. Within another full presidential administration, the American intelligence community will be recovered or lost. After that point, it will matter little who is president.

What to Do with the CIA

Protection of America's first interests requires the most robust and capable foreign intelligence machinery possible. As with anything else, money and size do not equate to value and usefulness. As for the

CIA itself, let's break it down by general function and see what can be done to keep what's needed and discard the offal. The CIA has run its course and should be dissolved in favor of something new. To start with, the organization should be split in two: a new intelligence service responsible for the collection and analysis of intelligence, and a separate service responsible for covert operations abroad. Those services should be small and efficient, and free from woke critical-theory people who contaminate the professionalism of intelligence. This takes leadership.

The CIA's primary job is to collect and analyze information from around the world, through every means possible, in order to provide unbiased, professional analysis for the president and his designees to make decisions. This is the law.

Most CIA secret intelligence is collected electronically and provided by other governments. Relatively little is from penetration agents or human sources—HUMINT—that the CIA runs on its own. The human intelligence networks that took decades to build, along with their trained and experienced handlers, collapsed in the anti-intelligence hysteria of the mid- and late-1970s and never recovered. CIA relies heavily on foreign governments, which usually provide selective intelligence to further their own purposes. This makes the United States especially vulnerable to covert foreign manipulation.

Of the CIA's roughly 22,000 employees, only about 1,500 are intelligence officers stationed abroad. Most of those intelligence officers are confined to American embassies, with relatively few in the field. Most of the rest are analysts, technicians, administrators essential to keeping the intelligence process running, and an unknown but substantial number of deadweight bureaucrats who serve no useful purpose.

Among the intelligence analysts who study the information collected and synthesize it into reports for decision-makers, there is a tendency to rely so much on open-source intelligence (OSINT)—public material that is freely available to anyone—that many strategic intelligence products read like something out of a think tank or news organization. So in this sense, the CIA employs a large army of analysts simply to read and write about things that anybody can write about. The intelligence community is increasingly committing resources to gather foreign intelligence on politically correct issues like climate change (what insider critics call "bugs and bunnies"), gender, and other matters of little or no value to decision-makers who do not subscribe to woke agendas.

The covert operations side of the CIA is comparatively small. Much of its excellent work is done with no recognition or credit. However, it appears that the agency, like the FBI, is given far too much credit, especially for non-combat operations to influence foreign decision-makers in ways that benefit the United States.

Without a grand strategy to shape America's role in the world, to defend effectively against foreign adversaries and enemies, the United States has no means of deciding what kind of intelligence community it needs, how it should be configured, how its people should be recruited and trained, how its duties should be tasked, and how it should be budgeted.

This lack of American strategic consensus limits a convincing "what to do" plan. As far as politicization and the transitioned culture of the CIA, the strategy should be to cull the agency of anyone involved in the clown show the agency has become before any employees can be considered for transfer to either of the two proposed new and smaller intelligence services. Any office, position, program, contractor, or official responsible for pushing critical theory must go. A new intelligence leadership will need to pull a lot of bureaucratic tricks to cull the deadwood and toxins from the agency.

Policymakers for decades have complained of the uselessness of many CIA intelligence products. CIA's strategic intelligence analysis has been poor for generations. It failed to predict the collapse of the

Soviet Union and the aggressive rise of the Chinese Communist Party. It failed to prepare American leadership to anticipate and confront the rise and spread of jihadist extremism and terrorism. It helped start a senseless war in Iraq by assessing that Saddam Hussein was building an arsenal of weapons of mass destruction. During the Iraq War, it failed to anticipate the rise of jihadism and the empowering of Iran in the region. CIA was one of only two intelligence agencies that could not determine where the Covid-19 pandemic originated. If this is actually true, God help us. Prior to the 2022 Russian invasion of Ukraine, CIA predicted that Moscow would be in control of Kyiv in one to four days.[1]

Intelligence collectors and analysts must be forced to do a better job through harder professional competition, and this means cutting their budgets and positions to weed out all but the most talented, creative, and courageous.

Every single member of the intelligence community who illegally leaks classified information should be investigated, arrested, and prosecuted. Enforcement of secrecy laws is seldom employed against those who leak to the media for personal or policy reasons, even though such leaks cost the American taxpayer billions of dollars, complicate or destroy the CIA's confidential relationships with people from other countries, and aid our adversaries to discern our sources and methods. Leaks allow anonymous intelligence agencies or personnel to contaminate the American news media and therefore public sentiment and debate, constituting threats to the integrity of citizens' political opinions and to the nation's democratic and legal processes.

Strict criminal penalties should apply to former intelligence personnel with access to secrets, including former directors of national intelligence and CIA directors, who leak classified information. Impartial enforcement of existing law will go a long way toward reducing the abuse of secret intelligence for political purposes.

Far too much federal government information is classified for no legitimate reason. Over-classification rewards incompetence and aids politicization because it enables wrongdoers to hide behind "national security" secrecy. If intelligence products are over-classified, they should be un-classified. And if they are unclassified, they are not legitimate products of a legitimate secret intelligence service. (This is different from de-classified, which is secret intelligence whose public release will not compromise sources or methods.)

Analytical products based purely on public or open sources—open-source intelligence, or OSINT in CIA speak—should be removed from the CIA completely, along with the thousands of analysts and bureaucrats who run them. CIA should be out of the business of producing unclassified material, unless the unclassified products are properly sanitized versions of the secret assessments provided to the president and his designees. And CIA should not be in the business of using intelligence resources on issues like the environment and climate change. Thus the CIA, or rather its successor agencies, can eliminate thousands more personnel from its rolls.

Not even the most vital secret intelligence can be trusted if it is compromised by ideological blinders, groupthink, and anything but the most exceptional analytical skills—to say nothing of the contaminating effect of critical theory, both in terms of personnel management and the willful bias that critical theory demands. These compromises are severe.

A president must repeal all the Obama and Biden executive orders that mandated critical theory and cultural Marxism, under whatever names. He must issue executive orders to abolish all intelligence professional and contractor positions that administer, promote, or enforce critical theory or cultural Marxism. Those individuals must not be administratively transferred to other positions. Without another position to go to, they will be compelled to leave the intelligence service.

Their security clearances must be revoked so that they can never work in the classified world again.

All ARG and ERG cell groups in the intelligence services must be banned as unprofessional and as dangerous risks to compartmentation and morale. Intelligence management must identify all personnel in the ARG and ERG cells, isolate them, and transfer them to positions where they can do no harm, or better yet to positions so unsatisfying that they will leave the agency. (It is almost impossible to fire them.) Once they leave the agency, revoke their clearances so they cannot gain other clearance-required jobs in government or private contracting. Require all private contracting companies to remove all critical theory/cultural Marxist personnel and policies if they wish to continue their lucrative intelligence contracts.

Congress must enact laws not only to defund but to make it a crime to use or reprogram any appropriated taxpayer funds to endorse or promote any form of cultural Marxism. The law must also ban any individual or corporation supporting cultural Marxism from receiving a government security clearance and federal intelligence contracts.

This is not a First Amendment–protected issue. Racism, anarchism, fascism, and other forms of extremism are presently grounds for denial of security clearances. Cultural Marxism must be added as another deal-breaker for recruitment of prospective intelligence professionals. Likewise, the intelligence community should disaccredit colleges and universities that act as feeder schools if those institutions deliberately cultivate prospective intelligence professionals in cultural Marxism.

CIA has done an excellent job in certain paramilitary and technological areas, which are beyond the scope of this book. The political correctness and wokeness that have swept the agency will end up damaging or abusing the agency's covert and technical capabilities, and will force the public to question their necessity.

Indeed, it started down that road a generation ago. As many did toward the Soviets, many intelligence managers and analysts mirror-imaged the jihadists after 9/11, meaning that they presumed the world thought as they did and didn't want to become politically incorrect by exploiting adversaries' own cultural taboos. No intelligence service can function with such built-in, and enforced, sociopolitical biases.

As for the FBI, all that applies and more. Especially since the bureau affects the lives of every citizen.

Chapter 37

What to Do with the FBI

With all the talk of "abolishing the FBI," few envision what would happen to our country if we were suddenly left without a federal service to fight interstate crime and child trafficking, conduct effective counterintelligence, and come up with the necessary technology and training for law enforcement and investigators.

A veteran FBI man with an extraordinary career that spanned from J. Edgar Hoover's days, through retirement, and for many more years as a contractor, has the best vantage point of all. Though he stops short of seeking the abolition of the FBI, Thomas J. Baker says the bureau cannot survive in its dual roles as a law enforcement agency and a domestic intelligence service. "The ethics of an intelligence agency is different from a law enforcement agency," he told a reporter. "In a traditional law enforcement agency, agents live every day for the time to come when they get on the witness stand and say nothing but the truth. But an intelligence agency deals with lies and disruption. It's a whole different mindset between the two."[1]

Something has to give. Here is an initial plan to get a national conversation started about what to do with the FBI.

The Federal Bureau of Investigation, as its name states, is only a bureaucracy. It is not a sacred institution. Its brand and mythology are not to be protected at all costs. It is a bureaucratic structure mandated to perform necessary functions to investigate federal crimes, combat foreign spies, and not much more. The FBI has no legal charter. No act of Congress, no law, created the FBI.

The FBI traces its founding to a July 26, 1908, memo by Attorney General Charles J. Bonaparte. The unsigned document is only a page long. Here is the text in full:

> All matters relating to investigations under the Department [of Justice], except those to be made by bank examiners, and in connection with the naturalization service, will be referred to the Chief Examiner for a memorandum as to whether any member of the force of special agents under his direction is available for the work to be performed. No authorization of expenditure for special examinations shall be made by any officer of the Department, without first ascertaining whether one of the regular force is available for the service desired, and, in case the service cannot be performed by the regular force of special agents of the Department, the matter will be specially called to the attention of the Attorney General, or Acting Attorney General, together with a statement from the Chief Examiner as to the reasons why a regular employee cannot be assigned to the work, before authorisation shall be made for the expenditure of any money for this purpose.[2]

That is the entirety of what the FBI calls its founding document. The myth and legend of today's FBI is built on a half-century of hard work and image-making by J. Edgar Hoover, no matter how much the bureau seeks to distance itself from him. Since the FBI was founded with a short memo by an attorney general, it can be dissolved with a short memo from a future attorney general.

When any government structure fails to do its job well, when the people within it fail to live up to the professionalism necessary to enforce the law objectively, and when that bureaucracy loses the public trust necessary to perform its lawful duties, it's time for a change.

The danger of considering an institution "sacred," as some do with the FBI, is that it becomes somehow beyond question, permanent, untouchable—indeed, sacrosanct. The FBI is no more sacred than the Bureau of Alcohol, Tobacco, Firearms and Explosives, or the Bureau of Land Management. But most of its functions are important.

The danger of protecting a brand at all costs is that, when the integrity of that brand has been compromised, the institution resorts to any form of deception and intimidation to protect the façade from even constructive criticism. Director Christopher Wray has filled J. Edgar Hoover's shoes in that regard.

It's time for such a bureaucracy to go. The bureau has become too large, too centralized, too opaque, too politicized, and too duplicative of other agencies to continue.

America needs federal law enforcement. It needs solid counter-espionage and counterintelligence capabilities to combat foreign spies and agents and to neutralize their operations. The country needs strong and professional capabilities against child trafficking, illegal narcotics trafficking, cybercrime, financial crimes, terrorists, and crimes against the federal Constitution. It needs some sort of federal mechanism to help states fight crime in their own jurisdictions.

That doesn't mean the FBI is still the answer. We already have a Drug Enforcement Administration. We have a number of counter-terrorism services. We have a standing cybersecurity organization with police powers. We already have a world-class financial crimes capability in a separate agency. And so on. And we do have many first-rate professionals in the FBI who are genuine public servants. Those professionals still have a role.

The FBI's reversion to a domestic intelligence service with police powers is incompatible with our constitutional form of government. Thomas J. Baker, the FBI veteran mentioned above, saw the entire metamorphosis of the bureau up close as he relates in his book, *The Fall of the FBI: How a Once Great Agency Became a Threat to Democracy.*

Time for FBI to Go the Way of OSS

After World War II, the country reassessed its entire national security structure, abolished certain agencies—even ones that performed with extraordinary success and heroism—and carefully considered something new. It abolished the Department of War, reorganized it, merged it with the Department of the Navy, and created the Department of Defense. It abolished its wartime foreign intelligence bureaucracy, the Office of Strategic Services, and later created an entirely new Central Intelligence Agency—being careful to vet the CIA staff to exclude the Communist Party members who had proliferated in the OSS. And so it's time for the FBI to go the way of the OSS, but without a centralized replacement.

Unfortunately, the realities of the world require our government to have most of the capabilities that the public expects the FBI to perform. To start a national conversation about what to do with the FBI, here is an initial proposal drawn up after years of consideration at the Center for Security Policy. This proposal does not claim to have all the answers. Others have come forward with their own ideas, including a purely domestic security service modeled after Britain's MI5 or Germany's BND. A European-style internal intelligence service is inconsistent with American founding principles and presents substantial opportunity for abuse of power through a new centralized apparat, especially one whose personnel are drawn heavily from the fatally flawed FBI. Even so, we can gain important ideas from careful consideration of the proposals.

What follows is a general blueprint to break up the FBI while preserving important national functions. It recognizes that legal authority, administrative and personnel issues, training, ethos, and so forth are far larger matters that deserve separate consideration. Since the FBI operates with no legal charter and was created by the executive branch and not an act of Congress, it can be dismantled unilaterally by any sitting president.

FBI Structure and What to Do with It

The latest major reorganizations in the George W. Bush and Barack Obama administrations divided the FBI into six major branches, each of which are divided into units called divisions. These branches and divisions are important to understand if we are to figure out what to do with the bureau. The six branches are:

1. National Security Branch
2. Intelligence Branch
3. Criminal, Cyber, Response, and Services Branch
4. Science and Technology Branch
5. Information and Technology Branch
6. Human Resources Branch

All branches perform or support an awkward and unstable combination of law enforcement and domestic intelligence functions that brought us to where we are today.

Let's look at each branch one by one. We can then see what functions complement or duplicate those of other agencies, and transfer those branches or divisions to those respective agencies and to the states, paring down the bureau as we go. The idea is for a quick transfer to eliminate the FBI, dealing with the other agency challenges later, while not creating any new agencies of any kind.

National Security Branch. The National Security Branch is arguably the most politicized and compromised component of the entire FBI. This branch must be broken apart, division by division, with relevant personnel, authority, equipment, and budgets transferred to other agencies and, where desirable, to states.

The National Security Branch contains a Counterintelligence Division, whose most famous chief was Peter Strzok. This division has seldom done well to combat foreign intelligence services in a strategic fashion. It has functioned as a fly-swatting operation, going after low-hanging fruit, not as a strategic tool to penetrate and disrupt hostile intelligence organizations from within. The most high-value FBI victories against deeply penetrated foreign spies generally have come from walk-ins and defectors from foreign intelligence services like the Soviet KGB and GRU and the Russian FSB and SVR as well as GRU, and not from painstaking, long-term counterintelligence penetration work. The personnel evaluation system put in place by Mueller, with its accounting-style box-checking demands and executive financial rewards, disincentivizes strategic counterintelligence work and empowers foreign spies.

The independent Office of the National Counterintelligence Executive, or ONCIX, was created in 2001, before Mueller, to address the problem. Unfortunately, after a promising start under non-FBI counterintelligence professionals, the office, since renamed the National Counterintelligence and Security Center (NCSC), was virtually taken over by Mueller's FBI and neutered as a strategic counterintelligence entity. The FBI Counterintelligence Division has become one of the most politicized elements in the bureau, despite Peter Strzok's departure in disgrace. Here's an interim solution:

- Transfer the FBI Counterintelligence Division to the NCSC under new leadership and a new ethos from outside the bureau, with a limited number of personnel billets to force undesirable FBI personnel out of the transfer. NCSC says its role is to "lead and support the U.S. Government's counterintelligence and security activities,"[3] so the FBI Counterintelligence Division is redundant. This is a dangerous move, though, because the present NCSC is both flaccid and politicized.
- Parcel out the Counterterrorism Division, the Terrorist Screening Center, and related elements of the National Security Branch to the National Counterterrorism Center (NCTC) and remove NCTC from the Office of the Director of National Intelligence into an independent and small counterterrorism agency. NCTC has its own problems that need addressing but is the only logical home for the terrorism-related units of the FBI.
- Move the Weapons of Mass Destruction Directorate of the FBI National Security Branch to the Bureau of Alcohol, Tobacco, Firearms, and Explosives, commonly known as ATF. This is a far from ideal solution given the ATF's own history and ethos, and the ATF itself should be abolished, but for the purposes of dismantling the FBI while keeping important functions, the ATF is a standing

law enforcement body with its own personnel trained in dealing effectively with weapons of mass destruction. ATF can be dealt with later.

These three steps will leave the FBI without a National Security Branch, while keeping the important public functions elsewhere in government. These steps will excise the most toxic branch out of the bureau.

Intelligence Branch. The FBI Intelligence Branch is responsible for the collection of information and its synthesis into analytical products and coordination with other agencies. The fact that the FBI has an entire Intelligence Branch shows that it is no longer a law enforcement agency but, indeed, a mutation of a European-style domestic intelligence apparat with police powers. There are legitimate reasons for different agencies in the federal government to have strong intelligence analysis, but when centralized into a dominant agency or bureau that analysis is subject to groupthink and political abuse. The Intelligence Branch is also opaque and armored against constitutional checks and balances like legislative oversight, which raises a host of problems, including quality control. Interim solution:

- Divide the Intelligence Branch along topical and functional lines and parcel the divisions out to other agencies with the legal authority and obligation to perform those varied work functions. Critics will say that such a move will recreate stovepipes and cause intelligence not to be shared. A positive response is that U.S. intelligence analysis must be competitive among different teams and leaders in order to serve the public interest, and the de-stovepiping of intelligence has not performed as planned. A less rosy rejoinder is that the FBI's domestic

> intelligence analysis record, as with other areas, shows politicization, groupthink, and overall less than stellar quality. The spate of "domestic violent extremists" who turned out to be federal agents or confidential human sources, and the many "known wolves" among terrorists and mass shooters, publicly indicate a fundamental problem that has gone unaddressed for decades.

Criminal, Cyber, Response, and Services Branch. The third branch, Criminal, Cyber, Response, and Services Branch, performs an amalgam of functions patchworked together since 9/11. This is an important branch of the FBI and, though manipulated politically by the Justice Department, is said to be not as politicized as the National Security Branch.

Just as a jerry-rigged patchwork is not an integrated body but is cobbled together from existing parts, this branch can be taken apart carefully without public danger. The Criminal Investigation Division of the branch does the important work of combating organized crime, transnational crime, certain violent crimes, and certain crimes against children, and of investigating public corruption, financial crimes, and violations of civil rights laws. However, the public corruption unit tends to attract the most politicized elements of the FBI. Interim solution:

- Transfer as many criminal investigative functions as possible to the states, with federal block grants to states that wish but cannot afford to perform these functions on their own as their state laws allow.
- Transfer the financial crimes unit to the very capable Securities and Exchange Commission.

- Transfer the remainder of the Criminal Investigation Division to the United States Marshals Service, the nation's oldest law enforcement agency, with few scandals in its history and little politicization. Ensure that the Marshals screen out their inherited FBI public corruption personnel with known records of politicization by limiting the number of billets available to (former) FBI personnel.

The branch's Cyber Division duplicates the functions of other agencies. Interim solution:

- Transfer the Cyber Division's security functions to the Cybersecurity and Infrastructure Security Agency (CISA) and move CISA out of the Department of Homeland Security to become an autonomous agency.
- Transfer the Cyber Division's cyber-intelligence functions and resources to the National Counterintelligence and Security Center (NCSC).
- Transfer the Cyber Division's law enforcement functions and resources to the very competent U.S. Postal Inspection Service.

The Response portion of the branch, called the Critical Incident Response Group, is a crisis management unit that puts the FBI at the center. Interim solution:

- Transfer the Critical Incident Response Group to the Federal Emergency Management Agency (FEMA), which needs a whole new rejuvenation of its own, and to states that seek those resources and responsibilities.

The Services component of the branch assists victims of terrorism and crime. A separate unit, International Operations, coordinates federal law enforcement abroad to investigate transnational crimes and to assist foreign countries in assisting American investigators. Interim solution:

- Transfer Services to other agencies like FEMA and the Department of Health and Human Services, and, with the support of block grants, to any willing state governments and private disaster relief and social counseling organizations, religious charities, and so forth (being careful to issue no contracts or funds to any private organization that facilitates illegal activity, including illegal immigration).
- Transfer experienced International Operations personnel to other agencies that presently perform law enforcement work abroad, or would do so under the proposed changes.

Science and Technology Branch. This small branch creates new scientific and technological methods, products, and training for the rest of the FBI's operations. It provides important support to state and local law enforcement. Its forensic sciences department is responsible for fingerprint, DNA, and other biometric analysis, scientific analysis necessary for criminal investigations, computer forensics, and safe transporting and preservation of evidence and hazardous materials. It also runs the FBI's world-class crime lab, FBI information services, the National Crime Information Center, and technical collection and analysis. Interim solution:

- This branch provides so many important uses nationwide that it should become an autonomous stand-alone center like FEMA, but it should be run by a bipartisan rotating board of state governors or their designees.

Information and Technology Branch. With its principal purpose being to manage FBI information and maintain and upgrade the bureau's information system, this branch can be abolished, with necessary talent and resources transferred to other agencies that assume the above FBI functions.

Human Resources Branch. By this point, all the other FBI branches have been transferred to other agencies. There is no more need for a Human Resources Branch. Interim solutions:

- The branch is the incubator of lax standards and wokeness in the FBI. Most of its staff have become so politicized that they are unsuitable for government service and should not be transferred anywhere.
- The sole exception is the FBI Academy, which sits in this branch. The FBI Academy has the valuable purpose of providing basic training to FBI agent recruits and other types of training. Since it offers almost no national security or counterintelligence training, the academy performs more of a law enforcement training function and should be transferred to the U.S. Marshals Service.

With these transfers, the United States will maintain its necessary federal law enforcement and national security functions without an FBI.

Other Issues

Dividing and scattering the FBI's key functions is easy to propose but very complicated to do. Many of the key problems have to do with personnel: substandard, weak, and bloated management at the top (few if any should be transferred anywhere except out); politicization and unprofessionalism in certain branches and field offices; a training and bureaucratic ethos at odds with the agencies that would inherit FBI functions; and a danger that an influx of FBI management into those agencies would have the opposite of the desired effect without strong and principled leadership.

Material and personnel resource transfers to other agencies should be reduced in size to force the attrition of redundant, non-essential, and substandard personnel at the discretion of the receiving agencies and under aggressive congressional and outside oversight.

As we redistribute and downsize the functions of the FBI central apparat, we face the problem of providing too much power to other agencies, especially elements of the hegemonic Department of Homeland Security bureaucracy. One of the virtues of transferring certain FBI functions to DHS is that it removes them from the hyper-politicized Department of Justice. DHS is a separate matter in itself. It too should be broken apart and abolished like the FBI, but first things first.

And then there is the very serious question of the power of the central government as a whole. Many FBI functions can be given up completely and left up to the states, funded where necessary by federal block grants that permit the states to spend the money as they see fit without federal interference. Block grants permit the states to expand their capabilities while retaining the federalist nature of government.

Like the OSS did in World War II, the FBI has performed extraordinarily valuable functions. It still does. As with the OSS, the FBI has become fatally flawed with personnel unsuitable for, or dangerous to, government service. While one can romanticize the OSS and the FBI, the fact is that neither was ever a "sacred" institution. Neither operated with a congressional charter. The idea of the FBI being sacred smacks of secret police–speak, for it was the Soviet KGB that called itself the "holy of holies."

The Federal Bureau of Investigation is just a bureaucracy and a brand. It must use obfuscation, deception, and intimidation to maintain its luster. It has failed to execute its constitutional potential. It has serially abused its authority and the public trust. It has become too politicized to function legally. It is a rogue organization that resists congressional oversight. And it is populating itself with new, politicized cadres who will make tomorrow's FBI far worse.

The only way to fix the FBI is to take it apart, parcel out the useful functions, and close down the rest. Now it's time for a good national discussion about how to do it.

Conclusion

Big Intel Is Bad Intel

A century ago, when Feliks Dzerzhinsky anointed the embryo of the Frankfurt School that would spread the gospel of DEI, the United States ranked far from first in his mind. America was barely a world power. After almost two years of brutal combat in the Great War, Americans wanted little to do with Europe and its problems and looked inward to build their own country. The United States had no foreign intelligence service. It had no domestic counterintelligence service.

Today, the ghouls of Iron Feliks, the cultural mass murderer Georg Lukács of Bolshevik Hungary's Red Terror, and the garroted Willi Münzenberg haunt the remains of Western civilization to tear down what still stands. Cultural Marxism, critical theory, and the other excreta of the Comintern's Frankfurt School have rotted American society from within. The FBI and CIA, built to defend the nation against subversion, resisted for decades, their human faults notwithstanding, but then fell almost in tandem. They failed completely to defend the nation against an ingeniously insidious Kremlin active measures strategic offensive, both when under Moscow's control and when it developed a life of its own.

Critical theory, the ideological matrix that now dominates the core missions of the FBI and CIA, requires a constant search for enemies, from fellow law-abiding countrymen to American constitutional institutions themselves. Critical theory dispenses with evidence, legal precedent and procedure, and equal justice under law. It cuts down, distorts, and manipulates every aspect of life toward a predetermined objective. It sets citizens against one another. By design its adherents consciously weaponize the law to achieve an ideologically engineered diverse, equitable, and inclusive end state. It causes people and the agencies in which they work to become arbiters of truth. Many of those just following orders are completely unaware, or find it personally expedient to proceed with their jobs.

Diagramming today's American intelligence community without labels might lead an old-school Sovietologist to guess it was an organizational chart of the old KGB, with every imaginable security and intelligence function permeating every corner of society.

And then came the merger with Big Tech, quantum computing, billions of cameras and microphones, and the overwhelmingly ubiquitous Internet of Things. Warnings of abuses, censorship, and illegal spying, brushed off as the apoplectic mania of the hateful and the paranoid, turned out to be true.

A combination of these transformations—the centralization of safely dispersed agencies, domestic intelligence with police powers, the merger with the world's most powerful tech and social media conglomerates, and the internal politicization of totalitarian mindsets among all professional personnel—created the most threatening machinery of human control outside Communist China.

The great institutions designed to protect us against the threat of Soviet Communism, in the end, absorbed and re-weaponized the most subversive Soviet plot ever launched. Even the most courageous G-Men and intelligence professionals caved in or quit. Or caved in *and* quit. Most stayed silent and watched it happen. They still do, just following orders and anticipating their pensions and post-career Big Tech jobs or federal contracting gigs.

During the final writing and fact-checking stages of this book, FBI traitor Robert P. Hanssen died alone in the miserable solitary confinement of his supermax prison cell.[1] He may have been the most destructive spy yet discovered in the FBI. Even though the scope of the damage he caused remains classified, it is difficult to see how Hanssen's crimes could have come close to the far greater and enduring evils of the critical theorists and cultural Marxists who have infiltrated our intelligence community and are on the verge of destroying it from within.

J. Edgar Hoover warned all along that something like this would take place if the citizens remained unaware and complacent. His track record was unmatched, and his name was reviled for it.

As today's cancel-culture FBI plans to erase Hoover's name from its planned megaplex headquarters while preserving Hoover's positive fictions about fidelity, bravery, and integrity, today's CIA lies to itself and to the public that Wild Bill Donovan was all about diversity, equity, and inclusion. The protectors of America's secrets, defenders of the nation's integrity, have become infiltrated with an ideology created from a century-old Kremlin active measures campaign. Implementing that ideology is part of their core mission now. They embrace it. They celebrate it. They are enforcing it.

We still have time to stop them.

Further Reading

Of the countless books on the CIA and FBI, many of my favorites are by authors with whom I disagree philosophically. Their research is impeccable, their approach sincere. They made me think.

Two contrarian histories rank among the most important works ever written on the subjects. Tim Weiner created two masterpieces after years of intensive original research, based entirely on primary sources, with no anonymous or secondary sources. Those works are *Legacy of Ashes: The History of the CIA* (Anchor, 2007) and *Enemies: A History of the FBI* (Random House, 2012).

Autobiographies and personal memoirs are always important but often self-serving, so none have made the cut even though many are priceless.

Some of the best biographies of the early American intelligence leaders are *Wild Bill Donovan: The Spymaster Who Created the OSS and Modern American Espionage* (Free Press, 2011) and *Disciples: The*

World War II Missions of the CIA Directors Who Fought for Wild Bill Donovan (Simon & Schuster, 2015), both by Douglas Waller. Two especially fine and very different biographies of the great Allen Dulles stand out. They are Peter Grosse's *Gentleman Spy: The Life of Allen Dulles* (Houghton Mifflin, 1994) and *Allen Dulles: Master of Spies*, by James Srodes (Regnery Publishing, 1999). Another indispensable biography, which spans the whole of World War II and the Cold War, is Joe Persico's *Casey: The Lives and Secrets of William J. Casey: From the OSS to the CIA* (Viking, 1990).

J. Edgar Hoover lived large as one of the most influential, controversial, and yes, popular Americans of the twentieth century. Many excellent and terrible biographies exist of the giant who built the FBI. My favorite excellent ones are wildly different from one another: *Young J. Edgar: Hoover, the Red Scare, and the Assault on Civil Liberties*, by Kenneth D. Ackerman (Avalon, 2007); Beverly Gage's colossal, eight-hundred-page, definitive *G-Man: J. Edgar Hoover and the Making of the American Century* (Viking, 2022); and one by Ralph de Toledano, who knew the FBI chief well and who much later took me under his wing, *J. Edgar Hoover: The Man in His Time* (Arlington House, 1973).

From a big-picture standpoint is the philosophical, strategically minded, and eternally valuable *Informing Statecraft: Intelligence for a New Century* (Free Press, 1992) by the incomparable, recently deceased Angelo Codevilla.

For a larger look at the effects of the Comintern's Frankfurt School and critical theory on our military, institutions, and society, I recommend *Irresistible Revolution: Marxism's Goal of Conquest & the Unmaking of the American Military* (2021) by Matthew Lohmeier, an officer purged from the very woke United States Space Force; former CIA analyst Stella Morabito's *The Weaponization of Loneliness: How Tyrants Stoke Our Fear of Isolation to Silence, Divide, and Conquer*

(Bombardier, 2022); and, for a vibrant overview, Michael Walsh, *The Devil's Pleasure Palace: The Cult of Critical Theory and the Subversion of the West* (Encounter, 2015).

About the Author

J. Michael Waller is senior analyst for strategy at the Center for Security Policy in Washington, D.C., and president of Georgetown Research, a private research company. He holds a Ph.D. in international security affairs from the University Professors Program at Boston University, where he received the University Professors Award for best dissertation and later received the University Professors Alumni Award. During and after the Soviet collapse from 1991–1994, he worked with human rights activists and lawmakers in Moscow to uproot and expose the KGB. It was in the course of his work in Moscow that he researched his dissertation, *The KGB and Its Successors Under Gorbachev and Yeltsin* (1993), a version of which was published as *Secret Empire: The KGB in Russia Today* (Westview, 1994).

For thirteen years, Dr. Waller was the Walter and Leonore Annenberg Professor of International Communication at the Institute of World Politics, where he developed and taught the only graduate program in the United States on political and psychological warfare. During the wars in Afghanistan, Iraq, and elsewhere, he was briefer and lecturer in psychological operations and information operations at the Naval Postgraduate School for the Army. He was an instructor for the 4th Psychological Operations Group (Airborne), for which he designed and taught the military's first forty-hour course in divisive operations. For years he has guest-taught at the John F. Kennedy Special Warfare Center and School at Fort Bragg.

Dr. Waller has lectured at the FBI Academy at Quantico, the National Intelligence University, National Defense University, Marine Corps University, and other intelligence schools and military commands. He helped develop a counter-jihadist training program for the FBI, for which he received a written citation for extraordinary service from FBI director Robert J. Mueller III.

He is a former congressional staffer, a former journalist, and a current feature and opinion writer. He has been published in American Greatness, The American Mind, the *American Spectator*, The Daily Beast, The Federalist, *Forbes*, *Investor's Business Daily*, *Military Review*, *National Review*, the *New York Times*, *Reader's Digest*, *USA Today*, the *Washington Times*, and the *Wall Street Journal*.

Notes

Epigraph

1. Benjamin Franklin, Letter to the Abbés Chalut and Arnoux, April 17, 1787.
2. Fulton J. Sheen, *Communism and the Conscience of the West* (Indianapolis: Bobbs-Merrill, 1948), 15.

Introduction

1. Robert S. Mueller III, *Report on the Investigation into Russian Interference in the 2016 Presidential Election* (Washington, D.C.: U.S. Department of Justice, 2019), https://www.justice.gov/archives/sco/file/1373816/download.
2. John H. Durham, *Report on Matters Related to Intelligence Activities and Investigations Arising Out of the 2016 Presidential Campaigns* (Washington, D.C.: U.S. Department of Justice, 2019), https://www.justice.gov/storage/durhamreport.pdf.
3. Ibid.; Kimberley A. Strassel, "Durham on Comey's Culpability," *Wall Street Journal*, May 18, 2023, https://www.wsj.com/articles/durham-on-comeys-culpability-fbi-russia-trump-dossier-intelligence-c4db4462.
4. Diana West, *The Red Thread* (Washington, D.C.: Center for Security Policy Press, 2019).

Chapter 2

1. See my further reporting on Representative Barbara Lee here: J. Michael Waller, "'I Was Known as Comrade Barbara.' Now, Congresswoman Barbara Lee Controls the State Department Budget," Center for Security Policy, January 26, 2021, https://centerforsecuritypolicy.org/comrade-barbara-lee/.
2. "Ana Montes: Cuban Spy," FBI, https://www.fbi.gov/history/famous-cases/ana-montes-cuba-spy.

Chapter 3

1. Here is the FBI history account of Hanssen: "Robert Hanssen," FBI, https://www.fbi.gov/history/famous-cases/robert-hanssen.
2. Louis J. Freeh, *My FBI: Bringing Down the Mafia, Investigating Bill Clinton, and Fighting the War on Terror* (New York: St. Martin's Griffin, 2005), 241.

Chapter 4

1. Leon Trotsky, *My Life* (1930), chapter XXII, available online at https://www.marxists.org/archive/trotsky/1930/mylife/ch22.htm.
2. See Kenneth D. Ackerman, *Trotsky in New York, 1917: A Radical on the Eve of Revolution* (Berkeley, California: Counterpoint, 2016), and excerpts by Linda Tenenbaum, "*Trotsky in New York, 1917: A Radical on the Eve of Revolution*, by Kenneth D. Ackerman," World Socialist Website, October 8, 2016, https://www.wsws.org/en/articles/2016/10/08/trot-008.html.
3. "Zimmermann Telegram (1917)," National Archives, https://www.archives.gov/milestone-documents/zimmermann-telegram.
4. For Trotsky's reaction to the Zimmermann telegram, see Ackerman, *Trotsky in New York*, 150–55.
5. Ibid.

Chapter 5

1. For the most authoritative history, see John J. Dziak, *Chekisty: A History of the KGB* (Lexington Books, 1987).
2. Beverly Gage, *G-Man: J. Edgar Hoover and the Making of the American Century* (New York: Viking, 2022), 3.
3. Ibid., 12–13.
4. Tim Weiner, *Enemies: A History of the FBI* (New York: Random House, 2012), 3.

5. House of Representatives, *Hearings Before the Committee on the Judiciary*, 66th Congress (Washington, D.C.: Government Printing Office, 1919), 44.
6. "Palmer Raids," FBI, https://www.fbi.gov/history/famous-cases/palmer-raids.
7. Kenneth D. Ackerman, *Young J. Edgar: Hoover, the Red Scare, and the Assault on Civil Liberties* (New York: Carroll & Graf, 2007), 155–63.
8. "Manifesto of the Left Wing Section of the Socialist Party of New York City," Exhibit I in testimony of Attorney General A. Mitchell Palmer, *Hearings before the Committee on the Judiciary*, House of Representatives, 66th Congress, 2nd Session, Serial 16, February 4 and 6, 1920, 57; J. E. Hoover, "Status of the Communist Party Under the Act of Congress Approved October 6, 1918," Exhibit K.
9. "Palmer Raids."

Chapter 6

1. Karl Marx, "Marx to Ruge," originally published in *Deutsch-Franzöische Jahrbücher* (1844), written September 1843, Marxists.org, https://www.marxists.org/archive/marx/works/1843/letters/43_09.htm; Karl Marx, "Letter from Marx to Arnold Ruge," originally published in *Deutsch-Franzöische Jahrbücher* (1844), written September 1843, Marxists.org, https://www.marxists.org/archive/marx/works/1843/letters/43_09-alt.htm.
2. Karl Marx, "Introduction," from *A Contribution to the Critique of Hegel's Philosophy of Right*, originally published in *Deutsch-Franzöische Jahrbücher* (1844), written 1843, Marxists.org, https://www.marxists.org/archive/marx/works/1843/critique-hpr/intro.htm.
3. James Bohman, "Critical Theory," Stanford Encyclopedia of Philosophy, 2005, https://plato.stanford.edu/entries/critical-theory/.
4. "critical theory," *Encyclopedia Britannica* (online edition), last updated August 18, 2023, https://www.britannica.com/topic/critical-theory.
5. J. Edgar Hoover, as compiled in James D. Bales, ed., *J. Edgar Hoover Speaks Concerning Communism* (Washington, D.C.: Capitol Hill Press, 1970), 267–268.
6. Ibid., 268.
7. Ibid.
8. Linda Tenenbaum, "*Trotsky in New York, 1917: A Radical on the Eve of* Revolution, by Kenneth D. Ackerman," Word Socialist Website, October 8, 2016, https://www.wsws.org/en/articles/2016/10/08/trot-o08.html.

9. Douglas Waller, *Wild Bill Donovan: The Spymaster Who Created the OSS and Modern American Espionage* (New York: Free Press, 2011), 34.
10. Sean McMeekin, *The Red Millionaire: A Political Biography of Willi Münzenberg, Moscow's Secret Propaganda Tsar in the West* (New Haven, Connecticut: Yale University Press, 1989).
11. For the authoritative work on Operation Trust, see Pamela K. Simpkins and K. Leigh Dyer, eds., *The Trust* (Arlington, Virginia: Central Intelligence Agency, reprinted by the Security and Intelligence Foundation, 1989).
12. Feliks Dzerzhinsky, "Pamyatka sotrudiikam' ChK," Cheka staff memorandum, 1918, in author's collection.
13. Ralph de Toledano, *Cry Havoc: The Great American Bring-down and How It Happened* (Washington, D.C.: Anthem Books, 2006), 26.
14. Ibid., 13. De Toledano converted from socialism to American conservatism after covering the Alger Hiss trial as a journalist. He became assistant Washington bureau chief of *Newsweek* and a prolific author, syndicated columnist, and historian. He earned lifelong enemies for his role in publicizing Hiss's treason and for developing friendships with Whittaker Chambers, Richard Nixon, and J. Edgar Hoover. His journalistic track record has withstood historical scrutiny. In his last work, *Cry Havoc* (2006), many of his original and most important sources are cited not in the text but, as with Ruth Fischer, in a bibliographical summary. De Toledano mentored the author in the early 1980s and told him of the Frankfurt School.
15. De Toledano, *Cry Havoc*, 31.
16. Stephen Koch, *Double Lives: Spies and Writers in the Soviet Secret War of Ideas against the West* (New York: Free Press, 1994), 205–36. Koch's lively account is especially valuable because he was able to interview Münzenberg's widow, Babette Gross, in the course of his research.

Chapter 7

1. As cited by Tim Weiner, *Enemies: A History of the FBI* (New York: Random House, 2012), 58–59.
2. "The FBI and the American Gangster, 1924–1938," FBI, https://www.fbi.gov/history/brief-history/the-fbi-and-the-american-gangster.
3. Ibid.
4. Weiner, *Enemies*, 58.
5. "The FBI and the American Gangster."
6. As cited by Weiner, *Enemies*, 59.

7. Douglas Waller, *Wild Bill Donovan: The Spymaster Who Created the OSS and Modern American Espionage* (New York: Free Press, 2011), 39–40.
8. *The Identification Division of the FBI* (Washington, D.C.: National Institute of Justice, 1981), https://www.ojp.gov/pdffiles1/Digitization/78671NCJRS.pdf, 5.
9. Sydney Mahan, "84 Years Ago Today, the FBI's Crime Lab Opened in DC," *Washingtonian*, November 24, 2016, https://www.washingtonian.com/2016/11/24/the-fbi-opened-its-crime-lab-here-in-dc-back-in-1932/.
10. "Ruth Fischer: A Life for and against Communism, 1895–1961," Wilson Center, March 24, 2011, https://www.wilsoncenter.org/event/ruth-fischer-life-for-and-against-communism-1895-1961.
11. Gary Bullert, "The Frankfurt School in America: A Transatlantic Odyssey from Exile to Acclaim," *Journal of Social, Political, and Economic Studies* (March 22, 2011), https://www.thefreelibrary.com/The+Frankfurt+School+demythologized%3F-a0251631883.
12. John Simkin, "Julian Gumperz," Spartacus Educational, September 1997, https://spartacus-educational.com/Julian_Gumperz.htm.
13. Tyler Brandt and John Miltimore, "Herbert Marcuse: The Philosopher behind the Ideology of Antifa," Foundation for Economic Education, February 1, 2019, https://fee.org/articles/herbert-marcuse-the-philosopher-behind-the-ideology-of-the-anti-fascists/.
14. Mark Bray, *Antifa: The Anti-Fascist Handbook* (New York: Melville House, 2017), 19–20.
15. Ibid., 20.
16. Ibid., 20–21.
17. Ibid., 24.
18. Kyle Shideler, Testimony Before the Judiciary Committee, Subcommittee on the Constitution, Center for Security Policy, August 4, 2020, https://www.centerforsecuritypolicy.org/wp-content/uploads/2020/09/Shideler-Testimony-Senate-Constitution-Subcommittee-080420202.pdf.

Chapter 8

1. Angelo M. Codevilla, "The Rise of Political Correctness," *Claremont Review of Books* 16, no. 4 (fall 2016), https://claremontreviewofbooks.com/the-rise-of-political-correctness/.
2. For the best short analysis of Machiavelli's influence on Gramsci, see ibid.
3. Antonio Gramsci, "Audacia e Fede" in *Avanti!*, 1915, translated and cited by Joseph V. Femia in Gramsci's *Political Thought: Hegemony,*

Consciousness, and the Revolutionary Process (Oxford: Clarendon Press, 1981), 88.

4. James Martin, "Antonio Gramsci," *Stanford Encyclopedia of Philosophy* (online edition), 2023, https://plato.stanford.edu/entries/gramsci/.
5. More than a thousand Comintern agents or assets became Catholic seminarians in the United States at that time, according to former Communist operative Bella Dodd's testimony, "Investigation of Communist Activities in the Columbus, Ohio, Area and the Philadelphia Area," hearings before the House Committee on Un-American Activities, 83rd Congress, 1st Session, June 17–18, 1953.
6. Herbert Marcuse, *Reason and Revolution: Hegel and the Rise of Social Theory*, reprint edition (Oxford, England: Oxford University Press, 1941; Boston: Beacon Press, 1969), frontispiece.
7. Allen Weinstein and Alexander Vassiliev, *The Haunted Wood: Soviet Espionage in America—The Stalin Era* (New York: Modern Library, 1999), 3–21.
8. Samuel Needham, "Tillich's Theological Influence on H. Richard Niebuhr (1894–1962)," Paul Tillich Resources, https://people.bu.edu/wwildman/tillich/resources/influence_niebuhrhr.htm.

Chapter 9

1. Willi Münzenberg to Ruth Fischer in Moscow, as Fischer related to Ralph de Toledano. See de Toledano, *Cry Havoc: The Great American Bring-down and How It Happened* (Washington, D.C.: Anthem Books, 2006), 27.
2. The FBI's official history colorfully describes the situation this way: "At the start of the decade, the public enemies were almost entirely homegrown—from 'Scarface' to 'Baby Face.' The next wave of villains would come primarily from afar, and they were in many respects bigger and badder still. They were hyper-aggressive fascist dictators, fanatical militarists, and revolution-exporting communists—along with their legions of spies, saboteurs, and subversive agents—who sought to invade, infiltrate, or even conquer entire swaths of territory, if not the world. They threatened not only the fate of peoples and nations, but the survival of democracy itself." "World War, Cold War, 1939–1953," FBI, https://www.fbi.gov/history/brief-history/world-war-cold-war.
3. "World War, Cold War, 1939–1953."

4. Jack Goldsmith, "How J. Edgar Hoover Went from Hero to Villain," *The Atlantic*, November 22, 2022, https://www.theatlantic.com/magazine/archive/2022/12/j-edgar-hoover-fbi-influence/671900/.
5. Beverly Gage, *G-Man: J. Edgar Hoover and the Making of the American Century* (New York: Viking, 2022), 285.
6. Goldsmith, "How J. Edgar Hoover Went from Hero to Villain."
7. Gary Bullert, "The Frankfurt School in American: A Transatlantic Odyssey from Exile to Acclaim," *Journal of Social, Political, and Economic Studies* (March 22, 2011), https://www.thefreelibrary.com/The+Frankfurt+School+demythologized%3F-a0251631883.
8. John Dewey, "Impressions of Soviet Russia," *New Republic*, November 20, 1928, https://newrepublic.com/article/104706/impressions-soviet-russia.
9. Alice Widener, *Teachers of Destruction: Their Plans for a Socialist Revolution—An Eyewitness Account* (Washington, D.C.: Citizens' Evaluation Institute, 1970), 189–90.
10. Willi Münzenberg to Ruth Fischer in Moscow, as Fischer related to Ralph de Toledano. *Cry Havoc*, 27.
11. Maurice Isserman, "When New York City Was the Capital of American Communism," *New York Times*, October 20, 2017, https://www.nytimes.com/2017/10/20/opinion/new-york-american-communism.html.
12. J. Peters, *A Manual on Organisation* (New York: Workers Library Publishers, 1935), Chapter 4, "Party Membership and Cadres," available at Marxists.org, https://www.marxists.org/history/usa/parties/cpusa/1935/07/organisers-manual/ch04.htm.
13. House Committee on Un-American Activities, *The National Lawyers Guild: Legal Bulwark of the Communist Party*, House Report No. 123, September 21, 1950, https://archive.org/stream/reportonnational1950unit/reportonnational1950unit_djvu.txt
14. Franklin D. Roosevelt, "Statement Placing the Federal Bureau of Investigation in Charge of Espionage Investigation," The American Presidency Project, University of California, Santa Barbara, https://www.presidency.ucsb.edu/documents/statement-placing-the-federal-bureau-investigation-charge-espionage-investigation.
15. Earl Browder, *The Second Imperialist War* (New York: International Publishers, 1940), available online at https://www.marxists.org/archive/browder/second-imperialist-war/index.htm.

16. J. Edgar Hoover, "Address before the New York Federation of Women's Clubs, New York, New York, May 3, 1940," in J. Edgar Hoover, ed., *On Communism* (New York: Random House, 1969), 102.
17. J. Edgar Hoover, "Remarks delivered at the Annual American Day Program of the American Legion, Arlington County, Virginia, April 26, 1940," in *On Communism*, 115–16.
18. Ibid.
19. J. Edgar Hoover, "Address before the Drake University Commencement Exercises, Des Moines, Iowa, June 3, 1940," in *On Communism*, 99.
20. De Toledano, *Cry Havoc*, 23.
21. Sean McMeekin, *The Red Millionaire: A Political Biography of Willi Münzenberg, Moscow's Secret Propaganda Tsar in the West* (New Haven, Connecticut: Yale University Press, 2003).
22. John Simkin, "Willi Münzenberg," Spartacus Educational, September 1997, https://spartacus-educational.com/GERmunzenberg.htm.

Part II

1. Robert Hayden Alcorn, *No Bugles for Spies* (New York: David McCay, 1962), 134.

Chapter 10

1. Tim Weiner, *Enemies: A History of the FBI* (New York: Random House, 2012), 106.
2. Beverly Gage, *G-Man: J. Edgar Hoover and the Making of the American Century* (New York: Viking, 2022), 286–87.
3. Erik Ofgang, "The CIA Wanted the Best and the Brightest. They Found Them at Yale," CT Insider, September 29, 2020, https://www.ctinsider.com/connecticutmagazine/news-people/article/The-CIA-wanted-the-best-and-the-brightest-They-17045591.php.
4. Weiner, *Enemies*, 106.
5. M. Stanton Evans and Herbert Romerstein, *Stalin's Secret Agents: The Subversion of Roosevelt's Government* (New York: Threshold Editions, 2012), 92–93. Also see Robert Whymant's sympathetic account, *Stalin's Spy: Richard Sorge and the Tokyo Espionage Ring* (New York: St. Martin's Press, 1996).
6. Evans and Romerstein, *Stalin's Secret Agents*, 89–98.
7. Ibid., 93–98.
8. Ibid., 250.

9. Ibid., 93–94.

Chapter 11

1. See his memoir, William Stevenson, *A Man Called Intrepid: The Secret War* (New York: Harcourt, 1976).
2. Ralph de Toledano, *Cry Havoc: The Great American Bring-down and How It Happened* (Washington, D.C.: Anthem Books, 2006), 124.
3. Ibid., 125.
4. John D. Wilson, "At Work with Donovan: One Man's History in OSS," CIA, https://www.cia.gov/static/8d638ba59d6abe97d6ae4d23efbbc8b0/At-Work-with-Donovan.pdf, 72.
5. Douglas Waller, *Wild Bill Donovan: The Spymaster Who Created the OSS and Modern American Espionage* (New York: Free Press, 2011), 55.
6. Communist Party USA membership remained strong after the Hitler-Stalin pact, as historian John Haynes noted from official data. See John Haynes, "CPUSA Loss of Membership after the Nazi-Soviet Pact," H-HOAC, April 17, 2019, https://networks.h-net.org/node/6077/discussions/4021026/cpusa-loss-membership-after-nazi-soviet-pact; Harvey Klehr, "American Reds, Soviet Stooges," *New York Times*, July 3, 2017, https://www.nytimes.com/2017/07/03/opinion/communist-party-usa-soviet-union.html.
7. Nellie H. Ohr, "Stalin's Russia by Chris Ward," *Russian History* 22, no. 3 (fall 1995): 324–26, cited in Diana West, *The Red Thread: A Search for Ideological Drivers inside the Anti-Trump Conspiracy* (Washington, D.C.: Center for Security Policy, 2020), 9–10.
8. Jonathan S. Gould, *German Anti-Nazi Espionage in the Second World War: The OSS and the Men of the TOOL Missions* (Oxfordshire, United Kingdom: Taylor and Francis, 2020).
9. Herbert Romerstein and Eric Breindel, *The Venona Secrets: Exposing Soviet Espionage and America's Traitors* (Washington, D.C.: Regnery Publishing, 2000), 300.
10. As a University of Oklahoma professor in the 1930s and early '40s, Halperin came under suspicion of being a Communist, at which point the OSS recruited him. When he died in 1995, the *New York Times* published a sympathetic obituary describing him as a "scholar." James C. McKinley Jr., "Maurice Halperin, 88, a Scholar Who Chronicled Castro's Career," *New York Times*, February 12, 1995, https://www.nytimes.com/1995/02/12/obituaries/maurice-halperin-88-a-scholar-who-chronicled-castro-s-career.html.

11. Allen Weinstein and Alexander Vassiliev, *The Haunted Wood: Soviet Espionage in America—The Stalin Era* (New York: Modern Library, 1999), 246.
12. Harvey Klehr and John Earl Haynes, *Venona: Decoding Soviet Espionage in America* (New Haven, Connecticut: Yale University Press, 2000).
13. J. Edgar Hoover, "Address at Annual Commencement Exercises, Holy Cross College, Worcester, Massachusetts, June 29, 1944," in J. Edgar Hoover, ed., *On Communism* (New York: Random House, 1969), 106.
14. Romerstein and Breindel, *The Venona Secrets*, 288–90.
15. Ibid., 283.
16. Hayden Peake, compiler, "Intelligence Officer's Bookshelf," *Studies in Intelligence* 58, no. 1 (March 2014), summarizing Raffaele Laudani, ed., *Secret Reports on Nazi Germany: The Frankfurt School Contribution to the War Effort* (Princeton, New Jersey: Princeton University Press, 2013), https://www.cia.gov/static/0b40310d227db6f2cb1d5b372f58e0e0/Intel-Officers-Bookshelf-58.1.pdf.
17. Romerstein and Breindel, *The Venona Secrets*, 285–86.
18. Ibid.
19. "Comintern Apparatus Summary Report," Investigation of Un-American Propaganda Activities in the United States (*Hearings Regarding Thomas Babin*), U.S. House of Representatives, Committee on Un-American Activities, 81st Congress, 1st Session, May 27 and July 6, 1949, cited in Klehr and Haynes, *Venona*. The Venona cables relating to Babin appear in Appendix A of *Venona*.
20. Klehr and Haynes, *Venona*.
21. Ibid.
22. Ibid.
23. Waller, *Wild Bill Donovan*, 224–25.
24. Former Soviet KGB officer Oleg Gordievsky, who defected to the United Kingdom, recalled a briefing twenty years earlier by the wartime chief of Soviet illegals in the United States, Iskhak Akhmerov, who allegedly handled Hopkins and had called him "the most important of all Soviet wartime agents in the United States." See Christopher Andrew and Oleg Gordievsky, *KGB: The Inside Story of Its Foreign Operations from Lenin to Gorbachev* (New York: HarperCollins, 1990). Herbert Romerstein and Eric Breindel identified Hopkins by deduction as a Soviet agent with the cryptonym "19" in *The Venona Secrets* (Regnery Publishing, 2000). Scholars Harvey Klehr and John Earl Haynes dispute the quality of the evidence and analysis of Andrew,

Gordievsky, Romerstein, Breindel, and another respected scholar, and conclude that "19" was State Department official Laurence Duggan. Additionally, Klehr and Haynes had access to later information from KGB notebooks and archives, which they detail with Alexander Vassiliev in *Spies: The Rise and Fall of the KGB in America* (New Haven, Connecticut: Yale University Press, 2009). For their critiques, see Harvey Klehr and John Earl Haynes, "Harry Hopkins and Soviet Espionage," *Intelligence and National Security* 29, no. 6 (2014): 864–79, https://www.tandfonline.com/doi/abs/10.1080/02684527.2014.913403; and John Earl Haynes and Harvey Klehr, "Was Harry Hopkins a Soviet Spy?," FrontPage Magazine, August 15, 2013, https://www.frontpagemag.com/was-harry-hopkins-soviet-spy-john-earl-haynes/.

25. Waller, *Wild Bill Donovan*, 225.

Chapter 12

1. *The Office of Strategic Services: America's First Intelligence Service*, CIA, May 2000, https://www.cia.gov/static/7851e16f9e100b6f9cc4ef002028ce2f/Office-of-Strategic-Services.pdf.
2. See Giles Milton, *Churchill's Ministry of Ungentlemanly Warfare: The Mavericks Who Plotted Hitler's Defeat* (New York: Picador, 2017).
3. John D. Wilson, "At Work with Donovan," CIA, https://www.cia.gov/static/8d638ba59d6abe97d6ae4d23efbbc8b0/At-Work-with-Donovan.pdf.
4. Richard Helms very kindly hosted me at his home years ago to inspire me firsthand about strategic intelligence. He told me of his prewar interview with Hitler, but he never said a word about his time in the OSS.
5. James Srodes, *Allen Dulles: Master of Spies* (Washington, D.C.: Regnery Publishing, 1999), offers a most extensive biography.
6. I am grateful to the late Bill Colby for walking me through his experiences at the OSS and CIA. I traveled with him to Russia in the early 1990s to help Russian lawmakers set up a Church Committee–style inquisition of the former KGB. Our attempt was cut short after President Boris Yeltsin attacked the Russian parliament in 1993, incinerating the intelligence oversight library that a group of us had created for the Human Rights Committee of the State Duma. Some of our work is referenced in *Demokratizatsiya: The Journal of Post-Soviet Democratization*, now published by the George Washington University.

7. The best biography to date of Casey is Joseph E. Persico, *Casey: The Lives and Secrets of William J. Casey: From the OSS to the CIA* (New York: Viking, 1990).
8. Late in life, toward the Cold War's end, de Toledano taught the author, as a college student, the influence of the Frankfurt School on American intellectual and strategic thought. He warned of the damage it would cause American culture, politics, law, and national security.
9. *The Office of Strategic Services: America's First Intelligence Service.*
10. Ibid.
11. Herbert Romerstein and Eric Breindel, *The Venona Secrets: Exposing Soviet Espionage and America's Traitors* (Washington, D.C.: Regnery Publishing, 2000), 293–94.
12. Ibid., 291–92.
13. *Underground Soviet Espionage Organization (NKVD) in Agencies of the United States Government*, FBI report, October 21, 1946, 163.
14. John H. Waller, *The Unseen War in Europe* (London: Tauris, 1996), 359.

Chapter 13

1. Harvey Klehr, John Earl Haynes, and Fridrikh Igorevich Firsov, *The Secret World of American Communism* (New Haven, Connecticut: Yale University Press, 1995), 259–86.
2. See Doug Waller, *Wild Bill Donovan: The Spymaster Who Created the OSS and Modern American Espionage* (New York: Free Press, 2011), 94.
3. Ibid.
4. Ibid.
5. Donovan testimony, 179, 182, cited in Harvey Klehr and John Earl Haynes, *Venona: Decoding Soviet Espionage in America* (New Haven, Connecticut: Yale University Press, 2000).
6. Herbert Romerstein and Eric Breindel, *The Venona Secrets: Exposing Soviet Espionage and America's Traitors* (Washington, D.C.: Regnery Publishing, 2000), 289–90.
7. Klehr and Haynes, *Venona.*
8. Ibid.
9. Ralph de Toledano, *Cry Havoc: The Great American Bring-down and How It Happened* (Washington, D.C.: Anthem Books, 2006), 125.
10. Ralph de Toledano, *Spies, Dupes, and Diplomats* (New York: Duell, Sloan and Pearce/Little, Brown and Company, 1952).
11. De Toledano, *Cry Havoc*, 125.

12. "Testimony of Elizabeth T. Bentley," Hearings Regarding Communist Espionage in the United States Government, Committee on Un-American Activities, House of Representatives, 80th Congress, 2nd session, 1948, 727.
13. John D. Wilson, "At Work with Donovan: One Man's History in OSS," CIA, https://www.cia.gov/static/8d638ba59d6abe97d6ae4d23efbbc8b0/At-Work-with-Donovan.pdf.
14. James Srodes, *Allen Dulles: Master of Spies* (Washington, D.C.: Regnery Publishing, 2000), 143.

Part III

1. "Longhand Note of President Harry S. Truman, May 12, 1945," Truman Library, National Archives, https://www.trumanlibrary.gov/library/truman-papers/longhand-notes-presidential-file-1944-1953/may-12-1945.

Chapter 14

1. John D. Wilson, "At Work with Donovan: One Man's History in OSS," CIA, https://www.cia.gov/static/8d638ba59d6abe97d6ae4d23efbbc8b0/At-Work-with-Donovan.pdf, 76.
2. Harvey Klehr and John Earl Haynes, *Venona: Decoding Soviet Espionage in America* (New Haven, Connecticut: Yale University Press, 2000), 181–82.
3. Herbert Romerstein and Eric Breindel, *The Venona Secrets: Exposing Soviet Espionage and America's Traitors* (Washington, D.C.: Regnery Publishing, 2000), 207.
4. Klehr and Haynes, *Venona*, 182.
5. Elizabeth Bentley, *Out of Bondage: The Story of Elizabeth Bentley*, reprint edition (New York: Ivy Books, 1988), 111.
6. Romerstein and Breindel, *The Venona Secrets*, 298, footnote 49.
7. Hede Massing, *This Deception* (New York: Duell, Sloan, and Pearce, 1951).
8. See M. Stanton Evans, *Blacklisted by History: The Untold Story of Senator Joe McCarthy* (New York: Three Rivers Press, 2007).

Chapter 15

1. Richard Helms, as told to Tim Weiner, *Legacy of Ashes: The History of the CIA* (New York: Anchor Books, 2008), 8.
2. J. Edgar Hoover, "How to Fight Communism," *Newsweek*, June 9, 1947, cited in Herman O. Bly, *Communism, the Cold War and the FBI Connection:*

Time to Set the Record Straight (Huntington House Publishers, 1998), 101–2.

Chapter 16

1. Georg Lukács, "Preface," The Theory of the Novel, translated from the German by Anna Bostock (London: Merlin Press, 1971), 10. Others have translated Lukács's question as, "Who will save us from Western culture?"
2. Angelo M. Codevilla, "The Rise of Political Correctness," Independent Institute, November 28, 2016, https://www.independent.org/publications/article.asp?id=8932.
3. Ibid.
4. "The Long Telegram [original], from George Kennan in Moscow to the Secretary of State, February 22, 1946," National Security Archive, https://nsarchive.gwu.edu/document/21042-long-telegram-original.
5. J. Edgar Hoover, "Lecture Prepared for Delivery at the Conference of Methodist Ministers, Garrett Institute, Evanston, Illinois, November 26, 1947," excerpted in J. Edgar Hoover, ed., *On Communism* (New York: Random House, 1969), 91.
6. J. Edgar Hoover, "The Communists Are After Our Minds," *The American Magazine*, October 1954, reprinted in *On Communism*, 106–7.
7. Art Swift, "Gallup Vault: J. Edgar Hoover, the FBI and American Communists," Gallup, May 10, 2017, https://news.gallup.com/vault/210107/gallup-vault-edgar-hoover-fbi-american-communists.aspx.
8. Herbert Marcuse, *One-Dimensional Man: Studies in the Ideology of Advanced Industrial Society* (Boston: Beacon Press, 1964).
9. Herbert Marcuse, "Repressive Tolerance," in Robert Paul Wolff, Barrington Moore Jr., and Herbert Marcuse, *A Critique of Pure Tolerance* (Boston: Beacon Press, 1969), 109.
10. Ibid., 110–13. The author acknowledges Jonathan Butcher and Mike Gonzalez, "Critical Race Theory, the New Intolerance, and Its Grip on America," Heritage Foundation, December 7, 2020, https://www.heritage.org/civil-rights/report/critical-race-theory-the-new-intolerance-and-its-grip-america.
11. Herbert Marcuse, *Counterrevolution and Revolt* (Boston: Beacon Press, 1972), 79.
12. Swift, "Gallup Vault."

13. Jack Goldsmith, "How J. Edgar Hoover Went from Hero to Villain," *The Atlantic*, November 22, 2022, https://www.theatlantic.com/magazine/archive/2022/12/j-edgar-hoover-fbi-influence/671900/.
14. Marcuse, *Counterrevolution and Revolt*, 99.
15. Rael Jean Isaac and Erich Isaac, *The Coercive Utopians: Social Deception by America's Power Players* (Washington, D.C.: Regnery Gateway, 1983), 221.
16. Ibid., 223–26.
17. Ibid., 237.
18. Ibid., 238–39.
19. Mike Gonzalez and Katharine C. Gorka, "How Cultural Marxism Threatens the United States—and How Americans Can Fight It," *Special Report* no. 262, The Heritage Foundation, November 14, 2022, https://www.heritage.org/sites/default/files/2022-11/SR262.pdf.
20. Felicity Barringer, "The Mainstreaming of Marxism in U.S. Colleges," *New York Times*, October 25, 1989, https://www.nytimes.com/1989/10/25/us/education-the-mainstreaming-of-marxism-in-us-colleges.html, h/t to Katharine Gorka.
21. "Speech of Nikita Khrushchev Before a Closed Session of the XXTH Congress of the Communist Party of the Soviet Union on February 25, 1956," Subcommittee to Investigate the Administration of the Internal Security Act and Other Internal Security Laws, Committee on the Judiciary, United States Senate, 1957.
22. Hoover, *On Communism*, 11–13.

Chapter 17

1. J. Edgar Hoover, *Masters of Deceit: The Story of Communism in America and How to Fight It* (New York: Henry Holt and Company, 1958).
2. J. Edgar Hoover, *A Study of Communism* (New York: Holt, Rinehart and Winston, 1962).
3. J. Edgar Hoover, "Remarks before the Supreme Council 33rd Degree of the Ancient and Accepted Scottish Rite of Freemasonry, Washington, D.C., October 19, 1965," cited in J. Edgar Hoover, ed., *On Communism* (New York: Random House, 1969), 98.
4. J. Edgar Hoover, "Communist Illusion and Democratic Reality," pamphlet, December 1959, reprinted in Hoover, *On Communism*, 118.
5. Ibid.

6. Herman O. Bly, *Communism, the Cold War and the FBI Connection: Time to Set the Record Straight* (Huntington House Publishers, 1998), 146.
7. Ibid., 141.
8. See John Barron, *Operation Solo: The FBI's Man in the Kremlin* (Washington, D.C.: Regnery Publishing, 1996).
9. The FBI released 109 heavily redacted pages of material on Levison. See "FBI Records: The Vault, Stanley Levison Part 01 of 109," FBI, https://vault.fbi.gov/Stanley%20Levison/Stanley%20Levison%20Part%2001%20of%20109/view.
10. We won't know for years what was really in the wiretaps. When Congress voted for Martin Luther King Day to become a national holiday, legislative sponsor John Conyers (D-MI), himself a longtime Communist Party acolyte if not a card-carrying member, prevented the public from knowing what was in the files by specifying in the national holiday legislation that the King archives would be under seal for the next fifty years.
11. Tim Weiner, *Enemies: A History of the FBI* (New York: Random House, 2012), 243–44.
12. Emma North-Best, "FBI Leadership Claimed Bureau Was 'Almost Powerless' against KKK, despite Making Up One-Fifth of Its Membership," MuckRock, December 8, 2017, https://www.muckrock.com/news/archives/2017/dec/08/fbi-kkk/.
13. Weiner, *Enemies*, 247–48.
14. See J. Michael Waller, *The Third Current of Revolution: Inside the "North American Front" of El Salvador's Guerilla War* (Lanham, Maryland: University Press of America, 1987).
15. "August 25 1956–Centralized Operations under COINTELPRO," 365 American Champions, August 25, 2018, https://www.americanchampions365.com/2018/08/25/august-25-1956-centralized-operations-under-cointelpro/.
16. Ibid.

Chapter 18

1. Ralph de Toledano, *Cry Havoc: The Great American Bring-down and How It Happened* (Washington, D.C.: Anthem Books, 2006), 300.
2. Tim Weiner, *Enemies: A History of the FBI* (New York: Random House, 2012), 88.
3. Ibid., 132.

4. "Longhand Note of President Harry S. Truman, May 12, 1945," Truman Library, National Archives, https://www.trumanlibrary.gov/library/truman-papers/longhand-notes-presidential-file-1944-1953/may-12-1945.
5. Weiner, *Enemies*, 134.
6. Laurence H. Silberman, "Hoover's Institution," *Wall Street Journal*, July 20, 2005, https://www.wsj.com/articles/SB112182505647390371?mod=article_inline.
7. As recalled by former Kennedy aide Ted Sorensen and recounted in Robin Lindley, "The Reflections of JFK's Closest Advisor, Ted Sorensen (Interview)," History News Network, Columbian College of Arts & Sciences, George Washington University, http://hnn.us/article/52263.
8. Ralph de Toledano, *J. Edgar Hoover: The Man in His Time* (Arlington House Publishers, 1973), 291.
9. Ibid., 306.
10. Weiner, *Enemies*, 241.
11. Ibid., 249.
12. Silberman, "Hoover's Institution."
13. Weiner, *Enemies*, 241.
14. De Toledano, *J. Edgar Hoover*, 300.
15. Silberman, "Hoover's Institution."
16. Ibid.
17. Ibid.
18. Evan Thomas, "Mr. God Goes to Washington," *Newsweek*, September 22, 1991, https://www.newsweek.com/mr-god-goes-washington-203460.
19. Max Holland, *Leak: Why Mark Felt Became Deep Throat* (Lawrence, Kansas: University of Kansas Press, 2012). Felt denied all along that he was the leaker and received a pardon from President Reagan. In 2005, shortly before his death, he admitted that he was indeed Deep Throat, which *Washington Post* reporter Bob Woodward confirmed. A twist for our purposes in this story is that the ghostwriter for Felt's memoir was former OSS man and *Newsweek* journalist Ralph de Toledano, who first told the author of the Frankfurt School.
20. *Final Report of the Select Committee to Study Governmental Operations with Respect to Intelligence Activities, United States Senate: Together with Additional, Supplemental, and Separate Views*, United States Senate Select Committee to Study Governmental Operations with Respect to Intelligence Agencies, 1976, available at https://archive.org/details/finalreportofsel06unit.
21. R. James Woolsey, as he told the author.

Chapter 19

1. Bittman was the author's graduate professor at the Disinformation Documentation Center at Boston University's College of Communication, and a reader for the author's master's thesis. Levchenko is a longtime acquaintance of the author since the 1980s.
2. Pacepa's memoir, *Red Horizons*, was generally unwelcome when it was first published because its revelations clashed with the intelligence and foreign policy establishment's prevailing views on Soviet disinformation and support for terrorism.
3. Some have attempted to discredit Bezmenov as tied to conspiracy theorists, but the defector has been considered authoritative by intelligence and policy professionals across the political spectrum, and his 1980s assessments stood the test of time. See Michael Carpenter, "Undermining Democracy: Kremlin Tools of Malign Political Influence," Testimony for United States House of Representatives Committee on Foreign Affairs Subcommittee on Europe, Eurasia, Energy, and the Environment, May 21, 2019, https://www.congress.gov/116/meeting/house/109537/witnesses/HHRG-116-FA14-Wstate-CarpenterM-20190521.pdf.
4. Yuri Bezmenov, cited in Judy Woodruff and Nick Schifrin, "The Long History of Russian Disinformation Targeting the US," *NewsHour*, Public Broadcasting Service, transcript, November 21, 2018, https://www.pbs.org/newshour/show/the-long-history-of-russian-disinformation-targeting-the-u-s.
5. Jigokucake, "The Age of Pigs—An Excerpt from Yuri Bezmenov's Lecture on Subversion," *Spiral Seas* (Substack), May 12, 2022, https://spiralseas.substack.com/p/the-age-of-pigs-an-excerpt-from-yuri?utm_source=%2Fprofile%2F60076943-jigokucake&utm_medium=reader2.
6. See the videos from 1983 and 1984 at www.bezmenov.net, and a four-hour compilation at The Truth Archive, "Yuri Bezmenov—All Interviews & Lectures HQ (1984–1983)," YouTube, April 1, 2019, https://www.youtube.com/watch?v=CRqiJSEj5UY. All Bezmenov quotations in this chapter are from these videos unless otherwise cited.

Part IV

1. James Rosen, *Cheney One on One: A Candid Conversation with America's Most Controversial Statesman* (Washington, D.C.: Regnery Publishing, 2015).

Chapter 20

1. Michael Warner, ed., *The Office of Strategic Services: America's First Intelligence Agency* (Washington, D.C.: Central Intelligence Agency, 2000), https://www.cia.gov/static/7851e16f9e100b6f9cc4ef002028ce2f/Office-of-Strategic-Services.pdf, 8.
2. George W. Bush, *The Department of Homeland Security*, June 2022, available at Department of Homeland Security website at https://www.dhs.gov/sites/default/files/publications/book_0.pdf; "An Act To Establish the Department of Homeland Security, and for Other Purposes," Public Law 107-296, 107th Congress, November 25, 2002, available at Department of Homeland Security website at https://www.dhs.gov/sites/default/files/publications/hr_5005_enr.pdf.
3. "ODNI Factsheet," Office of the Director of National Intelligence, February 24, 2017, https://www.dni.gov/files/documents/FACTSHEET_ODNI_History_and_Background_2_24-17.pdf.
4. Tim Weiner, "FBI's Historic Tug of War," *Politico*, April 1, 2012, https://www.politico.com/story/2012/04/fbis-historic-tug-of-war-security-vs-liberty-074713.

Chapter 21

1. Stephen Friend, interview with author, 2023.
2. Thomas J. Baker, *The Fall of the FBI: How a Once Great Agency Became a Threat to Democracy* (New York: Bombardier, 2022).
3. Stephen Friend, interview with author, 2023.
4. Steve Friend, "FBI Imitates Minority Report and Moneyball," Uncover DC, February 9, 2023, https://www.uncoverdc.com/2023/02/09/fbi-imitates-minority-report-and-moneyball/.
5. FBI field agent, interview with author, 2022.
6. Friend, "FBI Imitates Minority Report." For a full account of his experiences, see Stephen Friend, *True Blue: My Journey from Beat Cop to Suspended FBI Whistleblower* (New York: Post Hill Press, 2023).
7. Stephen Friend, interview with author, 2023.
8. Weaponization Committee (@Weaponization), "Mr. Baker retired from the FBI . . . ," Twitter, February 9, 2023, 2:15 p.m., https://twitter.com/Weaponization/status/1623762572804608000.
9. Baker, *The Fall of the FBI.*
10. Tim Weiner, *Enemies: A History of the FBI* (New York: Random House, 2012), 445.

11. Baker, *The Fall of the FBI.*

Part V

1. "Editorial: One U.S. Senator's 'Terrorist' Is Another One's 'Patriot,'" *Ely Times*, April 25, 2014, https://elynews.com/2014/04/25/editorial-one-u-s-senators-terrorist-another-ones-patriot/.
2. Paul Kengor, "How Barack Obama Fundamentally Transformed the United States," *National Catholic Register*, January 12, 2017, https://www.ncregister.com/news/how-barack-obama-fundamentally-transformed-the-united-states.

Chapter 22

1. Ken Jensen, "Hardly Small Change: Marcuse and Obama," *American Interest*, May 29, 2013, https://www.the-american-interest.com/2013/05/29/hardly-small-change-marcuse-and-obama/.
2. See Paul Robinson, *The Freudian Left: Wilhelm Reich, Geza Roheim, Herbert Marcuse* (Ithaca, New York: Cornell University Press, 1969).
3. Herbert Marcuse, "Repressive Tolerance," in Robert Paul Wolff, Barrington Moore Jr., and Herbert Marcuse, *A Critique of Pure Tolerance* (Boston: Beacon Press, 1969), 109.
4. Lawrence Lader, *Power on the Left: American Radical Movements since 1946* (New York: W. W. Norton, 1979), 213–15.
5. Ibid., 215.
6. See Dinesh D'Souza, *The Roots of Obama's Rage* (Washington, D.C.: Regnery, 2010), 91–92. Dinesh de-emphasizes Davis's Communist Party membership and describes Obama's main motivations as coming from his father, a Kenyan socialist radical who also saw Western civilization as construct of white supremacism.
7. Barack Obama, *Dreams from My Father: A Story of Race and Inheritance* (New York: Crown Publishers, 1995), 97.
8. Michelle Ye Hee Lee, "Frank Marshall Davis: Obama's 'Communist Mentor'?" *Washington Post*, March 23, 2015, https://www.washingtonpost.com/news/fact-checker/wp/2015/03/23/frank-marshall-davis-obamas-communist-mentor/. Researcher Cliff Kincaid was the first to reveal the Davis-Obama connection. He obtained the redacted FBI file on Davis through the Freedom of Information Act. Cliff Kincaid, ed., *The Frank Marshall Davis FBI File*, America's Survival, http://www.usasurvival.org/uploads/1/2/6/3/126369300/pages_from_davis_fbi_file_pdf.pdf. For a heavily

documented history of Davis and Obama, see Paul Kengor, *The Communist: Frank Marshall Davis: The Untold Story of Barack Obama's Mentor* (New York: Simon & Schuster, 2012).

9. Barack Obama, *A Promised Land* (New York: Crown, 2020), 10.
10. Obama, *Dreams from My Father*, 100.
11. See "Frantz Fanon's Critique: Marxism to Mao-Tse-Tung Thought," FrantzFanon.org, March 27, 2022, https://www.frantzfanon.org/Frantz-Fanons-Critique-of-Marxism-to-Mao-Tse-Tung-Thought.html; M. D. Lovett, "Forms of Fanonism: Frantz Fanon's Critical Theory and the Dialectics of Decolonization," *Journal of African American Studies* 15 (March 25, 2011): 412–13, https://doi.org/10.1007/s12111-011-9178-x.
12. D'Souza, *The Roots of Obama's Rage*, 91–92.
13. *Religion in the Public Sphere: Case Studies in Hope and Stress*, Record of Symposium Proceedings, Pulitzer Center, April 25, 2016, https://pulitzercenter.org/sites/default/files/07-18-16/e-book_religion_in_the_public_sphere.compressed.pdf, 60.
14. "Who Is Reinhold Niebuhr and What Is His Connection to James Comey?" NPR, April 13, 2018, https://www.npr.org/2018/04/13/602288646/who-is-reinhold-niebuhr-and-what-is-his-connection-to-james-comey.

Chapter 23

1. For example, Palmer served as an executive board member of the Communist Party USA–dominated U.S. Peace Council from 1983–1985. For the Communist Party connection to the WPC, see "The World Peace Council: A Soviet-Sponsored International Communist Front," CIA, https://www.cia.gov/readingroom/print/1355567 and "U.S. Peace Council," Wikipedia, https://keywiki.org/U.S._Peace_Council.
2. Mitch Dudek, "Alice Palmer, State Senator Who Mentored Barack Obama, Dies at 83," *Chicago Sun-Times*, May 31, 2023, https://chicago.suntimes.com/obituaries/2023/5/31/23744672/alice-palmer-state-senator-who-mentored-barack-obama-dies-at-83.
3. Ben Smith, "Obama Once Visited '60s Radicals," *Politico*, February 22, 2008, https://www.politico.com/story/2008/02/obama-once-visited-60s-radicals-008630.
4. "Weather Underground Bombings," FBI, https://www.fbi.gov/history/famous-cases/weather-underground-bombings.
5. Arthur M. Eckstein, "How the Weather Underground Failed at Revolution and Still Changed the World," *Time*, November 2, 2016, https://time.com

/4549409/the-weather-underground-bad-moon-rising/. See also Christopher F. Rufo, "How the 1970s Liberation Movement Led to Today's Identity Battles," *New York Post*, July 15, 2023, https://nypost.com/2023/07/15/how-the-70s-liberation-movement-led-to-todays-identity-battles/.

6. Ben Joravsky, "The Long, Strange Trip of Bill Ayers," *Chicago Reader*, November 8, 1990, https://chicagoreader.com/news-politics/the-long-strange-trip-of-bill-ayers/.
7. Lawrence Lader, *Power on the Left: American Radical Movements since 1946* (New York: W. W. Norton, 1979), 281–82.
8. Ibid., 283–84.
9. Earl Caldwell, "A Shotgun That Miss Davis Purchased Is Linked to the Fatal Shooting of Judge," *New York Times*, April 18, 1972, https://www.nytimes.com/1972/04/18/archives/a-shotgun-that-miss-davis-purchased-is-linked-to-the-fatal-shooting.html.
10. "Angela Davis on Protest, 1968, and Her Old Teacher, Herbert Marcuse," Literary Hub, April 3, 2019, https://lithub.com/angela-davis-on-protest-1968-and-her-old-teacher-herbert-marcuse/.
11. "Angela Davis," KeyWiki, https://keywiki.org/Angela_Davis.
12. Robert M. Gates, *Duty: Memoirs of a Secretary at War* (New York: Alfred A. Knopf, 2014), 585–86.
13. Lader, *Power on the Left*, 284.
14. Charles C. Johnson and Ryan Girdusky, "As College Student, Eric Holder Participated in 'Armed' Takeover of Former Columbia University ROTC Office," Daily Caller, September 30, 2012, https://dailycaller.com/2012/09/30/as-college-sophomore-eric-holder-participated-in-armed-takeover-of-former-columbia-university-rotc-office/.
15. "Black Panther Party," FBI Vault, https://vault.fbi.gov/Black%20Panther%20Party%20.
16. Johnson and Girdusky, "As College Student, Eric Holder Participated."
17. Giovanni Russonello, "Fascination and Fear: Covering the Black Panthers," *New York Times*, October 15, 2016, https://www.nytimes.com/2016/10/16/us/black-panthers-50-years.html. For full context, see Kyle Shideler, *Understanding Black Identity Extremism* (Washington, D.C.: Center for Security Policy, 2023).
18. Ben Smith, "At Columbia, Holder Recalls Protest Days," *Politico*, May 14, 2010, https://www.politico.com/blogs/ben-smith/2010/05/at-columbia-holder-recalls-protest-days-027002.

19. Hans A. von Spakovsky, "The Injustice of Eric Holder," The Heritage Foundation, September 18, 2014, https://www.heritage.org/crime-and-justice/commentary/the-injustice-eric-holder; Hans A. von Spakovsky, "Eric Holder's Legacy," The Heritage Foundation, April 29, 2015, https://www.heritage.org/crime-and-justice/commentary/eric-holders-legacy.
20. Andrew C. McCarthy, "Eric Holder, Racial Profiler," *National Review*, August 23, 2014, https://www.nationalreview.com/2014/08/eric-holder-racial-profiler-andrew-c-mccarthy/.
21. Daniel Arkin, "Eric Holder, Former Attorney General, Returning to Covington & Burling Law Firm," NBC News, July 6, 2015, https://www.nbcnews.com/news/us-news/eric-holder-former-attorney-general-returning-covington-burling-law-firm-n387331.
22. Hans A. von Spakovsky, "Every Single One: The Politicized Hiring of Eric Holder's Voting Section," The Heritage Foundation, August 15, 2011, https://www.heritage.org/civil-society/commentary/every-single-one-the-politicized-hiring-eric-holders-voting-section.
23. Ralph R. Smith, "Tallying Political Donations from Federal Employees and Unions," FedSmith, December 27, 2016, https://www.fedsmith.com/2016/12/21/tallying-political-donations-from-federal-employees-and-unions/.
24. Ibid.
25. "FBI Files Document Communism in Valerie Jarrett's Family," Judicial Watch, June 22, 2015, https://www.judicialwatch.org/communism-in-jarretts-family/.
26. "Frank Marshall Davis," KeyWiki, https://keywiki.org/Frank_Marshall_Davis.
27. "Valerie B. Jarrett," KeyWiki, https://keywiki.org/Valerie_B._Jarrett.

Chapter 24

1. The author worked with DIA officers and staff during Clapper's tenure as DIA director, and had an inside look into Clapper's management. These assessments of Clapper are from conversations at the time and overall at DIA between 1991 and 2022.
2. Ibid.
3. Ken Dilanian, "Intelligence Nominee's Contractor Ties Draw Scrutiny," *LA Times*, July 25, 2010, https://www.latimes.com/archives/la-xpm-2010-jul-25-la-na-clapper-contractors-20100725-story.html.

4. Todd Farley, "Ana Montes Is the Most Damaging Spy in US History," *New York Post*, January 14, 2023, https://nypost.com/2023/01/14/ana-montes-is-the-most-damaging-spy-in-us-history/.
5. "Cuba Spy Ana Belen Montes Released after 20 Years behind Bars," Reuters, January 6, 2023, https://www.reuters.com/world/americas/cuba-spy-ana-belen-montes-released-after-20-years-behind-bars-2023-01-07/.
6. "Ana Montes: Cuban Spy," FBI, https://www.fbi.gov/history/famous-cases/ana-montes-cuba-spy.
7. "DIA Official Warns about Cuban Spies," *Washington Times*, March 14, 2007, https://www.washingtontimes.com/news/2007/mar/14/20070314-110701-3092r/.
8. Interviews with former DIA officers who served under Clapper.
9. "Faces of Defense Intelligence: The Honorable James R. Clapper, Jr.," Defense Intelligence Agency, January 18, 2017, https://www.dia.mil/News-Features/Articles/Article-View/Article/1052063/faces-of-defense-intelligence-the-honorable-james-r-clapper-jr/.
10. John O. Brennan, *Undaunted: My Fight against America's Enemies, at Home and Abroad* (New York: Celadon Books, 2020), 7.
11. Shane Harris, "How the CIA Came Out of the Closet," Daily Beast, April 14, 2017, https://www.thedailybeast.com/how-the-cia-came-out-of-the-closet.
12. "Establishing a Coordinated Government-Wide Initiative to Promote Diversity and Inclusion in the Federal Workforce," Executive Order 13583, Executive Office of the President, August 18, 2011, https://www.federalregister.gov/documents/2011/08/23/2011-21704/establishing-a-coordinated-government-wide-initiative-to-promote-diversity-and-inclusion-in-the.
13. Noam Scheiber, "The Obama Whisperer," *New Republic*, November 9, 2014, https://newrepublic.com/article/120170/valerie-jarrett-obama-whisperer.
14. Carol Felsenthal, "The Truth about Valerie Jarrett, Mystery Woman of the White House," *Chicago*, January 31, 2014, https://www.chicagomag.com/Chicago-Magazine/Felsenthal-Files/January-2014/The-Mysteries-and-Realities-of-Valerie-Jarrett-Mystery-Woman-of-the-White-House/.

Chapter 25

1. John A. Gentry, "Demographic Diversity in U.S. Intelligence Personnel: Is It Functionally Useful?" *International Journal of Intelligence and*

Counterintelligence 36, no. 2 (December 2021): 564–96, https://www.tandfonline.com/doi/full/10.1080/08850607.2021.1994346; John A. Gentry, "Intelligence Learning and Adaptation: Lessons from Counterinsurgency Wars," *Intelligence and National Security* 25, no. 1 (2010), 75.

2. Patrick C. Neary, "Intelligence Reform, 2001–2009: *Requiescat in Pace?*," *Studies in Intelligence* 54, no. 1 (2009), https://www.cia.gov/static/c09c0295963fb5daa5ecd12937f2cd89/Intel-Reform-2001-2009.pdf.
3. Leon Panetta with Jim Newton, *Worthy Fights: A Memoir of Leadership in War and Peace* (New York: Penguin, 2014), 232–35.
4. Gentry, "Demographic Diversity."
5. Michael D. Shear, "Petraeus Quits; Evidence of Affair Was Found by F.B.I.," *New York Times*, November 9, 2012, https://www.nytimes.com/2012/11/10/us/citing-affair-petraeus-resigns-as-cia-director.html.
6. John O. Brennan, *Undaunted: My Fight against America's Enemies, at Home and Abroad* (New York: Celadon Books, 2020), 169.
7. Gentry, "Demographic Diversity."
8. Ibid.
9. Brennan, *Undaunted*, 251.
10. Gentry, "Demographic Diversity."
11. "National Committee to Abolish the House Un-American Activities Committee," KeyWiki, https://keywiki.org/National_Committee_to_Abolish_the_House_Un-American_Activities_Committee.
12. Jordan Michael Smith, "The Philosopher of the Post-9/11 Era," *Slate*, October 17, 2011, https://slate.com/culture/2011/10/john-diggins-why-niebuhr-now-reviewed-how-did-he-become-the-philosopher-of-the-post-9-11-era.html.
13. Diana West discusses this, with sourcing, in her monograph *The Red Thread: A Search for Ideological Drivers inside the Anti-Trump Conspiracy* (Washington, D.C.: Center for Security Policy, 2020), 44–51.
14. Chris Smith, "Mr. Comey Goes to Washington," *New York*, October 10, 2003.
15. West, *The Red Thread*, 46.
16. Ibid., 47.
17. Ibid., 48.
18. Ashley Feinberg, "This Is Almost Certainly James Comey's Twitter Account," Gizmodo, March 30, 2017, https://gizmodo.com/this-is-almost-certainly-james-comey-s-twitter-account-1793843641; Paul Elie, "A Few Theories about Why James Comey Might Call Himself 'Reinhold Niebuhr' on

Twitter," *New Yorker*, April 3, 2017, https://www.newyorker.com/culture/cultural-comment/a-few-theories-about-why-james-comey-might-call-himself-reinhold-niebuhr-on-twitter.

19. Z. Byron Wolf, "James Comey Confirms He's 'Reinhold Niebuhr' in the Strangest Possible Way," CNN, October 24, 2017, https://www.cnn.com/2017/10/23/politics/james-comey-twitter-account-reinhold-niebuhr/index.html.
20. James Comey, *A Higher Loyalty: Truth, Lies, and Leadership* (New York: Flatiron Books, 2018), 1.
21. Ibid., 13–14.

Chapter 26

1. "The U.S. Government's Woke Training," *Wall Street Journal*, December 30, 2022, https://www.wsj.com/articles/the-u-s-governments-woke-training-federal-employees-diversity-equity-inclusion-11672251764.
2. "Moving the Diversity Needle," FBI, https://www.fbi.gov/news/stories/fbis-first-chief-diversity-officer-a-tonya-odom-reflects-on-tenure-022621.
3. "A. Tonya Odom Named Assistant Director of the Office of Equal Employment Opportunity Affairs," FBI, October 6, 2020, https://www.fbi.gov/news/press-releases/a-tonya-odom-named-assistant-directo; "Moving the Diversity Needle."
4. "Moving the Diversity Needle."
5. "A. Tonya Odom Named Assistant Director."
6. "Moving the Diversity Needle."
7. Ibid.
8. Stephen Friend, interview with author, 2023.
9. Mike Gonzalez and Katharine C. Gorka, "How Cultural Marxism Threatens the United States—and How Americans Can Fight It," *Special Report* no. 262, The Heritage Foundation, November 14, 2022, 15–16, citing Bruce Gilley, Peter Boghossian, and James Lindsay, "Responding to Social Justice Rhetoric: A Cheat Sheet for Policy Makers," Parents Defending Education, August 2021, https://defendinged.org/wp-content/uploads/2021/08/Responding-to-Social-Justice-Rhetoric.pdf.
10. *Intelligence Community Equal Employment Opportunity and Diversity Enterprise Strategy (2015–2020)* (Washington, D.C.: Office of the Director of National Intelligence, undated), https://www.dni.gov/files/documents/Newsroom/Press%20Releases/2016EnterpriseStrategy.pdf.

11. "Intelligence Community Equal Employment Opportunity and Diversity Council Members," in *Intelligence Community Equal Employment Opportunity and Diversity Enterprise Strategy (2015-2020)* (Washington, D.C.: Office of the Director of National Intelligence, undated), 3–4.
12. Scott Uehlinger, "How the Intel Community Was Turned into a Political Weapon against President Trump," *The Hill*, April 5, 2017, https://thehill.com/blogs/pundits-blog/the-administration/327413-how-the-intel-community-was-turned-into-a-political/.
13. *Enterprise Strategy*, 6.
14. CIA (@CIA), "The Agency Network of Gay, Lesbian . . . ," Twitter, August 19, 2020, 12:15 p.m., https://twitter.com/CIA/status/1296118661871276038?s=20&t=3Xwmpf1zkea1Wouog7v8Ww.
15. *Enterprise Strategy*, 6.
16. Ibid.
17. Ibid.
18. Ibid., 7.
19. Ibid.
20. CIA (@CIA), "You can say General Donovan was . . . ," Twitter, December 3, 2021, 2:15 p.m., https://twitter.com/CIA/status/1466848460498292737?s=20.

Chapter 27

1. James B. Comey, "Intelligence Community Pride: Shaping Culture beyond Summits," FBI, June 8, 2016, https://www.fbi.gov/news/speeches/intelligence-community-pride-shaping-culture-beyond-summits.
2. "Scott McMillion Named First FBI Chief Diversity Officer," FBI, April 19, 2021, https://www.fbi.gov/news/press-releases/scott-mcmillion-named-first-fbi-chief-diversity-officer.
3. "DNI Clapper, FBI Director Comey, and DIA Director Stewart to Salute #LGBTSPIES at #2016ICPRIDE Summit," ODNI News Release No. 13-16, June 8, 2016, https://www.dni.gov/index.php/newsroom/press-releases/press-releases-2016/item/1599-dni-clapper-fbi-director-comey-and-dia-director-stewart-to-salute-lgbtspies-at-2016icpride-summit.
4. Ibid.
5. Ibid.
6. Comey, "Intelligence Community Pride."
7. Ibid.
8. Ibid.

9. James Comey, *A Higher Loyalty: Truth, Lies, and Leadership* (New York: Flatiron Books, 2018), 262.
10. "DNI Clapper, FBI Director Comey."
11. Timothy Barrett, "The Intelligence Community Comes Out in Austin," ODNI Gov Tumblr, March 16, 2016, https://odnigov.tumblr.com/post/141432568410/intelligence-community-comes-out-in-austin.
12. Interview with the author.
13. Robert S. Muller III, *Report on the Investigation into Russian Interference in the 2016 Presidential Election* (Washington, D.C.: U.S. Department of Justice, 2019), https://www.justice.gov/archives/sco/file/1373816/download.
14. John H. Durham, *Report on Matters Related to Intelligence Activities and Investigations Arising out of the 2016 Presidential Campaigns* (Washington, D.C.: U.S. Department of Justice, 2023), 2, hereafter referenced as Durham Report.
15. Durham Report, 4.
16. Ibid., 9.
17. Ibid.
18. Ibid.
19. Ibid.
20. Ibid., 10.
21. Ibid.
22. Ibid.
23. Ibid., 50.
24. Ibid. 9.
25. Ibid., 8.

Chapter 28

1. Curiously, Fusion GPS leader Glenn Simpson was working for the International Assessment and Strategy Center, a small consulting firm that did federal defense and security contracts, according to a page on the company's website that was deleted after Simpson became controversial.
2. "Soviet Involvement in the West European Peace Movement," Central Intelligence Agency, declassified report, undated, circa 1983, https://www.cia.gov/readingroom/docs/CIA-RDP85M00364R001001530019-5.pdf. KGB defector Oleg Gordievsky and MI5 historian Christopher Andrew say that the KGB rezident or station chief in London "tried to take credit, without much justification, for the well-publicized protests by CND." Christopher

Andrew and Oleg Gordievsky, *KGB: The Inside Story* (New York: Harper Perennial, 1991), 604.

3. "Major West European Peace Groups," diagram in "Worldwide Active Measures and Propaganda Alert [Redacted]," Directorate of Intelligence, Central Intelligence Agency, November 1987, declassified, at https://www.cia.gov/readingroom/docs/CIA-RDP88T00986R000100040002-8.pdf, 20.
4. Durham Report, 13–14.
5. Ibid., 12.
6. Ibid., 13.
7. Natasha Bertrand, "Hunter Biden Story Is Russian Disinfo, Dozens of Former Intel Officials Say," *Politico*, October 19, 2020, https://www.politico.com/news/2020/10/19/hunter-biden-story-russian-disinfo-430276.
8. Durham Report, 17.
9. Ibid., 17–18.
10. Ibid., 18.
11. Ibid.
12. David Satter, "The 'Trump Report' Is a Russian Provocation," *National Review*, January 12, 2017, https://www.nationalreview.com/2017/01/russia-donald-trump-intelligence-report-christopher-steele-russian-propaganda-disrupt/.
13. Ibid.
14. Ibid.
15. "'Perfectly Appropriate': Jake Sullivan Defended Steele Dossier in 2018 Interview," True Pundit, November 25, 2018, https://truepundit.com/perfectly-appropriate-jake-sullivan-defended-steele-dossier-in-2018-interview/.
16. Anthony Leonardi, "Documents Show Never-Trump Lincoln Project Founders Had Ties to Russia and Tax Debt: Report," *Washington Examiner*, July 21, 2020, https://www.washingtonexaminer.com/news/documents-show-never-trump-lincoln-project-founders-had-ties-to-russia-and-tax-debt-report.
17. Bertrand, "Hunter Biden Story Is Russian Disinfo." The original letter with signatories is linked with the *Politico* story: https://www.politico.com/f/?id=00000175-4393-d7aa-af77-579f9b330000.
18. J. Michael Waller (@JMichaelWaller), "CBS reported it months ago . . . ," Twitter, September 25, 2020, 11:02 p.m., https://twitter.com/JMichaelWaller/status/1309689773964001282?s=20.

19. For example, see David Molloy, "Zuckerberg Tells Rogan FBI Warning Prompted Biden Laptop Story Censorship," BBC, August 26, 2022, https://www.bbc.com/news/world-us-canada-62688532 and Jesse O'Neill, "FBI Pressured Twitter, Sent Trove of Docs Hours before Post Broke Hunter Laptop Story," *New York Post*, December 19, 2022, https://nypost.com/2022/12/19/fbi-reached-out-to-twitter-before-post-broke-hunter-biden-laptop-story/.
20. Michael Ginsberg, "IRS Whistleblower Confirms FBI Knew Hunter's Laptop Was Real in 2019," Daily Caller, June 22, 2023, https://dailycaller.com/2023/06/22/gary-shapley-whistleblower-fbi-hunter-biden-laptop-2019/.

Chapter 29

1. Eric Tucker and Ben Fox, "FBI Director Says Antifa Is an Ideology, Not an Organization," AP News, September 17, 2020, https://apnews.com/article/donald-trump-ap-top-news-elections-james-comey-politics-bdd3b6078e9efadcfcd0be4b65f2362e.
2. Spencer Case, "How Obama Sided with the Muslim Brotherhood," *National Review*, July 3, 2014, https://www.nationalreview.com/2014/07/how-obama-sided-muslim-brotherhood-spencer-case/.
3. Josh Gerstein, "DNI Clapper Retreats from 'Secular' Claim on Muslim Brotherhood," *Politico*, February 10, 2011, https://www.politico.com/blogs/under-the-radar/2011/02/dni-clapper-retreats-from-secular-claim-on-muslim-brotherhood-033259.
4. Tony Heller, "Nadler: Antifa Is a Myth," YouTube, August 30, 2020, https://www.youtube.com/watch?v=oLolk-FXeow, 0:06.
5. "Jerrold Nadler," Discover the Networks, https://www.discoverthenetworks.org/individuals/jerrold-nadler.
6. "Antifascist Working Group," Democratic Socialists of America, https://www.dsausa.org/working-groups/anti-fascist-working-group/.
7. Adam Shaw, "Biden Says Antifa Is an 'Idea,' Days after WH Moved to Label It a Terror Group," Fox News, September 30, 2020, https://www.foxnews.com/politics/biden-antifa-idea-what-we-know.
8. Tucker and Fox, "FBI Director Says Antifa Is an Ideology."
9. Kyle Shideler, Testimony before the Judiciary Committee, Subcommittee on the Constitution, Center for Security Policy, August 4, 2020, https://www.centerforsecuritypolicy.org/wp-content/uploads/2020/09/Shideler-Testimony-Senate-Constitution-Subcommittee-080420202.pdf, 2.
10. Ibid., 5.

11. Ibid.
12. Ibid., 14.
13. *Verfassungsschutzbericht 2019* (Berlin: Bundesministerium des Innern, für Bau und Heimat, 2020), https://www.verfassungsschutz.de/SharedDocs/publikationen/DE/verfassungsschutzberichte/2020-07-verfassungsschutzbericht-2019.pdf?__blob=publicationFile&v=11.
14. Ibid.
15. Ibid.
16. *Analyse, Radikalisierung im gewaltorientierten Linksextremismus* (Berlin: Bundesamt für Verfassungsschutz, 2020), https://www.innenministerkonferenz.de/IMK/DE/termine/to-beschluesse/2020-06-17_19/analyse.pdf;jsessionid=64B2170EC7132D6FC56E6A804C5328E2.1_cid365?__blob=publicationFile&v=2.
17. Noah Manskar, "Riots Following George Floy's Death May Cost Insurance Companies up to $2B," *New York Post*, September 16, 2020, https://nypost.com/2020/09/16/riots-following-george-floyds-death-could-cost-up-to-2b/.
18. Ari Blaff, "Six Antifa Extremists Arrested, Charged with Domestic Terrorism in Fiery Atlanta Riots," Yahoo News, January 23, 2023, https://news.yahoo.com/six-antifa-extremists-arrested-charged-151301053.html.
19. See, for example, Hilary Beaumont, "The Activists Sabotaging Railways in Solidarity with Indigenous People," *The Guardian*, July 29, 2021, https://www.theguardian.com/environment/2021/jul/29/activists-sabotaging-railways-indigenous-people.
20. See, for example, Andrew Mark Miller, "Antifa Sympathizers Celebrate Death of Washington State Sheriff's Deputy," Fox News, July 24, 2021, https://www.foxnews.com/politics/antifa-sympathizers-celebrate-death-of-portland-area-sheriffs-deputy.
21. "Domestic Terrorism," FBI, November 16, 2010, https://archives.fbi.gov/archives/news/stories/2010/november/anarchist_111610/anarchist_111610#:~:text=Law%20enforcement%20is%20also%20concerned,re%20investigated%20by%20local%20police.
22. Kyle Shideler, "FBI Director Faces Scrutiny over Refusal to Name Antifa as Organization," Center for Security Policy, September 18, 2020, https://centerforsecuritypolicy.org/fbi-director-faces-scrutiny-over-refusal-to-name-antifa-as-organization/.
23. Kyle Shideler, "2021 ODNI Annual Threat Assessment Includes 'Domestic Violent Extremists' for First Time," Center for Security Policy, April 15, 2021,

https://centerforsecuritypolicy.org/2021-odni-annual-threat-assessment-includes-domestic-violent-extremists-for-first-time/.

24. *Strategic Intelligence Assessment and Data on Domestic Terrorism*, Federal Bureau of Investigation and Department of Homeland Security, October 2022, https://www.fbi.gov/file-repository/fbi-dhs-domestic-terrorism-strategic-report-2022.pdf/view, 29–30.
25. Ibid., 42.
26. Kyle Shideler, interview with author.

Chapter 30

1. Nicholas Ballasy, "Schumer Warns Trump: Intel Community Has Many Ways to 'Get Back at You' (Flashback)," YouTube, September 26, 2019, https://www.youtube.com/watch?v=6OYyXv2l4-I.
2. Steven Nelson, "Trump Names Hand-Picked Panel to Supervise, Investigate Intelligence Community," *Washington Examiner*, November 21, 2018, https://www.washingtonexaminer.com/news/white-house/trump-names-hand-picked-panel-to-supervise-investigate-intelligence-community.
3. "FBI Hosts Sixth Annual 'IC Pride' Summit," ODNI News Release no. 16-17, June 15, 2017, https://www.dni.gov/index.php/newsroom/press-releases/press-releases-2017/3134-fbi-hosts-sixth-annual-ic-pride-summit-keynote-speakers-from-ic-congress-and-human-rights-campaign.
4. Ibid.
5. Ibid.
6. See Kyle Shideler, *Understanding Black Identity Extremism: Considerations for Law Enforcement* (Washington, D.C.: Center for Security Policy, 2023).
7. FBI (@FBI), "Throughout June, the #FBI . . . ," Twitter, June 30, 2018, 10:30 a.m., https://twitter.com/FBI/status/1013067235135574017?s=20&t=QPnaJOsD4WEpANSHtovc5g.
8. FBI (@FBI), "Yesterday, the #FBI was honored . . . ," Twitter, June 27, 2018, 8:55 a.m., https://twitter.com/FBI/status/1011956215281278976?s=20&t=QPnaJOsD4WEpANSHtovc5g.
9. FBI (@FBI), "Happy #PrideMonth from the FBI. . . . ," Twitter, June 1, 2019, 10:01 a.m., https://twitter.com/FBI/status/1134822186278109185?s=20&t=QPnaJOsD4WEpANSHtovc5g.
10. FBI (@FBI), "At the FBI, we know that . . . ," Twitter, June 1, 2020, 12:01 p.m., https://twitter.com/FBI/status/1267486368864841735?s=20&t=QPnaJOsD4WEpANSHtovc5g. The 2022 Pride Month art was more

subdued: FBI (@FBI), "June is #PrideMonth . . . ," Twitter, June 2, 2022, 5:11 p.m., https://twitter.com/FBI/status/1532469964329951232.

11. FBI (@FBI), "As #PrideMonth comes to an end . . . ," Twitter, June 26, 2019, 6:30 p.m., https://twitter.com/FBI/status/1144010038039777280?s=20&t=QPnaJOsD4WEpANSHtovc5g.
12. "What Is the FBI's Policy on the Use of Deadly Force by Its Special Agents?" FBI, https://www.fbi.gov/about/faqs/what-is-the-fbis-policy-on-the-use-of-deadly-force-by-its-special-agents.
13. Author's analysis of video of the incident, provided by former FBI special agent Kyle Seraphin.
14. "'Surreal' Photos of FBI Employees Kneeling amid Protests in DC Spark Confusion & Calls for 'Disciplinary Action,'" RT, June 6, 2020, https://www.rt.com/usa/491009-fbi-kneeling-dc-protests/.
15. Tarik Johnson, interview with author.
16. Chris Marquette, "Capitol Police Promotes Officers Who Got Jan. 6 Attack Spotlight," Roll Call, August 24, 2023, https://rollcall.com/2023/08/24/capitol-police-promotes-officers-who-got-jan-6-attack-spotlight/.
17. Houston Keene, "Gaetz Demands Answers on How FBI Agents Who Kneeled for 2020 Protestors Allegedly Got 'Plum' Promotions," Fox News, June 28, 2023, https://www.foxnews.com/politics/gaetz-demands-answers-fbi-agents-kneeled-2020-protesters.
18. James A. Gagliano, "The FBI Agents Association Rewarded Agents Who Took a Knee in Front of BLM, Proving the Rot Isn't Just at the Top," *New York Post*, October 19, 2022, https://nypost.com/2022/10/19/fbi-agents-association-rewarded-agents-who-took-a-knee-in-front-of-blm/.
19. Kyle Seraphin, interviews with author, May and September 2023; unsigned letter to Seraphin from U.S. Department of Justice, Federal Bureau of Investigation, March 31, 2013.
20. CIA (@CIA), "We're proud to be featured as one . . . ," Twitter, June 10, 2019, 2:51 p.m., https://twitter.com/CIA/status/1138156715332046849?s=20.
21. "Q&A with Former Acting Director of National Intelligence Richard Grenell on Pride in 2020," Office of the Director of National Intelligence, https://www.dni.gov/index.php/newsroom/news-articles/news-articles-2020/3464-q-a-with-former-acting-director-of-national-intelligence-richard-grenell-on-pride-in-2020.
22. Ibid.
23. Ibid.
24. Ibid.

25. *2020–2023 CIA Diversity and Inclusion Strategy*, CIA, https://www.cia.gov/static/c26da464843c5aee8217ef3919b19638/2020-2023-DI-Strategy.pdf, 9.
26. John A. Gentry "Demographic Diversity in U.S. Intelligence Personnel: Is It Functionally Useful?," *International Journal of Intelligence and CounterIntelligence* 36, no. 2 (December 2023): 564–96, https://www.tandfonline.com/doi/full/10.1080/08850607.2021.1994346.
27. *2020–2023 CIA Diversity and Inclusion Strategy*, 10.
28. Ibid., 9.
29. Ibid., 4.
30. "Executive Order on Combating Race and Sex Stereotyping," Trump White House, September 22, 2020, https://trumpwhitehouse.archives.gov/presidential-actions/executive-order-combating-race-sex-stereotyping/.
31. "Working at CIA: Diversity and Inclusion," CIA, https://www.cia.gov/careers/working-at-cia/diversity-and-inclusion/.
32. Central Intelligence Agency, "Humans of CIA," YouTube, March 25, 2021, https://www.youtube.com/watch?v=X55JPbAMc9g. There was some poetic justice to it all. Zora Neale Hurston, one of the early twentieth century's most prominent black American authors and an anthropologist and ethnographer, was somewhat of a radical when she wrote "How It Feels to Be Colored Me" in 1928. Before long she became what some described as a "counterrevolutionary," a political and cultural conservative, and a member of the Republican Party.

Chapter 31

1. FBI (@FBI), "A8: The FBI's strength is in its diversity . . . ," Twitter, November 8, 2017, 4:01 p.m., https://twitter.com/FBI/status/928366777804972038?s=20.
2. Federal Bureau of Investigation, *FBI Diversity Report*, revised May 2023, https://fbijobs.gov/sites/default/files/2022-05/Report_Diversity.pdf, 2.
3. Natasha Bertrand, "Inside the Biden Campaign's Pushback against Foreign Interference," *Politico*, July 20, 2020, https://www.politico.com/news/2020/07/20/biden-foreign-russia-kremlin-373277.
4. See J. Michael Waller, "Biden Makes Powerful Statement against Kremlin Election Interference, but Angela Davis Complicates Things," Center for Security Policy, July 24, 2020, https://centerforsecuritypolicy.org/biden-kremlin-russia-election-communist-angela-davis/.

5. "Angela Davis on Black Lives Matter Protests, Trump vs Biden & Defunding the Police (E891)," RT, June 15, 2020, https://www.rt.com/shows/going-underground/491798-angela-davis-usa-protests/, 19:00.
6. Ibid.
7. Ibid.
8. Ibid.
9. "Advancing Racial Equity and Support for Underserved Communities through the Federal Government," *Federal Register*, January 25, 2021, https://www.federalregister.gov/documents/2021/01/25/2021-01753/advancing-racial-equity-and-support-for-underserved-communities-through-the-federal-government.
10. Ben Gittleson et al., "Biden's 1st 100 Days: Promises Kept, Broken, or in Progress," ABC News, April 26, 2021, https://abcnews.go.com/Politics/bidens-1st-100-days-promises-broken-progress/story?id=77242864.
11. J. Michael Waller, "I Saw Provocateurs at the Capitol Riot On Jan. 6," The Federalist, January 14, 2021, https://thefederalist.com/2021/01/14/i-saw-provocateurs-at-the-capitol-riot-on-jan-6/.
12. "Diversity and Inclusion," CIA, https://www.cia.gov/careers/working-at-cia/diversity-and-inclusion/.
13. The author observed the Alger Hiss photograph while visiting the Carnegie Endowment for International Peace.
14. *National Strategy for Countering Domestic Terrorism* (Washington, D.C.: National Security Council, June 2021), 8.
15. The main mandatory reading was Ibram X. Kendi, *How to Be an Antiracist* (New York: One World, 2019). Bruce Golding, "Joint Chiefs Chair Gen. Mark Milley Defends Teaching 'Critical Race Theory' at West Point," *New York Post*, June 23, 2021, https://nypost.com/2021/06/23/gen-mark-milley-defends-teaching-critical-race-theory-at-west-point/.
16. *National Strategy for Countering Domestic Terrorism*, 8–9.
17. Libby Emmons, "FBI Falsely Claims Agency Never Investigated Parents at School Board Meeting," The Post Millennial, July 14, 2023, https://thepostmillennial.com/fbi-falsely-claims-agency-never-investigated-parents-at-school-board-meeting.
18. Joe Bukuras, "Acquitted Pro-Life Activist Mark Houck Reveals Details of 'Reckless' FBI Raid; Will Press Charges," Catholic News Agency, February 1, 2023, https://www.catholicnewsagency.com/news/253523/acquitted-pro-life-activist-mark-houck-reveals-details-of-fbi-raid-will-press-charges.

19. "Judiciary Committee Uncovers Multiple FBI Field Offices Coordinated to Prepare Anti-Catholic Memo," House Judiciary Committee, August 9, 2023, https://judiciary.house.gov/media/press-releases/judiciary-committee-uncovers-multiple-fbi-field-offices-coordinated-prepare.
20. *National Strategy for Countering Domestic Terrorism*, 9.
21. Ibid.
22. *Updated Assessment on COVID-19 Origins*, Office of the Director of National Intelligence, National Intelligence Council, October 2021, https://www.dni.gov/files/ODNI/documents/assessments/Declassified-Assessment-on-COVID-19-Origins.pdf, 1.
23. Ibid., 2.
24. Ibid.
25. *National Strategy for Countering Domestic Terrorism*, 9.
26. Ibid., 10.
27. Stephen Sund, who was United States Capitol Police chief on January 6, 2021, described the federal agencies' failure to warn the Capitol Police in his book, *Courage Under Fire: Under Siege and Outnumbered 58 to 1 on January 6* (Blackstone Publishing, 2023), passim., and in an extended interview with Tucker Carlson (@TuckerCarlson), "Ep. 15 Former Capitol Police Chief Steven Sund reveals . . . ," Twitter, August 10, 2023, 7:40 p.m., https://x.com/TuckerCarlson/status/1689783814594174976?s=20.
28. *National Strategy for Countering Domestic Terrorism*, 11.
29. Ibid., 12.
30. "Editorial: One U.S. Senator's 'Terrorist' Is Another One's 'Patriot,'" *Ely Times*, April 25, 2014, https://elynews.com/2014/04/25/editorial-one-u-s-senators-terrorist-another-ones-patriot/.
31. *National Strategy for Countering Domestic Terrorism*, 16.
32. Ibid., 20.
33. Ibid., 21.
34. Ibid.
35. Ibid., 23.
36. Ibid., 24.
37. Ibid., 26.
38. Kyle Seraphin, interview with author.
39. Tommy Waller, interview with author (no relation). Tommy Waller is now president of the Center for Security Policy.

40. Carmandy Graff (@GraffCarmandy), "More from the sinister . . . ," Twitter, March 21, 2023, 5:57 p.m., https://twitter.com/GraffCarmandy/status/1638298848790745088?s=20.
41. *National Strategy for Countering Domestic Terrorism*, 27.
42. Ibid., 28.
43. Ibid.
44. Ibid., 29.

Chapter 32

1. *Final Report of the Select Committee to Study Governmental Operations with Respect to Intelligence Activities, United States Senate: Together with Additional, Supplemental, and Separate Views* (Washington, D.C.: Government Printing Office, 1976), https://archive.org/details/finalreportofsel06unit.
2. "Spies Who Lie: 51 'Intelligence' Experts Refuse to Apologize for Discrediting True Hunter Biden Story," *New York Post*, March 18, 2022, https://nypost.com/2022/03/18/intelligence-experts-refuse-to-apologize-for-smearing-hunter-biden-story/.
3. Ray Bogan, "President Biden, Twitter, Others Were Wrong about Hunter Biden's Laptop," Straight Arrow News, March 29, 2022, https://san.com/cc/president-biden-twitter-others-were-wrong-about-hunter-bidens-laptop/.
4. "Public Statement on the Hunter Biden Emails," *Politico*, October 19, 2020, available at https://www.politico.com/f/?id=00000175-4393-d7aa-af77-579f9b330000.
5. Natasha Bertrand, "Hunter Biden Story Is Russian Disinfo, Dozens of Former Intel Officials Say," *Politico*, October 19, 2020, https://www.politico.com/news/2020/10/19/hunter-biden-story-russian-disinfo-430276.
6. "New Testimony Reveals Secretary Blinken and Biden Campaign behind the Infamous Public Statement on the Hunter Biden Laptop," Press Release, House Judiciary Committee, April 20, 2023, https://judiciary.house.gov/media/press-releases/new-testimony-reveals-secretary-blinken-and-biden-campaign-behind-infamous, citing "a transcribed interview with Michael Morell, a former Deputy Director of the CIA and one of the 51 signatories of the public statement."
7. Jeff Giesea, "Establishment Disinformation Is Killing Western Democracy," American Greatness, October 17, 2020, https://amgreatness.com/2020/10/17/establishment-disinformation-is-killing-western-democracy/.

8. Jerry Dunleavy, "Hunter Biden Laptop Letter Signers Embraced 'Russian Disinfo' *Politico* Headline, Emails Show," *Washington Examiner*, May 10, 2023, https://www.washingtonexaminer.com/news/hunter-biden-laptop-letter-russian-disinfo-politico-headline.
9. Emma-Jo Morris and Gabrielle Fonrouge, "Smoking-Gun Email Reveals How Hunter Biden Introduced Ukrainian Businessman to VP Dad," *New York Post*, October 14, 2020, https://nypost.com/2020/10/14/email-reveals-how-hunter-biden-introduced-ukrainian-biz-man-to-dad/.
10. John Douglas Weaver, who cofounded the Lincoln Project in 2019, registered with the United States Department of Justice as an agent of Russia on May 10, 2019. See "Exhibit A to Registration Statement Pursuant to the Foreign Agents Registration Act of 1938, as amended," U.S. Department of Justice, received by NSD/FARA Registration Unit May 10, 2019, 12:59:00 p.m., accessed at https://efile.fara.gov/docs/6677-Exhibit-AB-20190510-1.pdf. The Lincoln Project removed references to its advisory board members from its website. Sipher's Atlantic Council biography as of 2023 said that "he serves as a senior adviser to the Lincoln Project." See "John Sipher," Atlantic Council, https://www.atlanticcouncil.org/expert/john-sipher/.
11. "Public Statement on the Hunter Biden Emails."
12. Ibid.
13. Ibid.
14. Glenn Kessler, "The Hunter Biden Laptop and Claims of 'Russian Disinfo,'" *Washington Post*, February 13, 2023, https://www.washingtonpost.com/politics/2023/02/13/hunter-biden-laptop-claims-russian-disinfo/.
15. Ibid.
16. "Public Statement on the Hunter Biden Emails."
17. Kessler, "The Hunter Biden Laptop."

Chapter 33

1. CSPAN (@cspan), ".@SenTedCruz: 'Did any FBI agents . . . ,'" Twitter, January 11, 2022, 11:53 a.m., https://twitter.com/cspan/status/1608844425651965952?s=46&t=lrqB32DVoq_Edarg1lRS3g.
2. Alan Feuer and Adam Goldman, "F.B.I. Had Informants in Proud Boys, Court Papers Suggest," *New York Times*, November 14, 2022, https://www.nytimes.com/2022/11/14/us/politics/fbi-informants-proud-boys-jan-6.html.
3. Joseph M. Hannaman, "20 Federal 'Assets' Embedded at Capitol on Jan. 6, Defense Attorney Claims," *Epoch Times*, April 12, 2022, https://www.theepochtimes.com/us/case-filing-says-at-least-20-federal-assets-embedded-at-the-us-capitol-on-jan-6-4400120.

4. Tucker Carlson (@TuckerCarlson), "Ep. 15 Former Capitol Police Chief Steven Sund . . . ," Twitter, August 10, 2023, 7:40 p.m., https://twitter.com/TuckerCarlson/status/1689783814594174976.
5. Jack Date, "Former Capitol Police Chief Steven Sund Says Entire Intelligence Community Missed Signs of Riot," ABC News, February 6, 2021, https://abcnews.go.com/Politics/capitol-police-chief-steven-sund-entire-intelligence-community/story?id=75729882.
6. Steven A. Sund, *Courage Under Fire: Under Siege and Outnumbered 58 to 1 on January 6* (Ashland, Oregon: Blackstone Publishing, 2023); Tucker Carlson (@TuckerCarlson), "Ep. 15 Former Capitol Police Chief Steven Sund."
7. Andrew Kerr, "Federal Authorities Won't Say Why Armed Capitol Rioters Disappeared from FBI's Most Wanted List," *Washington Examiner*, January 6, 2022, https://www.washingtonexaminer.com/news/federal-authorities-wont-say-why-armed-capitol-rioters-disappeared-from-fbis-most-wanted-list.
8. Barnini Chakraborty, "FBI Informants Had Bigger Role in Whitmer Kidnap Plot Than Thought: Report," *Washington Examiner*, July 21, 2021, https://www.washingtonexaminer.com/news/fbi-informants-bigger-role-whitmer-kidnap-plot.
9. Tim Hains, "Cruz Grills FBI Director: The Guy in Charge of the Whitmer Kidnapping Entrapment Plot Got Promoted and Is Now in Charge of the J-6 Case?," RealClearPolitics, August 4, 2022, https://www.realclearpolitics.com/video/2022/08/04/sen_ted_cruz_grills_fbi_director_how_is_agent_who_ran_entrapped_fake_whitmer_kidnappers_now_working_on_j-6_case.html#!.

Chapter 34

1. Diana Glebova, "Exclusive: FBI LGBT Guidance Quietly Scrubbed after Employee Backlash, Whistleblower Says," Daily Caller, December 13, 2022, https://dailycaller.com/2022/12/13/exclusive-fbi-lgbt-guidance-backlash-agents/.
2. Federal Bureau of Investigation, *FBI Diversity Report*, revised May 2023, https://fbijobs.gov/sites/default/files/2022-05/Report_Diversity.pdf, 2.
3. Author's interviews with FBI whistleblower Stephen Friend, who was pulled off such cases, and with other FBI agents who requested anonymity.

4. Taylor Branch, "Affairs of State," *Washington Post*, October 30, 1988, https://www.washingtonpost.com/archive/lifestyle/magazine/1988/10/30/affairs-of-state/2babf1dd-ee5a-4eae-b244-e1f0d321018d/.
5. Beverly Gage, *G-Man: J. Edgar Hoover and the Making of the American Century* (New York: Viking, 2022), 534–35.
6. Tim Weiner, *Enemies: A History of the FBI* (New York: Random House, 2012), 106–7.
7. Cf. J. Michael Waller and Fredo Arias-King, *Nursing Injustices: An Unsparing Psychological Profile of Vladimir Putin Will Reveal a Deeply Vulnerable Kremlin Leader* (Washington, D.C.: Center for Security Policy, July 2021), https://centerforsecuritypolicy.org/wp-content/uploads/2021/07/Waller_AriasKing_Putin_July2021_Optimize.pdf.
8. Christopher Andrew and Vasili Mitrokhin, *The Sword and the Shield: The Mitrokhin Archive and the Secret History of the KGB* (New York: Basic Books, 1999), 1–22, 234–36; Andrew and Mitrokhin, *Active Measures and the Main Adversary*, 306–7; Gage, *G-Man*, 535–36.
9. Kyle Seraphin, Stephen Friend, and other suspended FBI agents, interviews with author in 2022 and 2023.

Chapter 35

1. Ronn Blitzer and Jake Gibson, "Biden DOJ Ending National Security Initiative Aimed at Countering China amid Complaints about Bias," Fox News, February 23, 2022, https://www.foxnews.com/politics/doj-ending-china-initiative-national-security-program-bias.
2. Ellen Nakashima, "Justice Department Shutters China Initiative, Launches Broader Strategy to Counter Nation-State Threats," *Washington Post*, February 23, 2022, https://www.washingtonpost.com/national-security/2022/02/23/china-initivative-redo/.
3. David Spunt, "Justice Department Pressured to End China Initiative Aimed at Targeting Espionage," Fox News, January 13, 2022, https://www.foxnews.com/politics/justice-department-china-initiative-doj-espionate-pressure.
4. Adam Sabes, "Chinese State Media Says GWU Is 'Asylum for Racism' for Allowing Anti-Chinese Government Posters," Fox News, February 12, 2022, https://www.foxnews.com/us/chinese-state-media-article-says-gwu-is-asylum-for-racism-for-allowing-anti-chinese-government-posters.
5. Ibid.
6. Emma Colton, "GWU President 'Personally Offended' by Art Slamming China's Human Rights Record, Has It Removed from Campus," Fox News,

February 7, 2022, https://www.foxnews.com/us/gwu-president-personally-offended-art-china-human-rights.

7. Josh Gerstein, "DOJ Shuts Down China-Focused Anti-Espionage Program," *Politico*, February 23, 2022, https://www.politico.com/news/2022/02/23/doj-shuts-down-china-focused-anti-espionage-program-00011065.
8. Ibid.
9. Former U.S. intelligence official, interview with author, 2022.
10. "Site Selection Plan: Federal Bureau of Investigation Suburban Headquarters," General Service Administration, September 22, 2022, https://www.gsa.gov/system/files/2022-09-22-FINAL-FBI%20HQ%20Site%20Selection%20Plan%20%28Signed%20and%20Redacted%29_0.pdf, 1.
11. Alicia Ault, "Why Is the Pentagon a Pentagon?" *Smithsonian*, April 10, 2017, https://www.smithsonianmag.com/smithsonian-institution/why-pentagon-pentagon-180962719/.
12. Alex Smirnov, "7 Interesting Facts about Russia," Russia Trek, November 20, 2010, https://russiatrek.org/blog/overview/fascinating-facts-about-russia/#:~:text=The%20Kremlin%20in%20Moscow%20is,the%20walls%20are%20twenty%20towers.
13. "Site Selection Plan," 10.
14. Ibid., 11.
15. Ibid., 7.
16. Jory Heckman, "Maryland Lawmakers Make One Fina Pitch to Build New FBI Headquarters in Their State," Federal News Network, March 8, 2023, https://federalnewsnetwork.com/facilities-construction/2023/03/maryland-lawmakers-make-one-final-pitch-to-build-new-fbi-headquarters-in-their-state/.
17. Sadie Gurman and Siobhan Hughes, "Republican Eyes Sweet Home for New FBI Headquarters in Alabama," *Wall Street Journal*, July 11, 2023, https://www.wsj.com/articles/republican-eyes-sweet-home-for-new-fbi-headquarters-in-alabama-479b19d8?mod=e2tw.

Chapter 36

1. Jim Sciutto and Katie Bo Williams, "US Concerned Kyiv Could Fall to Russia within Days, Sources Familiar with Intel Say," CNN, February 25, 2022, https://www.cnn.com/2022/02/25/politics/kyiv-russia-ukraine-us-intelligence/index.html; Jacqui Heinrich and Adam Sabes, "Gen. Milley Says Kyiv Could Fall within 72 Hours If Russia Decides to Invade Ukraine: Sources," Fox News, February 5, 2022, https://www.foxnews.com/us/

gen-milley-says-kyiv-could-fall-within-72-hours-if-russia-decides-to-invade-ukraine-sources.

Chapter 37

1. Jeff Mordock, "FBI Politicization Began under Mueller, Former Agent Says," *Washington Times*, August 10, 2022, https://www.washingtontimes.com/news/2022/aug/10/fbi-politicization-began-under-mueller-former-agen/.
2. "A Brief History," FBI, https://www.fbi.gov/history/brief-history#:~:text=It%20all%20started%20with%20a,of%20the%20Department%20of%20Justice.
3. *Strategic Plan 2018–2022*, National Counterintelligence and Security Center, https://www.odni.gov/files/NCSC/documents/Regulations/2018-2022-NCSC-Strategic-Plan.pdf.

Conclusion

1. Lindsay Whitehurst, "Former FBI Agent Robert Hanssen, Who Was Convicted of Spying for Russia, Dies in Prison," *Washington Times*, June 5, 2023, https://www.washingtontimes.com/news/2023/jun/5/former-fbi-agent-robert-hanssen-who-was-convicted-/.

Index

E

F

G